HOME-MADE KIDS

PRAISE FOR *HOME-MADE KIDS*

I found *Home-Made Kids* fascinating and so very accessible.
My children are coming into teenage and I shall be
dipping into this book regularly
Cassandra Jardine, The Daily Telegraph

The author knows well that many parents need to be told
straightforward things in plain language... this is an excellent
book thanks to its clear layout, excellent case studies
and theoretical underpinning
Times Educational Supplement

What a super book! I have dipped into it and there
really is some useful advice.
Nick Bevan, Headmaster Shiplake School, Henley-on-Thames

Packed with useful insights and good advice ... it will prove
very helpful to anyone looking after children
David Christie, St Edward}s Oxford

I have been dipping into it over the past month or so
and found it fascinating, well-written, clear and helpful.
Gavin Esler, Broadcaster

I found this book fascinating – Essential reading for parents and teachers!
Jo Petty, Director Dyslexia Teaching Centre, London

HOME-MADE KIDS

A Journey through Adolescence

Peter Gilchrist

illustrated by
Alan Turner MBE

Troubador Publishing Ltd
12 Manor Walk, Coventry Road
Market Harborough
Leics LE16 9BP, UK
Tel: (+44) 1858 468828
Email: books@troubador.co.uk
Web: www.troubador.co.uk

The Case Studies featured in this book are based on experience of actual cases, but are not representative
of any specific case. Names and places have been changed in all instances.

ISBN 1 899293 98 1

Typeset in 11pt Garamond by Troubador Publishing Ltd, Market Harborough, UK
Printed and bound by Cambrian Printers Ltd, Aberystwyth, Wales

t² is an imprint of Troubador Publishing

Contents

Introduction

This book began life as an Educational Psychologist's column in *The Daily Express*. On one hundred and three mornings, I sat before a blank page and wrestled to order my thoughts on a wide variety of subjects affecting our children, having worked with them and families for over thirty years. Surely the thoughts should flow more freely? It proved to be a fascinating adventure, not only in self-discipline, but seeing the theme, pattern and philosophy that gradually emerged over the two years. It was a useful exercise in keeping the material 'jargon free', accessible and, hopefully, entertaining. This is the approach that we have maintained in this book, sprinkling each chapter generously with case studies.

Each stage in a child's development has its own ups and downs, and its focus. We often wonder whether our children will ever pass the 'terrible tens' or the monosyllabic fourteens! Our role is to bring them to maturity, and some degree of independence, by their eighteenth birthday. There are many subtly different shades of management that apply to each stage, during this eighteen-year journey. It is one of the greatest tasks with which the human being is confronted. It is genuinely life altering. We are all products of our parents, yet few, if any of us, have any training in parenting.

It seemed absurd to allow these 'ponderings' over two years, to simply pass by, and not refine them into one place and, hopefully, one coherent philosophy, covering our lives over the many formative years we spend with our children.

The family as a team

The theme of 'families as a mutually supportive team' has become a fundamental focus. There are times, as parents, when we obviously have to adopt an authority figure role, take a lead and set an example, but as 'team leader', not 'hectoring bully'. This search for an effective family team, allows parents to incorporate the various ramifications of 'familyness'. Over the years, I have obviously included the traditional 'Oxo family', with both parents on their first marriage and two point five children, living in a stable community. However, I have also looked at single parents, gay relationships, and indeed, most structures within which children are brought up. The team concept has taken away the enormous burden of responsibility that so many of us as parents have felt. Our commitment is all that is required. Even young children should have their supportive role to play, and once they reach adolescence, they should be seen to be making a genuine contribution to the effective running of the team. It creates an atmosphere of mutual support and respect, and children grow up anticipating the roles they will have to play and the responsibilities they must share, however small, even in the early days. Nobody is allowed to be parasitic on the rest of the team..

Acceptance of a family as a team also allows us to look at 'the game of life' and how we are playing it. We can stand back and examine our roles as 'players' in this game, where this interaction may be breaking down, and, therefore, how the game might be played a great deal more effectively. So often, this reveals two separate 'referees', blowing the whistle at different times, one producing a red card, while the other simply ignores an offence. Any of us who have been involved in traditional team games remember well the bad tempered matches, when players were hurt, - almost always badly refereed. The same disenchantment applies to the mismanagement of the 'game of life'. As parents we need to decide who, in which circumstance, will be the 'referee', and who will be the supportive 'referee's assistant'. Inconsistency of management is a recurrent theme in families where behaviour is breaking down.

A family forum

As the column began to develop the philosophy of 'teamness', it became increasingly apparent that more and more families had little or no time, or structure, within which to exert this type of influence. I was horrified to read that little more than half of our population ever have a regular family meal, and almost a quarter have no table around which a meal could occur, in any event. Busy parents, and even busier children, pass each other like ships in the night, neither having any influence on the other. Not only were such children receiving no support or guidance, but the parents were benefiting all too little from the fun of being with their children as they grew and matured. The family meal, at least three evenings a week, became a vital focus, if a family forum was ever to be established. It became apparent that, without this, management was going to be desperately difficult and, at best, haphazard.

I am not suggesting that every meal should be an inquisition, or a lecture session. It should be a vehicle within which the attitudes of the youngsters and their parents become increasingly clear on vital subjects such as drugs, sex, alcohol, race, gender and so on.

I was very taken aback recently by Daniel, a vulnerable dyslexic boy, with heavy pebble glasses, who was having his books stolen from him, his school cap thrown in puddles. He was being kicked, pushed and verbally abused every single day of his school life. He had eventually arrived in the local police station in floods of tears, soaking wet, and dishevelled. He was terrified of returning home because he would be in trouble, yet again, for losing items of uniform, and, as his father had said, "Don't be so wet. Stand up for yourself, boy". Daniel's parents were far too busy with their professional lives to ever have family meals, and Daniel had to forage for himself. Daniel had tried, on several occasions, to sit down with his father and discuss his anxieties, but Dad was always too tired to be interested in school – "Talk to your mother, Daniel".

Daniel's parents had never noticed his pallor, and the dark shadows under his eyes. For a thirteen-year-old boy, he was far too often close to tears. and becoming increasingly monosyllabic. He finally arrived home with a welfare officer from the local police station, and his parents were shattered to find how desperately unhappy and threatened their son had become. This type of bullying needs sensitive management. and Daniel's parents had never allowed themselves time to observe the symptoms. After several periods of family counselling, they established a regular pattern of meals together, especially at weekends. We still had to deal with his father's tendency to use the meals as a chance to lecture, and give, what he felt, was 'helpful advice'. Now, at long last it has become a forum for simply sharing time together – becoming a team.

The column also focused on the considerable dilemma of working parents, and the pressures this puts on them, their fatigue, their time, their need for space for themselves at weekends, and, annually, the desperate need to manage the lengthy summer holidays. There are no easy solutions, but one thing is absolutely certain. If both parents work, then a considerable, deliberate investment of time in the children will be vital, particularly at the weekends, if a serious gap is not to be left in management. Parents roles may be threatened, and their ability to influence the development and happiness of their children, seriously compromised.

Pillars of Identity

Each one of us has several vital pillars that balance our identities, almost like a platform of life. It is the vulnerability of these very pillars that creates so much personal stress. For our children, in their early years especially, parents, siblings, a class teacher or possibly an extended family, are the principle supports of their developing identities. Shaky, inconsistent pillars can be particularly damaging. If we are inadequate, we may have little control over our replacement, who may well be a powerful but inappropriate peer.

By mid teenage, youngsters are striving to develop their own pillars of identity, with us as parents, drifting, properly, to the periphery. Not an easy adjustment, fraught with challenge. But a necessary part of development if they are to become substantial identities in their own right in adulthood. Our efforts in management are crucial if this vital process is to succeed.

Little has been written about the hurdles over which the adolescent must clamber as they create their own pillars. This book, therefore, is going to look at parenting, behaviour problems, and the educational needs of this fascinating group of young people.

Acknowledgements

No book has ever been completed without a team of people to help and support. In my case, none more so than Anna, my secretary, mentor, and she who typed all 97,000 words! Lynn Andrews helped in the early stages with the 'accessibility' of each chapter as it was prepared, and has, ultimately, spent many hours proof reading. I would also like to thank her for advice on the Asperger's chapter. Also thanks to Nick, her husband, for advice and support on marketing, Nuala for very thorough proof reading, and of course, my wife Rosemarie, whose love and support were invaluable. My brother also made a major contribution in the chapter concerned with ICT. Finally, thanks to Alan Turner, who has enlivened the book so much with his cartoons.

Part 1

Your Issues and How They Affect the Family Unit

Can You Be a Pal and a Parent?

I was talking recently to a distraught mother of two little boys, one of whom suffers from an attention deficit disorder (ADD), about a regular disruption to her evening. Most evenings her husband came home from work shortly after 7 o'clock, and, feeling that he must play his 'father's role', promptly regressed to 10 years of age with the two boys! Curiously enough, the interaction often ended when one of the boy's became too rough and inadvertently hurt his father. "I am not going to play with you guys if you can't be sensible!" By now the boys were so hyped up that it was impossible to get them to have a bath or even think of going to bed.

Where does 'friendship' fit with our role as parents? A 'pal', at best, is someone you would do anything for, of whom you are very fond, with whom you share interests. Even with close friends of our own age, do we truly share everything? It is a question of finding a platform for sharing in the enjoyment of one another's company, with an unspoken code reflecting what is 'OK' within this relationship.

Children need to find a similar balance. It is a mistake to feel we can pretend to be 15 again, let alone 9 years of age. To relate effectively, we need to be ourselves and nothing should be pretended. Furthermore, we can too easily become a gross embarrassment to the children. A boy commented, "I love my father coming to watch us play football but he is so embarrassing – he charges around in his tracksuit, as though he is a sub waiting to come on and play!"

We must also remember that children of different ages deal with the subtleties of language very differently. Below the age of 10, children are largely unable to deal with abstract thought and language. At this stage being there with a smile, ready to help and support, taking an interest in Johnny's football and Susan's appearance in the Christmas play are all immensely valuable, and demonstrate warmth, caring and the true role of a parent as a 'pal'. Indeed, it is important for the development of the children that they have effective relationships with both parents.

At a post 10-year-old level, before they move into the murky waters of adolescence, the sharing of hobbies and interests is an extremely valuable vehicle for developing friendships with our children. Not only do they value our approval and involvement, but these memories will be treasured many years later.

Sports are also a valuable parent-link with offspring. However, there is a hidden psychological danger. The father and son who play golf or tennis together may find themselves as competing 'stags' in the same herd. Do not forget that you are getting older and the young person is becoming fitter, more able and, hopefully, is learning from you. However, he may well become increasingly difficult to beat. I played doubles last summer against a father and son combination who refused to speak to each other throughout and the father stormed off at the end, without a word to any of us. It emerged that his son had beaten him earlier in the day! Losing is one thing, but losing to your child may not be easy to take and is something to deal with in a mature, not petulant, fashion.

We should also remember that in the early teens, children begin to evaluate all they have learnt from their background, and this needs to be understood and not resented. You hope that they will re-emerge at 17 or 18, reflecting the standards and attitudes that you will then share with them. Parents often complain, "My daughter and I shared everything and now she won't tell me what is going on in her life!" The truth is that the pre-adolescent, who feels secure, will often sit at the end of our beds talking happily about the events of the day. Nevertheless, the sharing is seldom reciprocated. Indeed, it would be unhealthy if it were. Children are challenging the pillars of their identities, which is more than likely to create short-term insecurity for their parents. Each will have become a pillar in the identity of the other over the years, but legitimate challenge is not rejection.

One of the most striking examples of this occurred when a 16-year-old girl made it clear that she 'did not want her father to join her during their visit to my office and explained that she had no respect for him.' It emerged that a very close relationship with her mother was continuing, but was beginning to make her feel very uneasy, particularly now that her mother had begun to discuss her father's sexual inadequacies. "I don't want to know about all that." It is such a mistake to malign a partner in front of another team member.

Children should grow up seeing us as friends, who care profoundly and would do anything for them, but we are, nevertheless, authority figures who will rescue them if they are in trouble and on whom they can rely, not simply 'pals'. We are vital pillars of their identity but children need to feel that these pillars are reliable and secure.

In middle to later teens, youngsters are often confronted by the rigours of public examinations, which all too often coincide with their first serious love. A time of confusion, difficulty with concentration, and even guilt. Remember what it was like for us. Do not question too closely. You will seldom be told the truth and all you do is dig the feelings of guilt in still further. Allow an open door as a confidant and, if necessary, a shoulder to cry on. It is a time when privacy is important. They need a room of their own, somewhere where they can work, play their music, relax and think. You are not being rejected if they want to stay up in their rooms for protracted lengths of time. Equally, do not forget that every generation thinks that it has invented sex, which tends to become a rather secret world in those adolescent years – not a place for us as 'pals'.

Throughout a child's life from the very early days, it is possible to show our love, our caring, our involvement, our approval of their activities and their enjoyment of ours. Remember to allow them to share your successes as well. Even unconditional love is about emotional giving and taking, but within clearly defined roles.

Eighteen plus may be the time for being a true 'pal'. You may have to accept somewhat differing views, but this no longer needs to be a challenge, but simply individual differences. You may now feel a subtle shift as roles begin to reverse and adult children become our friends and support, helping and encouraging us. We may even begin to learn from them!

2

How to Stay Amicable for Your Children's Sake After Separation

Often marriages struggle to stay together "for the sake of the children". I admire the persistence and self-sacrifice, and relationships do take work. It is a great comfort that an enormous number of marriages do survive. Marriage is an institution worth working for. We must also remember what crucial pillars of a developing child's identity we become.

However, it is hard to forget the image of Pamela, aged 8 years, clinging to the upper banister of the staircase, with 4-year-old Charlie on one arm and her beloved teddy on the other, listening to yet another row between her parents. Charlie was bewildered and his ill formed, uncertain memories led to our clinical work together many years later.

Parents do separate, regretfully, increasingly often. Marriages are not made in heaven and it sometimes becomes evident that two people are simply not suited to live together. It can be fairer to all concerned to begin afresh. Children do not need to live through continual rows, but they must understand, at least to some degree, what has happened and why one or other parent will no longer be living in the family home. It is vital that this remains a real relationship and that this vulnerable 'pillar' is not allowed to become too insecure and insubstantial. Above all, make it clear that it is not the child's fault. So many children experience terrible, but unwarranted guilt.

Be quite realistic. Couples do not usually separate amicably. There is almost always hurt and emotional damage lying within the causes of a separation and it is understandable that one or other partner may feel very bitter about what has occurred. The first step in dealing with the children's dilemma is to be as objective and honest as one possibly can, with their interests truly at heart. This is the time when the sacrifice "for the sake of the children" is well worth making.

Firstly, the children have to be told. We must bear in mind their ages. For a child of less than five, life is very black and white, and long philosophisings will simply be lost, or worse, misunderstood. Over the years they come gradually to terms with increasingly abstract concepts. However, a child of over ten will understand very much more about why relationships have not worked. They will need reassurance that their parents still love them and that they will continue to enjoy the friendship and support of both parents, despite the separation. Remember that they will be anxious lest one parent will be lost to them. It is impossible to go into full detail about the separation. It is usually best to say that you have decided that it will be impossible to live together, and it would only cause unhappiness for everyone if you attempt to do so. It will be easier if you live separate lives, in separate homes, but, above all, continue to love the children and be involved in their lives and development.

Accept your own feelings of guilt and misgiving. This is inevitable. Remember that they will not fully understand, and that tears and anger will be a most understandable reaction from them.

It is vital for the children that they feel that the loss can, in some way, be remedied by promises that will be kept, and by a 'contract' that will be built between them and their parents. The hurt and, at times, injured party may well not wish to be so generous to someone they feel has betrayed them, but, in the interests of the children, a deal must be sought. Emotional, psychological 'games' are so often a cause of misery for both the ex partners and their children. Promises are made and broken, understandings are reached which are never fulfilled.

Make a clear understanding about contact, exactly how and where this will take place. Do not promise something in the early stages that you cannot fulfil. Make it clear to all concerned that trust will have to be rekindled but there is a clear plan as to how this will be achieved. Children must be a part of the real lives of both parents, in their new homes. Ideally, they should have toys, and a part of their identity in each of their different bedrooms.

Especially for the hurt partner, it is very difficult not to blame and criticise in front of the children. It is understandable and may make you feel better in the short term, but it does damage to the children. Keep remembering that no matter how angry and hurt you may feel the children must come first, and it is important that they feel that it is an 'amicable' relationship, conducted in their best interests. Nothing distresses children more than half overheard fights about contact, forcing children to divide their loyalties. Remember not only will the children lose respect for your ex partner, but for you into the bargain.

They must feel that they can trust and respect you. Bed times, their general behaviour, pocket money, and so forth, must be consistent. This gives them a sense of security.

A second major issue, which may eventually emerge, will be the advent of a new partner. Separation is about beginning new lives, in new homes, and, possibly, with new relationships. This may seem hurtful to the other partner who may not want their role to be undermined by someone else, but it is vital that children grow to understand their parents in a real and developing context. Do not challenge contact purely because an ex partner has now found a live-in boyfriend or girlfriend.

An angry telephone call made it all too clear that a hurt mother was refusing to let her children's father come anywhere near them. "Why should he? He doesn't deserve the kids, treating me like this." It takes such strength to rise through this myopic world of hurt and hostility, to look clear-sightedly at the child's needs, which must be of paramount importance. The mother and I have since met and talked the issue through, and at least the first step has now been taken. The children will be able to see their father on a Saturday afternoon, once a fortnight. This is a beginning, but far from what the children truly need.

There are certain circumstances where, sadly, contact has to be heavily curtailed. If there has been a genuine history of physical or sexual abuse of the children, for example, it may be quite inappropriate for such a father or mother to have access to the children until matters have been thoroughly sorted out.

On rare occasions there is a genuine fear of abduction. It is in this context that we need to be sure, as a society, that we do not condone this type of behaviour and leave women feeling threatened. I worked with a case where the two daughters were not returned by their father after a weekend away. Pleading only led to further refusal until matters came to court 17 months later. Unfortunately, by then the children were established at school, had made local friends, and become used to father's large house, with its swimming pool. Mother lived quietly in Yorkshire. Sadly for the mother, the Court decided that the interests of the children were paramount and they were better suited to their father's home. It is no wonder that separated mothers feel anxious. It is up to the father in these circumstances to create an atmosphere of trust and security by fulfilling his commitments and the understandings as laid down by the court, from a very early stage.

Broken promises are one of the worst offences of the part-time parent.

Nevertheless, reduce the stumbling blocks to a minimum. This is difficult to do in the emotional heat of early separation, especially during the first twelve months when a new pattern of life is developing for all concerned. Look at issues together which may involve schooling, clothing, behavioural management, and particularly holiday times. How will these be shared? Will you allow your ex-partner to take your children abroad and so forth?

Above all, avoid shock moves. These are often understandable when a parent is afraid that their plans will be blocked. I am particularly concerned about changes of school, home, moves across the country or even abroad. Do remember that the absent parent has considerable rights in the lives of their children and it will only cause conflict if a move is committed before it is even discussed.

I remember going to Court a couple of years ago to discuss whether Roger should go to an all boys school, or be educated in a co-educational environment. This caused misery for the boy and by the time the wrangling had finished, it was uncertain whether he would be happy in either environment! The whole situation could so easily have been pre-empted, if discussion had taken place long before the situation became a major issue.

The aim should be at least weekly contact with the largely absent parent, with intervening telephone calls. The ease, happiness and readiness of contact is vital to the interest of the children. Certainly, it will lend a ready image of a relatively amicable separation with parents who care. Both parents need to be aware that the absent parent is a pillar of the children's identity, which needs to be kept intact if they are not to suffer emotionally. It is in the interest of both the parents and the children to encourage this stability. Resist the urge to further undermine an already vulnerable 'pillar'.

While it is unrealistic to say that arguments should be kept away from children within a marriage, it should be very much easier once parents are separated. Try to arrange a forum within which conflicts will be discussed miles from the hearing of the children:

- Trust and consistency are vital in the management of children with separated parents.

- Clear-cut understanding of the terms of contact is absolutely vital. It will not be easy; it will mean compromise; it may need discussion out of the hearing of the children, but they must feel that within your relatively amicable separation you are fully committed to their welfare and that there is apparent agreement between you, about how their lives will be managed.

- Both parties need to agree that life will be kept as genuine as is humanly possible.

- The issue of quality of life and, particularly, the possibility of new partners must be confronted early on. Contact should not be denied because a parent has found a new partner. The visit will be a more realistic experience for the child, because they will see the parent against an honest background. Nevertheless, one cannot but respect the anxiety of the other parent who feels that they might be supplanted. This very seldom happens if honesty and generosity are the prime motivators.

- Agree basic management strategies. For a child to learn that either parent can be manipulated and turned into a source of 'goodies' seriously challenges respect for that parent. Think about pocket money, homework, bedtime, TV watching and table manners, which are all focal points for this type of conflict. A child needs to feel that life is reliable and management similar throughout the 7-days of the week. They should not have to play different roles, depending on who they are living with, teaching them almost to live a lie. Remember how valuable you are as a pillar of your child's identity, but insecure, unreliable pillars provoke stress.

WEEKEND PARENT'S ROLE

As the part-time parent, there is a subtle but fundamental decision to be made. Do you want to continue being a parent, or are you prepared to drift to 'uncle' or 'aunt' status? If you are occasionally seen, not for long, but always with a bag of goodies and you never insist on discipline of any kind, please do not expect to be regarded as fulfilling a parent's role, or remaining for long as a worthwhile pillar of the children's identity.

- Make time available. You have two instead of seven days in which to carve your role as a parent. These two days are your chance to make a mark on your child's life. Fathers so often under-estimate their true value to developing children. Be there for them and regard this commitment as being of the highest possible priority. Children grow so quickly. You only have one chance.

- If possible, have a special room set aside for the child/children where they can leave marks of their identity behind them. They need to feel that they are 'coming home' when they come back to you. This is so different from simply 'visiting Mum or Dad'.

- I have seldom heard a child refer to their father as a 'Git', but it happened recently when a nine-year old complained to me that her bicycle had broken down, her skateboard was bust, she did not have enough games for the GameBoy and 'Auntie' was being difficult about what television she could watch. I asked her what she meant and she said, "Oh, I can get anything I want out of Dad. He doesn't care, as long as I am happy and shut up." You cannot buy children. Treats, properly timed and appropriate, are not spoiling; giving way to every whim and fancy, often against a background of whinging, most certainly is. It damages the children and has a wrecking effect on their respect for parents.

- Ensure that activities are age appropriate. You may thoroughly enjoy a steak in a first class restaurant, but it may be a crushingly dreary occasion for a 14-year old child. You want to see the local football match, but does your daughter? Do not try to do too much and over pack the weekend.

- It can be valuable to let them bring a friend for the weekend, so that they can create their own entertainment for some of the time. This is your chance to enjoy their company and offer moral support in their development.

- To maintain a realistic but caring environment, some module of homework should be undertaken with you during the weekend. Equally, there is no reason why one domestic chore should not be kept as their personal responsibility. We all have commitments, even from a young age.

- Keep occasional telephone contact, letters, cards and so forth for the mid week. A child's success at school, for example, needs to be relayed as quickly as possible. This support will encourage the child, to the benefit of all concerned.

- You will have to deal with the attitudes of new partners and if a second marriage takes place, possibly with stepsiblings. This is far from easy, but it needs to be made quite clear, from a very early stage, that the child concerned is a fundamental part of your life, a pillar of your identity and not simply a hangover from a previous relationship.

- Try to be open-handed with all the children. The worst experience I have had was in a family of three children where the father would have two of them to stay, but not James. "I don't want him in my home. Anyway, my new wife can't stick him." The boy's feeling of rejection at having heard this comment was difficult to deal with. Angry and bitter – he certainly was!

This difficult world must be made as honest as is humanly possible and this needs generosity from all concerned. The children need to feel that they are still a vital part of our lives, not excluded from it.

3

Single Parents and Divorce

Research suggests that single parent families are particularly vulnerable, and instances of illness, learning difficulties in school, behavioural problems with children, and so forth, seem to be greatly magnified. In some ways, this is hardly surprising, when you consider the enormous task involved in bringing children from birth through to early adulthood. Even with both parents and an extended family, the task is far from easy, and none of us is adequately trained for the experience.

Single parent families fall largely into two separate groups: those with single parenting as a result of divorce or bereavement, and others where the mother, or occasionally the father, has elected not to marry but to care for the children on their own. The origin of single parenting may be different but the outcome is very similar. There is, in reality, no reason why a single parent should not bring up happy and successful children. However, the family needs more structure and organisation when only one adult has to carry the responsibilities.

Where children grow up with both parents, but then lose one through bereavement or divorce, we must remember that the remaining parent and the children have suddenly lost a vital pillar of their identity on whom they depended. This creates an enormous psychological hole and the parent will suddenly find themselves 'wearing two hats', instead of one, and not having the periods of respite to which they had become accustomed. The children, used to sharing their love, and being supported by both parents, are now in a diminished emotional environment, and, in the case of divorce, with only occasional contact with the missing parent.

For the elected single parent, there has been no pillar to lose. Tasks may be more difficult from the outset, but they do not have to face the colossal psychological adjustment to a loss.

COPING STRATEGIES

Whether you are a single parent and always have been, but have now hit a particular crisis, or you are a new single parent struggling to come to terms with loss, never be afraid to admit vulnerability and seek appropriate counselling help. A support system can be extremely helpful, a resource to which an individual can return, possibly on many occasions. When major issues need to be faced and dealt with, it is helpful to have another person with whom to share the dilemma.

Counselling support is particularly valuable, and, indeed, very important, not only for the adults but for the young people in the family as well. This is particularly true when a couple are on their way to divorce, and times are unhappy and emotionally highly charged. There is so much to be dealt with that adults tend to become very inward looking and self-centred, and the children's emotional needs tend to be forgotten. Once divorce is in the air, young people are often terrified by the potential loss. The question is often asked – "If Dad really loved me, he wouldn't just leave me like this." Not very rational, but an understandable emotional response.

In essence, to be a successful single parent, adults need to be strong, well resourced and very clear in their thinking and planning with their children. Decision making, particularly with older children, sharing of problems, the mutual search towards solutions, are made achievable largely around a shared family meal. It is healthy for children to assist in this type of problem solving and it tends to make them more committed to the eventual outcome.

Children in single parent families often enjoy experiences impossible in two parent circumstances. They may become aware of a parent achieving successes of which the children can be proud. They also see new loves and new relationships close at hand, and this, too, can establish a very healthy role model, particularly if the youngsters are honestly and openly involved in the circumstances.

It is a time when young people need to contribute as team members, robustly, openly and honestly. It is no time for 'passengers'. It is a terrible mistake to assume that children need to be spoilt "because of all they have been through". Each needs to contribute, help and support and to be given full credit for having done so. In essence, the entire 'team' is needed for successful day-to-day living.

THE NEED TO ADJUST ATTITUDES

1. The first step for the entire family is to stop perceiving single parenthood as a pathological cultural failure, as a result of which all concerned will inevitably suffer. This need not be the case. Many single parents treasure their autonomy and independence, are very positive about the future, both for themselves and their children, and have often commented to me that they are very glad that they are free of the endless family arguments that had too often been a part of their earlier experience.

2. There is no room for doubt or uncertainty. You have to accept that you are the authority figure in the family. You are an important pillar of your children's identities. They need to trust and respect you. They have to perceive that you are the individual who prescribes the rules for their particular 'game', and have sanctions available to deal with breaches. Remember that to say 'no' can be a sign of strength, love and respect. However, to say no nine times and then give way and convert to a yes, is to undermine both adult and child.

3. Try to avoid overload and becoming swamped. Plan your time carefully, using extended family support, if it is available, and ensure that the children carry their share of the work load, to create space for you. Keep reminding yourself and the children that you are a team. Well trained, well organised teams function most effectively. Above all, rid yourself of guilt and do not allow children to pressure you.

4. Remember that your own physical and emotional health is important, to yourself and your children, because if you become vulnerable this will be extremely unsettling for the rest of your team. It follows that proper nutrition, exercise, stimulation, creating a degree of reasonable space for yourself and allowing yourself to develop new relationships is crucial to your sanity, and the balance of your family. These can be times when sessions with a counsellor can be extremely valuable, giving you space to simply talk through issues, with no chance of recrimination or criticism.

WATCH OUT FOR MINEFIELDS

There are one or two minefields into which all parents can easily stumble, but particularly those coping entirely on their own. This may become the case where an only child is involved. Firstly, it is tempting to share everything with the child and turn them into a 'quasi adult', almost a peer. They are going through their developmental stages, and are coming to terms with life through childish eyes, and, certainly below their teen years, are not even seeing things in the same subtle, sophisticated adult terms as the parent. There are too many children burdened by the cares of the family that they frankly do not understand but which will simply panic them and increase their own guilt. Not only is this unhealthy for the child, but it tends to create an almost inevitable apparent rejection when the youngster moves into their middle teens. They then become, naturally, much quieter and more secretive, withdrawing into themselves to re-evaluate all that they have learnt over the years. This is normal.

Secondly, it is easy and normal to live vicariously through our children. We long to see them successful, partly for themselves, but also so that we no longer need to face that dreadful feeling of guilt. We want the best for our children. Above all, we want them to have much that we were unable to experience. Possibly, but at what cost?

Jonathan

I remember Jonathan, who, according to his single parent mother, was destined for Oxford and an academic career. She had no partner to help balance her ambitions for Jonathan. He was a very bright boy, but dyslexic, only fifteen years of age, and was going to struggle with his literacy orientated GCSEs. Jonathan might just have made it to Oxford, but he too had begun to live in his mother's dream world. He found himself increasingly in conflict with fantasy and reality. The more he worked, studied and revised, the more at one level he realised that he was on a totally hopeless collision course with failure, whilst on the other, the dream persisted. The result was that Jonathan began to dream more and more and work less and less. Psychosomatic stress and anxiety symptoms began to appear. He found school attendance more and more difficult. Jonathan and his mother looked continually for someone to blame for his failure to thrive. She was even considering suing the school. In all truth, the target of four A grade A Levels and Oxford was vastly over ambitious for a boy with his profile, and was fraught with almost inevitable failure. A more realistic appreciation of expectations would have taken Jonathan to perfectly acceptable A Levels, and on to college.

SUPPORT SERVICES

We have already discussed the value of counselling for both parents and children. Do not be over critical of the use of babysitters, child minders, and especially the use of extended families, particularly grandparents, who are often very fulfilled by being able to help in the nurturing of the next generation. However, grandparents are not as young as they used to be, and be careful not to overload them with the demands that you make on them.

You need to be fulfilled and a job may well be important, both for fulfilment and provision of sufficient funds to support the family. You also need personal space. This is a psychological requirement. It may be when the youngsters are at their homework or after they have gone to bed, when they are younger. You need this for your own sanity.

Finally, even bearing in mind all the tremendous demands that are made on a single parent, remember the most valuable resource in the world for your children is your undivided time. If you can cut a small window of time in each day for each of your children, where they begin to look forward to it, and see themselves as rather special, then so much the better. This is the point when the overuse of support services can become damaging. It is vital that you are not marginalized from your children and that other people are laying down the law, insisting on standards, and you are simply peripheral to the experience. It is very difficult to re-trench when children are in their early teens. You need to be the primary influence in their lives.

LOVE AND THE SINGLE PARENT

You may fall in love and develop a new relationship. It may be possible, even likely, that a new partner will become a major factor in the children's lives, and eventually a new pillar of their identity. It is important not to hide this love away in a corner of your life. The children need to know that you are human, involved in a happy and successful relationship, and that there is much for them to learn from the experience. Let them share in your happiness.

If your new love moves into the house with your family, remember how symbolically important this will be to the children. It is important not to rush this stage before a relationship is sufficiently mature.

The converse is true if you introduce a new and rather permanent love too late. Rather than seeing the individual as an important ingredient in their psychological makeup, they will interpret this as an intrusion and a possible threat to you, as well as a source of considerable vulnerability for them. They now have to share you and may well resist allowing your new partner to become a pillar of their vulnerable identities.

There is no denying the enormous challenges of being a single parent, and there are countless examples of outstandingly successful children from exactly this background. It can and has been done.

CONTACTS

FAMILIES NEED FATHERS
154 Curtain Road.
London WC2 3AR
General Advice: 020 8886 0970
Office: 020 7615 5060
www.fnf.org.uk

NATIONAL FAMILY MEDIATION
For separating or divorcing couples« Can help couples make joint decisions about a range of issues.

9 Tavistock Place,
London WC 1H9SN
Tel: 020 7585 5995
Fax: 0207585 5994
www.nfm.u-net.con

NATIONAL STEPFAMILY ASSOCIATION
3rd Floor, Chapel House,
18 Hatton Place,
London EClN 8RU
Tel: 020 7209 2460
Fax: 020 72092461
Counselling Service: 0990 168 588

PARENTLINE PLUS
Endway House
Endway, Hadley,
Essex SS7 2AN
Tel: 01702 559900
Fax: 01702 554911
Helpline: 0808 800 2222
www.parentline.co.uk

RELATE
Herbert Gray College,
Little Church Street,
Rugby CV21 5AP
Tel: 01788 575241
Fax: 01788 555007
Helpline: 08706012121

RELATIONSHIP COUNSELLING, PSYCHOSEXUAL THERAPY, EDUCATION & TRAINING
www.relate.org.uk

LONDON MARRIAGE GUIDANCE
Tel: 020 7580 1087

MARRIAGE CARE
Tel: 0545 575921

NATIONAL COUNCIL FOR DIVORCED & SEPARATED
Tel: 0114231 3585

FAMILY CRISIS LINE
Tel: 01485 722533

ASIAN FAMILY COUNSELLING SERVICE
Tel: 020 8997 5749/ 020 8967 5390

AFRICAN CARIBBEAN FAMILY MEDIATION
Tel: 020 7738 6090

GINGERBREAD
Support and practical help for lone parents and their children via a national network of local self-help groups.
www.ffinfferbread.org.uk

NSPCC CHILD PROTECTION HELPLINE
Tel: 0808 800 5000 (helpline)
Free helpline that provides counselling, information and advice to anyone concerned about a child at risk of abuse.
www7.nspcc.org.uk

NATIONAL ASSOCIATION OF CHILD CONTACT CENTRES
Centres offer neutral meeting places where children of separated families can enjoy contact with one or both parents, and sometimes other family members, in a comfortable and safe environment when there is no viable alternative.
www.naccc.org.uk

NATIONAL COUNCIL FOR ONE PARENT FAMILIES
Information for lone parents on a variety of issues including benefits, tax, legal rights, housing maintenance and CSA, and returning to work.
www. oneparentfamilies.org.uk

WOMEN'S AID FEDERATION ENGLAND
Help for women experiencing physical, emotional, or sexual violence in the home.
www.womensaid.org.uk

MAMA (meet-a-mum)
Support for lonely mums or pregnant women
Tel: 020 876 80123 (7-lOpm)

MUSLIM WOMEN
Confidential service for all Muslim women
Tel: 020 8904 8193

JEWISH MARRIAGE COUNCIL
Tel: 02082036311

4

Step Parents

A mother described, six months into her new marriage, the desperate friction and jealousy which she was experiencing with 14-year-old Deirdre, her new husband's teenage daughter. She was bullying her daughter, Janet, and even more, her 10-year-old son David, and was thoroughly uncooperative and oppositional.

The mother was trying to make her new marriage work, and felt that Deirdre was doing all she could to undermine it. This situation is, sadly, not unusual. We sat together for several sessions, looking carefully at the dynamics of the family of which she was now a part. Deirdre's mother had left, after having a torrid affair, wanted to settle into her new love, and, most unusually, wanted no further contact with Deirdre. Deirdre felt betrayed. The youngster discussed her fury with me and we arranged counselling for her. To lose a pillar of your identity is bad enough, but to be betrayed must be devastating.

The concept of a 'team' is a vital target at which to aim, but never pretend that all is necessarily well. Your new relationship may be a happy and exciting event, but do remember that the courtship, which is a natural part of your relationship, may seem a little odd and quirky to the children. New partners require gentle introduction and the children need time to gain acceptance.

Cliff

Cliff had a particularly difficult introduction to his new stepmother. He was 16 and the stepmother, only 26, brought with her a 3-year-old child. His father left his mother to run off with this new girl. Cliff's mother had become so depressed that she felt unable to look after Cliff. He moved in with his stepmother, but bitterly resented this young woman who was attempting to supplant his beloved mum. He felt that he was betraying his mother and took out his sense of betrayal on his 3-year-old stepsister. He also felt that this new woman was undermining his love for his father, who now seemed to show much less interest in him. It subsequently became apparent that his father was attempting a 'balanced view'. He was forgetting that he was perfectly entitled to feel love for his son, and must now do all in his power to make the boy feel that, despite all that had occurred, he was still very much loved.

James

We had similar problems with 12-year-old James. He and his father had visited the local football team most Saturdays and shared much in common. The marriage had broken down, and, as a result, James now saw his father almost as an 'uncle' figure with whom he had only intermittent contact. Unfortunately, his mother experienced considerable friction with her ex husband. They were unable to talk to each other in a civilised way, and she was doing all she could to impede contact. Matters were complicated by her new partner, who was rather older with two boys of 15 and 17 to whom he was very close, but their interests were not shared with James. Hence, he was isolated from his father and he was marginalised within his new family.

We sat down together to resolve the anger and conflict that was burning within this family. We decided, like it or not, contentment and success would only come from team building and drawing the threads together. But this would take a great deal of effort. We discussed the dynamics affecting all the boys. The new stepfather, while accepting that he would always have a very special bond with his own children, was working on contact with James, trying to develop some shared interest with all three boys.

Management strategies must be the same for all the children, and accepted as appropriate by both parents. It is vital to avoid the 'my children, your children' syndrome. It has to be accepted that step parents cannot be expected to instantly 'love' stepchildren – it may develop in the future. This does not stop us working towards a relationship of liking, friendship, and shared interests. Above all, the stepchildren must not feel that they are excluded, marginalised or resented. If they feel that they have been dealt with even-handedly, they are far less likely to drive a wedge between the new couple.

Dee

Dee married a man twenty years older than herself, who had three teenage girls, and she herself had a 10-year-old son, Theo. She moved into an extremely affluent background into which she was totally absorbed. Indeed, she became the 'trophy wife'. The lifestyle was different. Everything she needed was provided for her without asking. Plans were put in hand for Theo to be removed from his Primary school to a major Prep school – but unfortunately, no discussion was had with either her or Theo.

Theo exploded, locked himself in his room and refused to even discuss going to the Prep school. It was at this point that my telephone rang. We met and talked about the true nature of partnership. Theo's stepfather began to realise that if he wanted this new relationship to work, and the love for his new partner to blossom, he would have to make compromises and accept the needs of all concerned.

We have now agreed a compromise school, which Theo has visited, and is perfectly happy to attend, and neither the Primary nor the original prep school are issues. Curiously, having worked with all three key parties, Theo now feels that he is respected as an individual by his stepfather, who has actually been prepared to have regard for his wishes. However, this was only on the proviso that he was prepared to make 'adult' suggestions for the resolution of the problem, rather than being negative. It also empowered his mother to feel that she was a true member of this new partnership.

Above all, it is vital to remember that while stepparents are often building a new life and leaving their hurt behind, the children have to accept the arrival of new competitors on their 'patch' and may not yet have resolved their own hurt. Children cannot simply be transplanted. Who do they feel they are betraying? Who has hurt who? How do they come to terms with an entirely different home of which they do not feel a fully integrated part? How are they to deal with children already in that home who have established their status within it? You have new, young 'animals' struggling for position within a brand new hierarchy. Respect the children, their needs and their hurt. Do not be afraid if stepchildren have to be friends first, but bridges must be built if this is to be achieved. Love may come later. Do not be afraid to love your own natural children and to let them know that this is very much the case, despite the change in circumstances. Fundamentally, take a balanced approach to the development of a new team and management of the children, equally balanced in the hands of both stepparents, and avoid the 'my kids, your kids' syndrome.

This is far from an easy emotional, psychological issue. Counselling often helps a great deal. It allows all concerned, adults and youngsters, to express their insecurities, uncertainties and their anger, deal with it and put it in place. With well-handled counselling, all concerned should feel that their problems have been listened to, and this defuses that feeling of betrayal, resentment and jealousy. Above all, it opens a bridge of communication which allows for dialogue to take place in the future, when further hurdles arise.

5

How Robust Should Our Support be for Our Children?

Children need to feel that we care and are involved in their activities. They love to know that we approve of their interests, their academic attainment and their success at sports. The busy parent who never sees a child's sporting efforts, or even watches them in a school play, inevitably creates an image in the child's mind that not only do they not care, but that parental time does not need to be wasted on them. It is no good explaining that you are busy at work or, even worse, "I have to make the money to allow you to do these things, you know."

Caring needs appropriate demonstration. At times sacrifices have to be made. We can then sit down and discuss a child's A-level choices, or visit a performance of the school orchestra. Children benefit so much from feeling that they have an ally who knows about their problems, and who takes joy in their successes.

However, support can easily go over the edge. "You are a regular player on the Third XV rugby team now. The Firsts next year, OK?" Even more worrying, is the A-level discussion which sets possible university placement at an A-level pass mark which is likely to be quite beyond the young person concerned. It is vital to know their capacity and a close look at GCSE results will give a clue. We are all disappointed and, at times, devastated by failure. If a young person senses that this is almost inevitable months ahead, it is hardly any wonder if they become neurotic, anxious and, at times, hostile. It is so important that we enjoy our children's successes, but do not heap an additional sense of failure and disappointment upon them if they have not quite achieved their target. Their failure must not be our failure.

I was talking to a 35-year old mother in my office some months ago about her impending divorce and how she felt she should manage the emotional needs of her two children. She had been very close to her own mother who had died two years earlier. They had a mutual interest in Drama and had taken part in several plays together. This had allowed them to become very close and although the plays had drifted into the past since her marriage, the woman commented to me, "I wish I could talk all this through with my Mum." What a shame this need was expressed far too late.

John

Support for our children's activities helps to create a valuable relationship bridge. 17-year-old John had somewhat unexpectedly been promoted to the First XV in his school and was thrilled to have made it quite so young. His father, who was a businessman 'workaholic', frequently travelling abroad, was often too tired to spend much time with the children when he was at home. John's comment was, "I wish I could tell my Dad about this, but he wouldn't be interested."

John felt that he could not rely on his father. Without the confidence that this support might have generated, when problems arose, the natural instinct would be for John to gravitate towards a friend whose advice would inevitably be given against a background of comparatively little experience. You need to be there for your children when they need your help.

- A child with a very average IQ, who actually achieves an E Grade in A-level Economics, for example, deserves a major celebration. It is important to set realistic targets.

- Touch line support at sporting events confirms in the mind of our children that we care, are prepared to give up time, approve of the activity and regard it as an important part of their lives. Especially for the under-functioning, less academic child, this can be particularly important.

- The support needs to be appropriate and controlled. It is totally understandable if we become excited and even heated during a match, but unruly, aggressive and rude comments are completely out of place.

Parents spend their lives nurturing their children towards adulthood, who, by their middle teens are already evaluating what they have learnt over the years and are beginning to struggle to piece together their own identity. The standards and examples that have been set are a vital part of this process. 'Out of order' behaviour not only embarrasses children, but, once the embarrassment has worn off, suggests that such behaviour may even be appropriate.

THE OVER-SUPPORTIVE PARENT

For some reason the autumn tends to bring a rash of over-supportive parents, especially fathers. Team games that are over in little more than an hour are an ideal vehicle for fathers to don a heavy coat and scarf, preferably of an old team for whom they never actually played, and charge up and down the unfortunate youngster's touch line.

Charlie and Neil

In fairness to Charlie's father, he had given up a great deal of time to take the boy to training sessions, always supported his matches and was immensely proud of his son. Unfortunately, three weekends ago, Dad was banned from the Under 14's rugby touchline for the rest of the season! The team had been losing and he had been noisily abusive from the touchline, ultimately raging at his own son in particular when he failed in a vital tackle. His voluble reaction caused such embarrassment that the referee came across and warned him and eventually reluctantly instigated the ban. The boy was mortified and there would be no further touch-line support for the rest of the season.

We invest so much love and fascination in our children's development that it is easy to over-react.

It seems that these incidents go in pairs. Charlie's friend Neil had a Dad who elected himself supernumerary coach to the team. He had not been banned but he had certainly been told to remain quiet. His problem was that he was spotting vulnerabilities in the opposing defence and advising the team how to take advantage of these vulnerabilities. He was, in fact, 'cheating' by giving unfair advice, when even the coach was forbidden from giving touchline assistance. He felt that he could usurp the rules. Once again, the motivation was admirable but the exercise lamentable. It is important for parents not to embarrass the kids.

Children are vulnerable if they feel that their parents are standing out or are different in some way. Only very occasionally will a child admire a parent's eccentricities.

The shame from Charlie's perspective was that he valued the time with his father. Time shared just between the two of them. His father's support from the touchline initially meant a great deal. It not only showed that his father cared, but also that he, above all, regarded football as a high status activity within the family. Furthermore, it created a relationship bridge for them at home. They would discuss the successes and failures of their local team, tactics, strategies and equipment, and yet the bond had now been shattered for the remainder of the football season.

Jon

A delicate situation arose with Jon, who had some rugby ability. He was vulnerable, shy and felt that he was failing in most facets of his school life. His father approached the master in charge of rugby and made it clear that his son must be chosen for the team. Unfortunately, his manner was sufficiently aggressive to alienate the teacher concerned, who then refused to have the child even at training sessions! It is vital that we do not attempt to interfere with team choices.

However, the fact that your child would love to be involved in an activity in some way could be discussed with the member of staff concerned. This worked well for another lad whose cricket would never allow him to stray beyond the outfield, but who became the regular scorer with the first team. Once or twice a season he was given a game as sub when someone was injured, but, in the main, he was delighted to be part of the group. It may be possible for your son or daughter to be a sub. Once a teacher has become sensitive to the need, they will often do their level best to allow a child to play, even if only for five or ten minutes at the end of the match. It gives a child a boost and sense of membership.

Sean

Sean's parents were aware of the considerable support that Tim Henman was given by his parents and felt their son should follow in his footsteps. However, there was a significant talent lag. They instigated endless coaching, painful for Sean who never seemed to progress. Unfortunately, he had been told that until he had the technical side of his game sorted out, he would not be allowed to play even friendly matches. He became totally alienated from tennis and eventually gave up.

In essence, games are for playing and enjoying. As a parent, do not take it so seriously that you drive the enjoyment out of it.

It is also worth bearing in mind the difference between over-demanding and a reasonable sense of responsibility.

Julie

Julie was a budding actress, but asked her parents not to come to any of her plays in the future. They were mortified. She tried to imply that their presence inhibited her, but in the end the truth came out. The problem was her mother's rather raucous laugh, often when no one else in the audience was laughing. Her over loud comments could be heard on stage! Julie heard another cast member asking a teacher to request 'a little peace and quiet from that woman in the audience'.

Their presence needed to be warmly supportive and unobtrusive, giving pleasure to Julie, as well as themselves.

6

Keeping Your Cool

'Keeping your cool' is much easier for some personalities than for others, but even the most robust individual will snap if put under sufficient pressure. The danger arises when our response to anger goes beyond the norm, and violent, out of control behaviour follows.

Sarah

I met Sarah in my office, with her third child, a baby of four months. She had been in a steady relationship for some six years but her partner was now serving a three-year prison sentence and it seemed unlikely that their relationship would be rekindled. Sarah felt betrayed. In many ways, she was projecting her anger at her partner onto her third child. Sarah's temper tended to be at boiling point before she even addressed the needs of the baby. Even normal frustrations precipitated screaming and violent shaking of the baby. She was extremely worried by her own behaviour. I suggested that Sarah should become involved with a counsellor skilled in dealing with anger management.

Sarah needed to deal with her pent up emotion if she was to develop a more stable relationship with her children.

Mike

Mike's case was rather different. He was a keen rugby player. His problems emerged most Saturday evenings when he came home from a rugby match, cheerful, but easily frustrated by the behaviour of his small sons. Joseph, at seven, was big enough to offer a physical rough and tumble challenge. However, Mike hit the boy far too hard, knocking him out and he had to be hospitalised. This led to the referral. Mike had not yet grown up and appreciated that he was a 'father' with family responsibilities. Furthermore, he became worryingly disinhibited by alcohol. He began to work on his behaviour, and his response to the three or four pints which tended to follow rugby matches.

Bobbie

Bobbie, a mother of two, nearly damaged her new baby. Her problem was post-natal depression. Depression following the birth of a baby is far from unusual, but often misunderstood and insensitively managed. In this instance, both Bobbie and her husband had been to see a family psychiatrist who was proving very effective in managing Bobbie's depression.

Even understanding the nature of the problem was a great relief to both of them, with the significant reduction in guilt.

MANAGEMENT

We all live in a busy world and often fail to address the factors that are over-tiring, distressing and even depressing. The simplest way to learn to keep your cool is to examine the factors which actually create stress in your life.

- As soon as loss of control begins to emerge in a family as a problem, it is important that partners sit down and look at management. Do not simply attribute blame and expect the 'weaker' partner to seek help on their own. It is almost certainly a joint issue which needs joint management. Families are a 'team' and it is important that all the members play their part.

- It may well be that the marriage has drifted into an unresolved state of conflict. Particularly in the interest of the children, matters need to be properly resolved. A counsellor can often be a useful support.

- Often the beleaguered feeling of having to cope, almost unaided, is what leads to a sense of depression and despair.

- If marital conflict is at the root of depression and anxiety and it proves virtually impossible to sit down and discuss issues, then counselling through an organisation such as RELATE may prove extremely valuable. So often it is the misunderstandings and inability to appreciate one another's points of view, that leads to marital rifts and understandable anger. Never be embarrassed to seek help for anger management.

- Analyse your 'hot spots'. In many ways, our lives are a 'psychological game'. It helps a great deal to know the moves which are being made within this game. Are 'hot spots' more likely during times of pressure at work? Are alcohol or drugs involved? Is it always a build-up during school holidays when a mother feels largely unsupported by her partner?

A strategy is vital:

- The very acknowledging of the 'hot spot' and its need for management is a major first step in the process.

- Have clear management strategies with your children. It is important that you know exactly how you will respond to children who may sense your vulnerability and have a habit of going 'over the top' almost as a response to their own insecurity. Visualising how you will respond when the pressure builds is a great start.

- Above all, avoid 'locking horns' and going into verbal battles. An articulate, manipulative child may well have the better of the argument, which will only increase your frustration and anger.

- Try to withdraw – make a cup of coffee and tell the child you will deal with the problem later.

If you are on the receiving end... If loss of control is becoming a regular feature within the family, it must be dealt with. Do not just sweep it under the carpet, even for the sake of peace and quiet. Some people have rages beyond their capacity to manage, they may need medical help. If a partner seems completely out of control, with no real frustration to explain it, if there is an uncanny feeling, after the outburst, that they cannot recall exactly what has happened, then in a peaceful moment, discuss it together and be sure that proper medical advice is sought. This type of behaviour can often be prevented altogether with appropriate management.

- If an outburst occurs, withdraw and avoid engagement. Most people who have lost control try to drag others into 'the game'. They are picking a fight. Do not play the game with them. It may be difficult, but the dust will settle more quickly and then the situation can be discussed rationally. Never attempt to discuss any kind of help or support while your partner is out of control. This will inflame matters still further.

- Be aware of the significant impact of drugs and alcohol. Alcohol can have a depressing and disinhibiting effect which allows anger to express itself without the usual social controls. If alcohol is beginning to dominate an individual's life, it may be necessary to seek appropriate counselling. Drugs present similar problems and a similar resolution.

- You can often help to prevent a loss of control by being aware that your partner is experiencing stress. Be aware of sudden mood swings which are not typical. Have there been changes of personality and emotional balance? Are they basically far moodier than they have ever been before? It may be far from easy to unearth exactly what is troubling an individual and they may not be happy to discuss it with a partner for fear of causing further upset. Nevertheless, they should be encouraged to seek counselling support to resolve the stress. Both partners may well become involved in the process.

Controlling behaviour and emotions is a vital part of coping in our culture. Anger can be managed but its persistent appearance should not be ignored. Have the courage to face the issue and deal with it.

7

Jealousy – Can we be Jealous of our Children?

Jealous of our own kids? But we are adults – we are mature! Surely it is absurd to say that we can be jealous of our own children? Equally, why on earth should our children be jealous of us?

The truth is we never lose our 'inner child'. We are fundamentally human beings who pass through a serious of life experiences and often react with a stunning level of immaturity.

For the majority of newly married couples the first baby tends to arrive after eighteen months to two years. Remember the emotional build up to the engagement and marriage. The early months of adjustment are far from easy, but they often bring a sense of sharing and closeness on which the marriage may rest for years. However, just as this point is reached the wife becomes pregnant. This may put tremendous pressure on her if she is trying to hold down a demanding job. Already there is stress within the relationship. Sexual contact may dwindle in the months leading up to the baby's birth. This in itself can be a source of frustration for both partners – then the baby arrives. The husband returns home in the evening expecting undivided attention, to find that there is a noisy invader who is taking up a great deal of his wife's time and leaving her exhausted. The new, fundamental pillar of his identity now has to be shared. It is hardly surprising that an enormous number of men are very jealous, especially of a first baby.

We worked recently with the troubled mother of a new baby who seldom saw her husband before nine in the evening, often rather the worse for drink, and thoroughly grumpy. She was beginning to feel that she has two children in the house, not just one! They needed to talk about it together, not just let the issue fester. It may even be a time for joint counselling to fully understand the dynamics of what is happening.

Freud made much of the relationship that often develops between mother and son, and father and daughter. These are usually perfectly healthy and very rewarding relationships that bring a great deal to both parties, but we need to be careful that we are not allowing a relationship of this kind to drive a wedge between husband and wife. We may find ourselves ganging up with children against the other parent who is struggling hard to make the rules within the family work. It is hardly any wonder if this causes jealousy, anger and frustration. Remember that the family is a team and it depends very heavily on its leadership, usually from the two partners. If this leadership is undermined, it leaves the other team members feeling insecure.

It is important to be aware of the vulnerable child, the child who needs our time and attention, but having fought for it, attempts to marginalise other members of the family to safeguard the relationship. Once we are aware that these 'games' can be played so easily, it is rather more possible to stop them developing and avoid the conflict that this sort of manipulating can often cause.

Adolescence is a classical time for jealous conflict within families. As fathers, how often do we criticise our daughter's first serious boyfriend? Are we really critical, or are we simply alarmed that they are now beginning to find another man more important to their lives? Is one of our 'pillars' being threatened by an outsider with sexual intent? It is appropriate that they should move forward into the next stage of their life, but it is not altogether surprising if a father feels anxious and unsettled by the experience.

Mothers have their problems too, of course. They suddenly find their daughter involved with a serious boyfriend with whom everything seems to be "as it used to be for us". By all means be envious, that is only natural, but do not let jealousy undermine your relationship with your son or daughter. Be proud. You have brought them to this level of maturity.

I was talking to a teenage girl who was furious with her mother and very jealous. She was a delightful girl, but not especially physically attractive, who had now fallen in love with a young man for the first time in her life. In trepidation, she had brought the boy home, only to be very confused by her mother's irritable, and apparently jealous, reaction. She was stunned a week or two later to find her mother dressing in short skirts and 'making up', reducing her thirty-eight years of age to 'twenty-five' and flirting with the boyfriend. She was shattered when her boyfriend admitted, "I'd love to have sex with your Mother!"

Older teenagers and young adults still living in the family 'nest' bring their own special problems. They have developed their own expectations of life and are often earning their own money. They have few responsibilities and, pound for pound, often have a great deal more money in their pockets than their parents, who are struggling to create a new life together now that the children have grown up. It is all too easy to be envious of the apparently struggle-free existence of maturing children who readily become non-contributing, rather parasitic and unreasonably demanding members of the household.

A post school youngster living in their parents' house where certain rules apply, should not continue to do so unless they are prepared to adhere to these rules. They should be prepared to 'pull their weight' as part of the team, both around the house and in terms of financial contribution. It is vital that they are seen as fully contributing members of 'the team' if they are to stay once they reach maturity. It is far too easy for the young 'bull' in the herd to challenge the leader and make life very unpleasant for the whole group, making little or no real contribution, but expecting total support.

8

What Do You Do if a Parent Prefers One Child to Another?

Tim

A mother became increasingly worried that her husband showed a very clear preference for his son Tim, then aged 15. The lad was in an academic grammar school, a talented sportsman, and already playing the lead in the school play. Certainly a 'star', and one who needed encouraging, but not at the expense of his two sisters.

Tim had become thoroughly spoilt, over indulged, and unpleasantly arrogant with the world at large, but, particularly, with his two sisters. He had lost his sense of generosity, could do no wrong in his father's eyes, and was beginning to feel that his unpleasant attitude was even appropriate.

However, his mother's concern revolved around the girls becoming increasingly resentful as they saw time, money, and very obvious love lavished on one member of the family, though only a passing interest taken in them. Katie, who was then eighteen, could not wait to leave home. Her mother felt, quite understandably, that it was unfair that her relationship with her daughters should be compromised by her husband's attitude to his son. If progress was to be made in this family, they would need to move quickly. Time was running out.

The parents needed to work with a Psychologist or Counsellor to develop a clear insight into the dynamics that were ruling the family. There is little that any of us do that does not have consequences. I very much hoped that Tim's father would begin to see the consequences already stemming radically from his behaviour. Maybe there was still time to adjust.

Sarah

I spoke to Sarah, who was twenty-nine, and a very successful Vet. For years she was the apple of her parents eye at school. They watched every step she took, they were constantly involved in the school, excessively efficient in organising her life and clearly living vicariously through Sarah, a sensitive young woman, well aware of the impact that this adoration was having on her much younger brother, Mark. She began to feel increasingly smothered in her later years in school, and more and more worried by the clinging, obsessional behaviour of her parents. She went to university, but very seldom came home during the vacations. To her parent's horror, she became pregnant in her third year. Often the case, neurotic love can turn sour and there was now a major rift within the family. Far too much was invested in one individual. I can still hear the echoes of "How could she do this to us, after all we have done for her!" Her brother Mark was also aware that far too much of his time as a little boy had been spent trying to undermine and irritate Sarah, to the point where this too became an obsession and distracted him from his own interests.

However, personality types in families differ. How often do we hear "My daughter and I are just too alike!" It is no wonder if some personalities 'gel' better than others. The issue is how we deal with these differences in relationships.

It is also fair to assume that children do not, in reality, share the same family environment. Sarah and Mark, who we were discussing a moment ago, were thirteen years apart in age. The family had moved, the father was in a different job, the mother was moving into her middle years by the time Mark was born. Sarah had been an adored only child for far too long. Our children arrive at different ages and stages in our own lives. Our lives change dramatically over the years, physically, emotionally and materially.

There are also typical issues that affect our reaction to our children. Birth is a traumatic experience for all concerned, and illness at that time, either physical or emotional, may lead to lack of bonding between mother and child. Depression is not unusual following the birth of a baby, either. Fathers react very differently to the arrival of a new baby and are often jealous. This is especially true of a first baby.

I was working with a Lawyer and his wife. The arrival of a baby would almost certainly break their marriage. They decided to be childless and both developed their careers. The wife changed her mind, felt that she wanted to fulfil herself, but had not discussed it with her husband and allowed herself to become pregnant by ceasing to take the pill. If they stayed together, her husband would have to work very hard to deal with his resentment. In this case, the father was going to struggle to even like this baby, or any other!

It helps to balance our approach if we realise the damage that we can so easily cause. As we have mentioned earlier, an over favoured child becomes understandably spoilt. Furthermore, they have to live with the enormous weight of responsibility on their shoulders. A young person of seventeen said to me, "What on earth will my father think if I don't get A grades in my A Levels?" Undue pressure from the family to succeed often creates stress that may well undermine the very success that they seek.

Secondly, exaggerated affection will usually cause resentment in the other siblings and even the spouse. It is inevitable that others in 'the team' will feel marginalised. They may not even realise that this is happening at a conscious level. You may have to deal with apparently need-less petty squabbling, jealousies and unexpected rows with your partner. Remember that this undue devotion understandably challenges love for any other members of your family.

Finally, fifteen year old Toby said to me; "I admire my older brother James who is such a good rugby player. I would love him to coach me and to go and see his matches, but he knows I am Dad's favourite and just does not want to be my friend." Managing this situation is far from easy. There is nothing wrong with being in tune with one or other member of the family. Sense it, enjoy it, but do not make the preference obvious. Share your time and love, carefully and methodically – it will be in the interest of all. Balanced management is very much the most effective. Treat parenting 'professionally'. The whole family needs support. Remember that from a nurtured, unselfish base, the stars shine more brightly. In a family, we are, each one of us, pillars of identity of the other team members. No one wants to feel threatened or, even worse, unloved by one of those vital pillars.

9

Do Grandparents Spoil?

Grandparents usually know the joy of sharing their grandchildren, and, hopefully, they enjoy and benefit from the experience.

Why is it that so many parents complain bitterly of the interfering, undermining effect of grandparental influence? I have never yet met a grandparent who would, in any way, wish to hurt their grandchild. So why the conflict?

Grandparents forget the enormous struggle they went through to create boundaries and a disciplinary framework for their children. Increasingly these days, even the routine of regular mealtimes is beginning to drift, and parents are struggling to re-establish these vital family forums.

Bedtime is often a matter of considerable squabbling and irritation, with tired children and even more tired parents. The same can be said for school attendance, homework disciplines, and general domestic behaviour.

We then face the thorny issues of pocket money, sweets and drinks, exactly what is and is not allowed and what degree of risk taking is a parent prepared to allow?

Darren

Darren's parents only allowed him out on Saturday nights, and at fourteen, they felt he should be back by ten o'clock. He normally stayed every six or eight weeks with his grandparents who knew the rules for a weekend. Shortly before Christmas, he persuaded them, quite against the wishes of his parents, to allow him to go out on two consecutive nights, with no curfew at all. On the second night, he was brought home drunk by the Police, and his parents subsequently found a small amount of marijuana in his jacket pocket. He has been given a warning by the Police and no further action will be taken.

His parents are, understandably, furious. They feel let down by the grandparents. If the grandparents felt unable to control Darren, they should have said so, and stopped his weekend visits until such time as he could prove that he could be trusted.

THE FAMILY 'TEAM'

It is essential that the extended family is seen as part of 'the team' whose responsibility is the life and welfare of the child. Rules need to be agreed and observed by all who have any interest in the child's management. It is very unkind to the child to rock their security by constantly moving the behavioural goalposts. It can also be a real danger for the grandparent. It can breed an attitude of "what can I get away with". Grandparents would never wish to be seen as 'Patsies', always giving way when pushed. While they should acknowledge the parental rules, they may also wish to impose a few of their own. This needs to be understood quite clearly by the child.

I have a particular clinical concern with ADD, and its management.

Simon – Attention Deficit Disorder (ADD)

Simon's ADD has been managed by controlling his diet, and he is now not allowed to eat chocolate, drink Coca Cola, or fresh orange juice. There is no doubt that all three exacerbate his ADD significantly, and at ten years of age, it makes him almost impossible to manage. His parents wondered for some weeks why Mondays were often such appalling days. It emerged that Sundays were often spent with his grandparents, who thought that his parents and the psychologist were being mean and 'punishing' him in some way, by denying him his Coca Cola and chocolate. With a conspiratorial whisper, they passed chocolate to him quietly during the day and even left some in his pocket for the return journey home!

David – Attention Deficit with Hyperactivity Disorder (ADHD)

David's ADHD was so severe, that the paediatrician prescribed Ritalin. His grandparents did not approve, but neither did they fully understand the need for medication. They did not discuss the issue with the boy's parents, let alone the doctor. They simply refused to give him his medication whenever he visited them. Matters came to a head when his parents went away on business for a fortnight, during which time he lived with his grandparents. His ADHD came back in florid form in school, almost leading to his expulsion.

It is vital that grandparents or other relatives do not make unilateral decisions about the needs of the children, without close discussion with the parents.

Grandparents have a marvellous, warm, supportive role to play with grandchildren, reinforcing their successes, encouraging their development, often an influence that leaves a profound effect on young people much later in their development. Furthermore, these days, many parents are busy, and the respite that grandparents are able to give, by sharing time with their grandchildren, can be a huge support.

We must all remember the vital need for communication. Grandparents need, and usually want to be, part of 'the team' bringing up the child. They must be seen in this role, but must know exactly what the rules are. If there is an element with which they do not agree, this should be discussed. Sometimes, boundaries can be made flexible, with the full knowledge of the parents. This is particularly true of bedtimes, and pocket money, especially at weekends and holiday time. Life can be generous and a little easier at these times with grandparents, but they must maintain the parents' standards and be proud they are a part of the team. They are in 'loco parentis', but must not undermine parents and leave them to 'unpick' the resulting chaos.

10

The Travelling Parent

Being a travelling or occasionally absentee parent implies stresses for both partners, and constantly varying emotional dynamics for the children. It is easy for a father to arrive home after a period away, only to insist on changing the ground-rules that his wife has struggled for so long to establish. The undermining of authority and management can be distressing, not to mention a source of manipulative behaviour for any family.

Brad

A parent who happens to be a Member of Parliament is never an easy balance to strike. In our culture it is particularly difficult for a mother who is in politics. We worked in recent times with a relatively new Member of Parliament, whose husband is a solicitor. She tends to be away for varying periods, often a week or ten days at a time, and her husband has never been a very effective father figure. Fortunately, the two older children are now young adults, in careers of their own, but the remaining son, Brad, at seventeen, is becoming increasingly resentful and angry. His parents argue, in an attempt to self justify, "at seventeen he is quite old enough to look after himself, particularly with the support of an au pair!" However, he resents this young woman, not much older than himself, apparently having disciplinary control over him, which he completely rejects.

Youngsters have needs, and we fail to meet them at our peril. We are struggling to find a 'deal' which will allow Brad's mother and father to see that their fundamental parenting role is fulfilled, before Brad loses his way entirely. The pillars of Brad's identity are rocking precariously. Brad saw a direct conflict in the 'need' for an au pair, but where were his so-called 'caring parents'?

Val

Val has an even more difficult problem to face, with a father who is a travelling salesman and a mother who works in a pub from 5.30 most evenings. She lets herself in with a latchkey, dumps her schoolbooks, and then disappears onto the streets with her friends. Parenting roles in this family are not being fulfilled, nor does there seem to be any intention of doing so. Val will become further remote from this family unless the couple concerned are prepared to accept that they have a parenting function, and that problems will inevitably follow their failure to acknowledge this.

David

David, who was only five, was the only child of an army Captain and his wife. David's father had spent a great deal of time away from home, and was previously in Northern Ireland. He was away from home for many weeks, and even months, at a time. He arrived home on leave, delighted to see his wife and small boy, but tense and rather tired. When I spoke to him, he was distressed that his arrival always began a spate of bed-wetting and tantrums in his boy. "I look forward to seeing him. Why does this happen every time?" He asked. We looked more closely and found that, hardly surprisingly, David had become very used to having his mother all to himself, resented the 'intruder' and was jealous of the time that now had to be shared. It took rather longer to unearth the fact that David's father was almost as jealous. He had little experience of small children, was fond of his wife, and was irked by the amount of time that she had to spend with an increasingly difficult little boy. This made him irritable, and arbitrary in the way he managed the child.

His mother was now busier and David was no longer having his evening story, neither was his mother sitting on the sofa with her arm around him, watching TV in the evenings. She commented, "But it has all been explained to him". The message David had heard was very clear – it's your father's fault! His mother was now out in the evenings on a regular basis, and he was having to come to terms with baby-sitters. David was particularly irritated by a change in the mealtime regime. His mother usually allowed him to leave the table as soon as he had finished, but his father insisted on him sitting right through the meal, including the parental coffee. He was bored, irritable, and he usually ruined the meals. Curiously, his father had doubled his pocket money, but rather than being pleased, David saw through the attempt to buy him off.

We established a clear 'management contract' agreed by both parents, to cover the times when David was on his own with his mother, and when the family were together. David began to feel less left out and the tantrums diminished as a result.

In essence, children need to feel that they are part of the team and that each member cares for the other, and above all, that the adult members of the team are able to offer support and care, as well as rescuing them in a crisis.

However, there are various classical stumbling blocks during each day. Meal times are a classical time of childish manipulation, so keep them consistent. What is your attitude to TV watching, GameBoy, and all the other diversions? Do you allow them? If so, when and for how long. Bedtime – if it is 8.30, reading and lights out at 9.00, then that is the deal. It is fruitless if a parent has returned from a long trip and now says, "Oh, why rush them off to bed. Let them stay up and watch telly". Pocket money – when do they get it, how much should it be, how do they spend it and what do they spend it on? Personal hygiene – hairstyles, especially long hair in boys, makeup for girls, jewellery, are all bones of contention which can easily become unnecessary emotional battlefields. How do you respond to disobedience, lying, stealing, and even more important, challenging and rude behaviour?

I would suggest that the family team resolve exactly how each of these will be dealt with. Management should be consistent, whether the parents are together or there are periods of separation. It is difficult for children if they can get away with behaviour with one parent, only to find that the other objects. Parents who are periodically separated must forge a very clear contract, that ensures the children feel that they have a unanimity of support and can trust and rely on those looking after them.

Remember that crises will occur when you are away from home. Your partner must deal with them as best as they can, and you must support their best efforts when you return, and not simply criticise. Above all, do not change the rules when you return. Support each other – do not undermine. Do not push the children out when you come home. Deliberately create a 'window of time' in which your children can share you. You do not want them resenting you every time you come home, because you marginalise them.

While you are away, remember the immense value of phone calls to the kids, e-mail messages, post cards. It is an assurance that you love and care for them, even when you are away from home.

11

Passive Smoking

We have been aware of the serious risks involved in addictive nicotine use/abuse for many years. The unfair impact of passive smoking is a more recent issue. Why should those who choose not to smoke be endangered by others? There is increasing evidence that constant exposure to second hand smoke can be damaging, let alone unpleasant.

Sam

> A delightful mother, whose children I had seen clinically over the years, wrote that she was finding herself cast in the role of arch hypocrite. A gregarious, very socially busy woman, she had begun smoking as a teenager and now smoked at least forty a day. She was a confirmed addict to nicotine and had tried a dozen times to stop, but seldom survived the very early stages of withdrawal. She found a part-finished packet of cigarettes in her sixteen-year-old daughter, Sam's, bedside table. Sam was only too ready to admit that she smoked socially, but was proud of the fact that she never brought them to school!

Sam's mother and I sat down and shared a strategy discussion, much of which she would attempt to reconstruct with her daughter. She accepted that her husband used to smoke and had given up, but this was largely because it was affecting his competitive squash. Smoking was affecting his breathing and he was not going to be able to compete in the top flight if he continued.

The evidence against smoking is now beyond dispute, especially the link with lung conditions, but it extends far further than this. Furthermore, there is increasing evidence of damage caused by passive smoking. Much of the harm can, unfortunately, be passed on to innocent bystanders caught in the 'waft' of stale smoke.

This forced Sam's mother to look at her youngest child, David, now five, who was very asthmatic, particularly bad at the change of seasons in the autumn and spring. There is no doubt that her cigarette smoke made him much worse. Indeed, he could not remain in the room if anyone was smoking. An extraordinarily dangerous environment for an already vulnerable five-year-old boy.

Sue

Sam's thirteen-year-old sister, Sue, a non-smoker, was upset when her very first boyfriend complained that her clothes always seemed to smell of stale smoke. This was particularly true in the wintertime when the stench 'clung' to the heavier materials used in overcoats, jackets, etc. Sue felt that he was talking about her personal hygiene and was very upset, especially when she realised it was not her, but the fault of those who said they loved her!

It very soon became apparent that Sue's mother was vulnerable and that the only possible chance of success was to have an 'adult/adult' dialogue with her daughter. When her mother began discussing the issue with Sam, her daughter admitted that it had been far from a joke when her young man had complained that her breath smelt and that 'snogging' was rather like kissing a wet ashtray! The pros, cons and vulnerabilities were discussed, leaving Sam to make her own judgement. 'Nagging' was certainly not going to work. Sam began to accept that her mother was now addicted and had tried many times to give up, was unable to but very much wished that she could.

They discussed the social circumstances in which her mother's smoking had begun. She admitted that in her early teens it had been an attempt to look more 'grown up'. To look 'cool'. I suggested that Sam, on her way to school, should look at the teenagers puffing away on their cigarettes standing on the railway platform. Do they look grown up, or do they look rather ridiculous, aping something they simply are not?

Her mother commented that cigarettes had helped her to relax, especially if she went to a pub with friends, over coffee at the end of meals, or sitting at home watching TV. Cigarettes were socially a useful support. However, it was not long before she only felt relaxed if she was smoking. Twitchy edginess forced the nicotine desire upon her.

She made a domestic compromise. The sitting room and upstairs in the bedrooms, bathroom, etc, were all to remain cigarette free. I was still concerned about the kitchen where the entire family gathered for breakfast, and she eventually agreed that there would be no smoking until everybody had left for work or school, and she put in an extractor fan. Not a total success, but enough to convince Sam that her mother was in earnest.

Bruce

Seventeen-year-old Bruce stumbled into a very unexpected dilemma. His boarding school would allow beer and cider in the upper sixth common room, and cigarette smoking with parental consent. His father, a rational, intelligent parent, himself a smoker, sat him down and asked him "Why do you want to? What pressures are making you feel that you must? Are you prepared to be a social puppet, manipulated by your friends?"

Bruce was not prepared to allow this to pass so easily – "What about you? What sort of example do you think you set?" The issue of 'passive' smoking arose. Bruce commented "You're abusing the rest of the family and our friends by smoking and are a hopeless example to us all. Do you honestly not mind injuring us?" His father's chest had been giving him trouble for some time. "What happens if you die? Where does that leave us?" asked Bruce. His parents had argued "It's too late for us, but not for you". Bruce felt that this simply would not do – far too feeble.

Bruce agreed that he would drop his request for a letter to the school allowing him to smoke, and agreed never to start, if they would give up.

His parents had to agree the argument against passive smoking. They had no choice if the dialogue with an intelligent boy was to have any substance. They agreed quickly to no further smoking in rooms that were jointly used. In fact, they designated a little back study as a 'smokers room' where they could retreat with a newspaper, smoke, watch TV, listen to music, and so forth. Then it was up to others to join them if they wished. The room rapidly became revoltingly smelly, and the whole situation untenable.

On his next visit home, Bruce was aware that his parents were doing their level best to stick to their smoking room, but were often far from successful. There was clear evidence of cigarette butts in an ashtray in the lavatory and, despite recent cleaning, the curtains in the living room smelt again.

Bruce confronted his parents with a straight choice. "Either your warnings to me are serious or they are not. If they are, are you prepared to make a major sacrifice to encourage me to stay away from what is obviously a dangerous habit? Let's see the colour of your love!"

Threatening, but horribly persuasive. His mother has given up and his father has agreed to smoke only when he is out of the house. Bruce has accepted this compromise, and is dealing perfectly happily with the social pressures in school, as he feels much stronger for having examined the dangers and asked for an example to be set at home. He is still critical of his father damaging his own health and hopes he will eventually influence him to stop.

When working teenagers choose to embark on an ill advised smoking career, but no other family members indulge, it is not unreasonable to ban smoking from the house. The passive smoking issue would inevitably affect the entire family – even the smell hanging in the curtains is thoroughly offensive if smoking is permitted anywhere in the house.

I wonder how often in our lives as parents we have to "clean our pot thoroughly before we can risk calling the kettle black!"

CONTACT

ASH
Smiking quitline: 0800 002200
(Mon–Fri 12 noon to 7pm)

Part 2

The Family as a Team and You are the Manager

12

Discipline – Spare the Rod

Fundamentally, life is a 'game' with complex rules. The bad tempered, injury prone, rugby match is often the one that is badly refereed. A lawless society is likely to be unhappy and insecure. The same is true of our children.

We must all know our boundaries. It is important that these boundaries are consistent. If a child can push a foot 'over the edge' one day and nobody notices, but the next day he is punished for precisely the same offence, this is not only unsettling but a very reasonable cause for grievance.

I remember a child I interviewed once surprising me by envying a neighbour's daughter who had been smacked for climbing a tree. "At least her Dad cares," she said!

As with the Law, it is the likelihood of being caught and the immediacy of retribution that tends to bring the benefits. This is what makes a combined, unified parental front very important.

Sanctions. Most children enjoy watching the television or playing with their computer. Once again, its removal for just a few, specified number of minutes, may well achieve a remarkable impact. Taking it away for the whole evening, or for days, is less effective. The child learns to cope without it and, above all, one of your key sanctions has been removed. Where there are other children in the family, sibling pressure will increase the value of this technique. Nobody likes having their favourite programme 'turned off' in the middle. Remember the child must have heard you and should be given two warnings before taking this step. They must learn that if a boundary is breached, a sanction will inevitably follow. Our aim is to throw the responsibility for the sanction firmly into the lap of the child. If 'A' happens, 'B' will be the response.

In the world of consistency, there are three techniques for the pre teenager that are easy and relatively painless to use. The first two are sanctions for dealing with behaviour that is frankly 'out of order', having warned the child a couple of times, but found no satisfactory response. The final one, and possibly the most valuable, is a behaviour modification programme to reinforce the positive.

Time out – if a child is being particularly difficult, rude, or non-compliant, it is important not to allow the behaviour to escalate to the point where we, as parents, also lose control, with

41

the obvious risk of physical violence. Indeed, 'that quiet voice that Dad only uses when he is angry' is the most effective of all. After the second, possibly even quieter warning, the child should be sent to their room for a maximum of three minutes. It is critical that the period of time is brief, so that life can return to normal as quickly as possible. It is not meant to be a punishment that hurts, but simply an assertion of authority, a right to control and a clear statement that a boundary has now been breached. We may not wish to be over controlling as individuals, but there is a responsibility with our children to establish boundaries, however wide, and see that they are adhered to. With 'time out' the conflict has ended before there is a crisis, the child has time to reconsider and then return to the family, above all, without any discussion or recrimination.

Two strategies to watch for:

- The bright child may well be halfway up the stairs before even being told to go to their bedroom – "Oh, I was going anyway". The second cunning manoeuvre is to simply refuse to come out of the room at the end of the three minutes. It is vital to avoid discussion. Do not perch on the top stair, trying to persuade the child that it is now appropriate to return to the family. This simply adds attention-seeking fuel to the fire.

- If they do not want to come out, leave them there until they are happy to join the family. This technique is quick and very effective.

- The point will often be reached when the second warning, in the lowered voice, possibly with a raised finger, will be enough to remind the child that they are likely to be removed from the family for a few minutes. This may well be sufficient.

- If 'games playing' starts, it is a subtle, subconscious admission by the child that your technique is working. They are trying to manoeuvre you out of using it! Keep at it! If, for example, they imply that they want to be in their room anyway – don't be fooled.

Reinforcement. Possibly the most effective way of dealing with discipline is to reinforce the positive. I would suggest deciding on a weekly amount of pocket money and then dividing it into nightly allotments. Establish a jam jar at the child's bedside and at bedtime the coin will 'clink' happily into the jar. This can, of course, also be used as a sanction, especially, for example, in the evening if homework has not been completed, or there is difficulty getting the child to go to bed.

However, the pocket money is basically a 'reinforcement' for a good day when all has gone well, and, once earned, cannot be taken away. Decide on a criterion level of savings that is agreed by all. This good, positive behaviour, will now justify an hour of the undivided time of one or other parent during which to visit the shops and spend the savings. I should emphasise – this is private, special, high quality time, not to be shared with anyone else. The value of the 'tokens' each evening assumes tremendous importance, but their target must be honestly met. This process is more effective if this is the only weekly source of pocket money. Remember, the 'special hour' only happens if it is truly merited.

13

Pocket Money

The issue of pocket money arises in most families, and I suppose it is fair to say that by ten or eleven years of age, most children in this country are given some form of pocket money. It is quite impossible to be specific about the amount of money that is appropriate for an individual child as so much depends on the circumstances of the family.

In essence, there are two phases in a child's development to which pocket money applies. In the early years, it is important that they should learn the value of money and that it is an important token in our culture to be exchanged for the goods that we want. Above all, they need to learn that there is a very clear limit to what they can afford and that, at times, they may even have to face the trauma of saving! It is never too early for a child to learn that money is not easily come by and needs a degree of care and judgement in its spending. It can be an invaluable vehicle for teaching children that if there is something they want that is beyond their means, they must look towards legitimate ways of boosting their funds. This may be waiting and saving, or asking for jobs around the house for which additional payments can be made.

In the teenage years, pocket money often moves closer to an allowance and the amount concerned usually increases significantly. At this point, it is vital that there are clear rules laid down in the family as to exactly what the young person is expected to use their money for. Does it include bus fares to school, school lunches, items of clothing, money to fund their social life, and so forth? The amount needs to be calculated with care, and with proper adult/adult discussion with the young person concerned, and only increased, possibly at birthdays or when the case for additional expenditure is well made. We all have to learn to live within our resources and adolescence is a very good training ground for exactly this.

The over materialistic child is not unusual, especially in this fashion accessory conscious world. Marketing in clothes shops is increasingly aimed at remarkably young children and even the cell phone has now become a young person's fashion accessory. There is often little regard for the item's true worth, or need, or even whether it is truly attractive. 'Keeping up with the Jones' now affects our ten year olds!

Sean

Sean, recently turned eleven, was referred to me for his objectionable, over demanding behaviour in school, and the difficulty his parents had in controlling

43

him. He would only co-operate around the house if he was paid for doing so. He even had to be given 10p to have a bath and go to bed!

However, we had to look further for a full explanation, as his behaviour had been similar long before he had discovered the latest childish craze. Prior to that, he had saved the money, and kept it clinking in a drawer in his bedroom, rather like a magpie. He was not attempting to exchange these 'tokens' for goods in any way, but feeling better for their very presence. For what was this neurotic behaviour compensating? After several sessions with Sean's parents, it gradually emerged that alcohol was playing far too great a part in the family life, which often led to noisy and sometimes violent rows late at night. To Sean's added confusion, by the time the alcohol wore off the following morning, his parents seemed to have forgotten the violence of only hours before. The acquisitive behaviour began to appear more clearly as the neurotic, insecure response of a frightened, lonely little boy. Sean's father is now a regular attender at AA, his mother is receiving counselling and Sean is gradually learning to trust the world around him.

With the over acquisitive child, it is important to ask why they want these glittering coins. They are not all like Sean.

Sharon and Steve

Sharon's case was very different – dramatically so. She was referred because she was mildly dyslexic. As a side issue, in discussion with her teachers and parents, it became evident that she was stealing regularly from her mother's handbag. She constantly moaned about not having enough pocket money, was caught stealing from her teacher's desk, and now she and her friend, Steve, were in trouble for bullying other children in the playground and extorting money from them. This behaviour was surprisingly out of character in many ways, and it was difficult to see exactly why they wanted all this money. They were neither hoarding it, nor did they seem to be any better off, in a material sense. It took the arrest of a seventeen-year-old boy for drug peddling, at the school gates, to unearth the truth. On one occasion, three months earlier, Steve had brought a very small amount of marijuana into the school and he and Sharon had been smoking it, nervously, behind the gym. This older boy had threatened to tell the Police that Steve was 'trafficking' in drugs, and that Sharon was also involved. They were having to pay their way on a weekly basis to keep this young man quiet. The arrest of the older boy, and Sharon and Steve's ready admission to the Police and to the school, cleared the air considerably.

We have to be very careful not to condemn 'money' out of hand, because it plays an essential part in our culture. As adults, it has to be earned, and our lifestyle depends on our success in doing so. Saving carefully for the future, whether through insurance or pocket money, is regarded as socially desirable. It is obviously not the money, but why and how it is being gathered and spent, that is the issue.

Finally, we need to look very carefully at our own values in life and, indeed, those of older children in the family. It is easy to be critical of an acquisitive child, only to find that the father's attitude is not far from that of Arthur Daley. Far too many adults equate the value of life around them, the pictures on the walls, meals, the car, even their home, against the price ticket associated with it. I heard parents talking in my waiting room the other day about the car a neighbour had bought, a rather lovely old sports car. When the father heard that it had only cost £9,500, his face dropped, and he commented, "Oh, well, I suppose he will be able to afford something better in the future". His fourteen-year-old son was appalled. He thought the sports car which was beautiful, had great 'class', and had survived nearly twenty years, still looking beautiful.

Children learn from us and much of what they learn is sound and helpful in their development. However, remember they are like sponges. Furthermore, they instinctively learn that behaviour parents feel is appropriate must be equally appropriate for them. Are we quite sure that we are not forever talking about our last 'deal' and the money we made, the price of the house next door, the better value holiday and, indeed, putting a price ticket on everything. Children will simply grow up doing the same.

Remember the value of the family as a team. Increasing pocket money as children grow older, is a useful part of the learning experience. For extra jobs around the house, a small payment is also perfectly justified. These should be tasks that would be undertaken by us, were it not for the help that the child is giving and, therefore, some small compensation is quite appropriate. However, if an evening meal is being prepared by the mother and the father is helping her or will later on help to wash up, there is no reason why one of the children should not lay the table, and the other one clear it, as part of the team working together. It would be quite inappropriate for either child to be paid. It is important that they grow up to realise that mutual support and caring is a vital part of the human experience and should not have a price label associated with it. Our children need to appreciate the subtle differences between unpaid 'team work', in which the whole family play a part, and additional pocket money earning tasks.

14

Expensive Football Strips

I have from time to time received letters of complaint from parents who were frustrated by the whinging, complaining behaviour of their sons who were keen football fans. They would buy new strips for them at Christmas time only to find that another would emerge in early May, and they were under continual pressure to find yet another £30.

Psychologically, 'club' membership is as much about acceptance by a group, as it is being involved in the actual activities of the club itself. Most of us need to feel that we belong.

John

John complained that he could not possibly go to a match dressed in the old strip, when those around him would have the new one – did they really want him to stop being a fan? Were they prepared to ruin the only thing that really mattered to him?

The pressures were enormous. Parents often find the implied 'tribalism' difficult to understand and are even made rather anxious by it.

Every team in the country, from the mighty to the least, would regard their fans as a crucial part of their performance. From the fans come the enthusiasm, the drive and the boost to their adrenaline that they need to perform at their best.

David

David, 13, is paraplegic and limited to a wheelchair. For him, becoming a football fan of his local team has been the making of him. The team shows a great interest in the boy and his disabilities. Indeed, he has been adopted as a team 'mascot'. For him, Saturdays during the winter months are very special. He struggles into his team's strip, and finds a place close to the pitch where he sits with considerable pride and watches his team play. For David, identifying with his team is therapeutically vital.

Damien

Damien, 12, who was possibly more typical, was failing in school and in constant trouble with both his teachers and, occasionally, the police. Then he found that he had a talent for football and now plays regularly on the school team. This new enthusiasm has encouraged him to identify with his local football team, and he was given the team strip for a Christmas present. He now feels a 'member' of a new group, all of whom share exactly the same enthusiasm. He has also learned to cope with the adult world, particularly on away matches when the fans travel by coach, youngsters and adults together.

The instinctive 'tribalism', innate in most of us, is fostered in a safe, harmless way. Fear of this tribalism is largely because we are not members ourselves and are therefore excluded. We must be careful not to exclude this type of group interaction purely because a tiny minority have misbehaved in the past. We all need to feel that we belong.

Diana

Diana was a 15 year old, who played football for her school, and found herself in considerable 'gender conflict' in her desire to become a fan of the local professional team. However, more and more girls and women are becoming supporters, as the football grounds become more fan friendly and safer places to visit. Diana has now become 'a member' and, like her brother, has been bought the strip. Unfortunately, in this family, there are now two children 'nagging' about the need to have the latest outfits. I suggested to the parents that they should look at what is involved. We rang up a couple of football clubs and discovered a similar pattern. Both clubs told us that they change their home and away strips every two years, although they alternate.

Hence, the reality of "constant changes of strip" is not entirely borne out. However, careful purchasing is crucial if we are to avoid unnecessary spending.

Parents need to know that the home and away strip will change every two years and, therefore, the expense will be limited to a home strip one year and an away strip the next. Each shirt should then be worn for virtually two years, and most children have grown so much in that time that they need a larger size.

We need to organise appropriate outfits for the autumn, as it is most unlikely to change during that season. Only buy mid season if there are at least eighteen months or so still to run before the strip is renewed. Children should be persuaded to wait so that they are properly equipped for the beginning of the next season, with two years to run on the strip.

Shane

Shane, 15, posed a particularly awkward problem. He was becoming difficult and very upset at not being allowed the new strip because it was to change in a few weeks time, at the beginning of May. He had found friends extremely difficult to make and membership of this supporters group had given him his first inroads into effective social integration. For this boy, the issue of fan membership was a crucial part of his personality development, especially at 15 years of age, which tends to be a challenging time in any event.

Shane was eventually persuaded to be more mature in his discussion about his new strip. He explained that there was a special Cup match that he wanted to go to, and could not join the group unless he had the proper strip. In this special instance his parents gave Shane a series of jobs to complete around the house to allow him to buy the strip for himself. It was vital in Shane's case that the whole discussion was held at an adult/adult level, and not at a whinging, manipulative child and a beleaguered parent level. Every time we give way to manipulative, nagging behaviour, we reinforce the possibility that it will occur again.

I am constantly advising young people about group activities where there is a specific aim involved. The Boy Scouts, local drama groups and, of course, being a fan of a local football club, are all possibilities. The key is that there is an instant dialogue available as every single member shares a common interest.

Establish dates in the diary when new strips will be issued

15

Christmas, and Surviving It

Christmas tends to have an expensive and sometimes emotional build-up. It should be a time of contented sharing, especially of that precious commodity – time. A predictable family ritual. Forward planning helps a great deal.

There is much that we can do to pre-empt unnecessary difficulties at Christmas. Youngsters love the day to be a predictable ritual and not a rather chaotic shambles. They feel so much safer if the routine is adhered to.

Why not begin your Christmas with a proper family meal around the table on Christmas Eve. Remember, quite apart from the presents, it is 'quality time' together that is so precious. The most relaxed Christmases are usually the well planned ones. Time together is the true Christmas gift.

Difficult though it may be, I feel that the issuing of Christmas presents on Christmas Day should be a relatively measured affair, giving each member of the family a turn and allowing each recipient to express their pleasure and surprise at what they have been given. There is nothing more shattering than watching a child shredding endless Christmas paper, rejecting present after present without even acknowledging who they were from. Too many children are becoming spoilt and over materialistic, and are losing some of the real human values in life.

Michael

> Michael, aged 11, was given an electronic game but could not make it work in the first two minutes. It was smashed by lunchtime. Present opening in this family had been a 'feeding frenzy' of Christmas paper, little regard for the giver and petulant frustration from Michael. He grumbled that the game was not quite the one he had wanted.

All this could have been prevented had his parents been prepared to become involved in the magic of Christmas Day, and helped Michael enjoy his game. Spare long life batteries would have helped! There is nothing more infuriating than a new game that will not work because the maker did not provide batteries.

The Christmas meal is often the focal point of the day. Be sure that everyone has a role to play. They can tidy up the wrapping paper, lay the table, help peel potatoes, and so forth. It is important that each team member is allocated a specific job, well before the event. The feeling of involvement is good for everyone, but there is no reason why one family member should provide for all the others. Monitor their jobs and be proud of what they have achieved. Make it quite clear that it would have been impossible to have a successful Christmas meal without their input.

Diet can have a devastating effect on a child's activity level, but with the excitement of Christmas, it can make them almost unmanageable. The key elements to avoid are the fizzy drinks (especially the colas), chocolate, flavoured crisps and fresh orange juice. Excessive chocolate not only makes some children over-active, but can make them sick and unable to face their Christmas meal!

Christmas is a time for everyone and not just the children so a couple of beers or glasses of wine is a perfectly normal part of the proceedings. Bear the repercussions of drinking too much in mind. You may become tired and sleepy. Your fuse may shorten and you may find the frustration of over-excited kids increasingly difficult to tolerate.

Keep one or two presents for each member of the family until the evening. Then there will be more excitement still to come and you will not be faced with a welter of anticlimax too early in the day! Leave the presents prominently displayed so that the family remains constantly aware of their presence.

The folklore of Santa Claus has given many children great delight. Try to persuade the older children that they have had their time when life was fun and full of magic – don't spoil it for the others.

Major Christmas presents have often taken much thought and expense in the buying, and even the wrapping and labelling. It is probably best that these are clearly identified as demonstrations of thought and love, quite separate from the magic of Santa. After all, how can a child thank a parent with an enthusiastic hug if they are convinced that the 'giver' has flown off on his rounds!

In essence, our two major commitments for a successful day are a willingness to give a great deal of our time to the children, and thorough pre-planning.

- Encourage turn taking in gift opening.

- Have some degree of organisation associated with present time

- Time your Christmas meal and alcohol consumption so that you control your own mood – don't always blame the kids.

- Share the Christmas chores.

- Keep a few presents for later in the day

- Plan to fill the quieter moments in the day.

WHEN CHRISTMAS GIFTS BECOME A NIGHTMARE

"How can I tell my 12-year-old daughter that she is not going to get a mountain bike for Christmas? She tells me her friends all have one, and feels that she is now responsible enough to have her own bike."

First and foremost, our philosophy with children should reflect the essential nature of the family of which they are a part. I fully appreciate the immensity of peer group pressure, but it is of tremendous importance that children, from an early age, realise that they are part of a 'team' that has its own norms, its own strengths and maybe its own vulnerabilities. Most children's parents have limited financial resources. The "Oh, but my friend has got one" line must, therefore, be rejected out of hand. What is possible within your team? Once the child is beginning to look at their own family and its resources, the whole discussion becomes rather more meaningful.

As Christmas becomes increasingly commercialised it is important to reintroduce children to the human interaction – the giving and receiving of gifts. It is fundamentally a way of saying: "I love you; I have thought about you and I feel you might like what I have bought for you." It is equally important, when someone has taken so much trouble, that we show appropriate pleasure in receiving the gift.

David

David's father had backed himself into a corner. His 18-year-old son had passed his driving test in May and had hinted that he would like his own car – not unnaturally. He had then suggested that maybe he could ask for this as a Christmas present. His Father had commented, "Oh, we'll have to wait and see, won't we?"

Be careful of anything that even implies a promise if you are not able to fulfil it. Never allow vague, half promises to grow in the mind of the youngster.

David's father did not have the money to buy a worthwhile car for his son and his son was in no position to run it, insure it, or tax it. However, the family was now in uproar because David was claiming that his Father had 'promised' him his car and was letting him down.

A deal was eventually reached between David and his father. If David saved £250 from his weekend job, his father would put the rest of the money towards a cheap second hand car and would help to insure and tax it for the first year, but his son would have to run it thereafter. At least a package had been worked out, but the situation should never have reached that point.

- It is important for all the family to remember they are part of a team. Each member has their rights to the available budget but it is not a bottomless pit and needs to be fairly apportioned. Post Christmas financial hardship can unbalance the entire team and it is particularly unfair if an extravagant gift for one family member has culminated in this state of affairs.

- Children are entitled to "chance their arm" and ask for expensive gifts – they may be lucky. Vitally, if the answer is to be 'no', it must be said immediately and with the clear agreement of both parents. Never allow a wedge to be driven between parents.

- Establish a clear budget limit. If £25 is available for each of your children's Christmas gifts, then this is clearly the budget limit within which they must make their choices. It makes it so much easier to say no without any fear of being unkind or unfair, if one family member has suggested wildly exceeding the budget limit. It would be different if a child had earned £25 for themselves in the weeks coming up to Christmas and then asks for a more expensive gift, on the grounds that they will contribute half. This type of commitment by a child is greatly to be encouraged.

- Beware the 'guilt trip'. It is natural for children to use all their guile's to persuade us to buy way beyond our resources. There is often an implication of withdrawal of their love if we fail to oblige, or that we are singling them out for particularly unfair treatment, or making them look ridiculous in front of their friends. Alternatively, we may be accused of being 'lousy' parents. The ball bounces back into the youngster's court if a budget limit that has been clearly established is now being breached.

The "I wanna ..." philosophy seems to be becoming increasingly prevalent. Let's get back to friendship, fun and the pleasure of giving and receiving at Christmas and move away from materialism.

KIDS BORED AFTER CHRISTMAS

There is much 'hype' leading up to Christmas, tremendous over-excitement, a glut of gifts and the inevitable anticlimax.

Jevon

"I suppose we will be on our own again" –– "I'm fed up" – "Even school is better than this!" said twelve-year-old Jevon, as early as Boxing Day. Unfortunately, his parents were going out to lunch with friends and Jevon was left behind with his older sister to cater for themselves. The unspoken assumption of 'togetherness' over Christmas had been shattered.

Our primary aim at Christmas should be to enjoy each other's company. It is important to remember that the essential quality of Christmas is the giving of our undivided time, as much as it is the presents. The subtle approach in this post-Christmas period needs to be an amalgam of involvement and encouraging self-sufficiency in the children. Make them think for them-selves and, above all, think of others, especially the old and the lonely.

This is also a crucial time to keep the ritual of the family meal, providing a valuable plat-form for discussing plans for the following day.

Janice

Janice, 12, asked for a special meal as her birthday happened to fall on the 28th of December. This led the family to decide that each day they would plan the meal for the following day and each member would choose in turn, and help with the buying of the ingredients and the preparation of the meal. If they cooked, they did not have to wash up, but could simply sit and enjoy themselves, while the rest of the family did the clearing away.

Already, meal times in this 'down period' after Christmas were beginning to have an increasing value for the entire family.

Always try to round the day off with an activity in which the whole family can be involved. Don't necessarily struggle with new games – it is often far easier to dive headlong into the old familiar Monopoly or card games. It is also time to be particularly selective about the television. Choose a catalogue of programmes or suitable videos and encourage everyone to restrict excessive TV watching. While you have the time, before the year begins to gather pace, encourage self-sufficiency and family interaction rather than too much staring at a television screen.

16

The Very Bright Younger Sibling

Rhonda and Jamie

Rhonda, just 8, was a delightful girl with fair hair and sparkling blue eyes. When I met her, she was able to conduct an almost adult conversation. She was in the school choir, played a major part in the school play, and felt that the third Harry Potter book was even better than the first! Jamie, who was three years older, was probably equally bright, but dyslexic. He was a solitary boy, whose reading was still far from age appropriate. Jamie tended to sit quietly for hours, working with his Lego. For Jamie, there were many areas of conflict. When he was involved with his homework he found his bright sister giving him advice and helping him to read questions that he had not fully understood. He welcomed the help but then felt humiliated. Recently, he had been reading to his mother in the evening, when Rhonda looked up and congratulated him for reading so well and then returned to her Harry Potter book. Even at meal times, Rhonda seemed to be linguistically 'a yard faster'. Jamie was given a new game for Christmas, which Rhonda won on three out of the four occasions and Jamie stormed off to his bedroom in a tantrum. He returned from his 'mood' to find his grandparents in the sitting room talking to Rhonda and admiring the work that she had brought home at the end of term. They hardly noticed his return.

This is not an unfamiliar dilemma, but unfortunately, it was driving Jamie further into a hole and making him less willing to take risks. Despite extensive remedial support, his progress was slowing down. The children's parents were searching for a strategy to deal with Jamie's dilemma. Ironically, we decided to look first at Rhonda and her strengths, interests and needs. I felt that it was very important to establish a profile of Rhonda's needs, to be absolutely sure that when we came to consider Jamie, we were not putting him into competition with his able sister. Equally, in our desire to help Jamie, we did not want to find ourselves compromising Rhonda.

We went on to consider 'multiple intelligences'. Our culture conditions us to admire certain types of ability, with little or no regard for skills that fall outside this framework. Academic intelligence seems to be of paramount importance. However, Jamie mentioned on his first visit that he was learning to play the viola. He was invited to bring his instrument on the next visit. This boy turned his viola into a 'magical' instrument as he flooded the office with his music.

This brought us to search for even more areas of endeavour in which Jamie could shine. He was showing considerable talent for football but, sadly, his remedial lessons often coincided with his games periods in school. Our first step was to change this pattern and ensure that his football was encouraged. His father started taking him to support the local club; he was bought new boots, and a team strip – which he virtually slept in!

Don and Julie

We had a similar experience with Don whose IQ was only 70*, in a school for the moderately learning disabled, who struggled to compete with his very able sister Julie. He had a fascination with fishing and wildlife in general. He even learned to tie his own trout flies, but these activities were not regarded as important as he grew older. To encourage his talent, his family framed versions of his colourful flies and they were used extensively as Christmas presents. Don went on to learn more about wildlife and became a local reference on the subject. He still has a reading age of only 9!

Our first practical exercise in managing this painful dilemma of a balance between children of different abilities was to look very carefully at time allocation. The able are inclined to be very demanding, understandably so. Their interests are many. However, your time is a major token of your love and concern for your children. An imbalance in the allocation of time is a silent comment that is hard to avoid. Once you have begun to 'carve out a place in the sun' for the less able member of the family, it will be easier to see where appropriate investment of time can be made to create this balance.

Jack

Jack, 13, developing his interest in football, found his father on the touchline with a video camera, producing edited close-ups of his son tackling, dribbling and, above all, scoring an all-important goal. This allowed multiple watching at home and easy reinforcement of the family's interest and concern for Jack's sport.

Do not disguise problems. They are part of family life and their management is a demonstration of your care and concern.

A father rang me to tell me that their very able son wanted to join the drama group which was his older sister's only source of recognition. We looked together at priorities. There are times when this 'precious place in the sun' has to be protected and this was one of them. We concluded that on no account should the gifted son be allowed to impose himself on that particular drama group. They found another group for him to join, but he had, by then, completely lost interest! The truth was that he simply wanted to compete with his sister and show her, once again, that he could dominate. It was this rather destructive form of competition that we needed to avoid.

---

*The average IQ is 100, and the 'average range' 85–115.

In essence, we each have our place and time. For many of us, we need to break away from traditional, and cultural expectations as the only criterion by which we judge success. We all need to find a corner of life where we can enrich ourselves and even bring a little enrichment to those around us.

CONTACTS

BRITISH MENSA LTD (JUNIOR BRANCH)
Tel: 01902 772771

BRUNEL ABLE CHILDREN'S EDUCATION CENTRE (BACE)
Tel: 020 8891 0121 ext 2415

NATIONAL ACADEMY FOR GIFTED AND TALENTED YOUTH
Warwick University
Tel: 024 7657 4213

NATIONAL ASSOCIATION FOR ABLE CHILDREN IN EDUCATION NACE)
Tel: 01865 145657

NATIONAL ASSOCIATION FOR GIFTED CHILDREN (NAGC)
Tel: 01908 673677

SUPPORT SOCIETY FOR CHILDREN OF HIGHER INTELLIGENCE (CHI)
Tel: 01386 881 938

17

A Place in the Sun for Each Twin

Since Cane and Abel, the issue of 'twinship' has raised a series of thorny issues. The bond between twins can range from hatred to a profound, lifelong devotion. They are two individuals, born to the same parents, who will endlessly compete for the same attention. There are two types of twin. Non-identical twins are no more alike than any other siblings in the same family. Identical twins share the same genes and are frequently extraordinarily alike.

The twin sister of a child I was working with had just died, and the identical twin was devastated. At 18 years of age, she was unable to cope without the intensity of the relationship and support that they shared. The twins had grown up almost as one. They shared everything together and did not allow themselves to be influenced by the outside world. They seldom made other relationships of any standing and, indeed, competing relationships had caused immense conflict on the rare occasions when they had occurred.

Nevertheless, twins can share considerable advantages. Language development is often quicker and easier for twins than single children, as they stimulate one another. They also learn about co-operative play more easily than their peers, and often develop to a point where they have less and less need of other children and survive quite happily in their own cocoon. This is particularly true of identical twins. There are implicit strengths, but dangers in these circumstances. By the way, do not be concerned by the strange private language twins often invent. This stage passes.

Friends and relatives tend to be much attracted by the 'twinship'. They often talk about the children as 'the twins'. In the rushed world of managing the lives of small children, it is often easier to buy everything in pairs, so that the twins look identical and the 'twinship' in itself becomes reinforcing. Often the children have an increasing desire to continue to look alike.

I have found clinically that there is often a tendency for one twin to be more dominant than the other. One will often talk for both and be more successful and confident in class, leaving the second twin languishing in the shadows.

I remember years ago suggesting that identical twin girls of 11 should be placed in separate classes and treated differently. Within four months, their mother was extremely concerned because the dominant twin had become less sure of herself, and the less dominant one had emerged with improving language skills, greater self confidence and was now insisting on her own 'place in the sun'. In the short term, the other twin was much shaken by the slipping of her dominance. Fortunately, matters settled within another six months or so, and both children began to develop as happy individuals and yet shared a great deal of contented time together.

I feel, philosophically, that each of us has just one life and, if we are lucky, it presents us with an exciting variety of options. It is a great shame if 'twinship' closes down some of these possibilities. Treat twins as different human beings, with their own lives to make. This is particularly true for identical twins. Often people cannot distinguish one from the other. Avoid dressing them identically. Look at the possibility of slightly different hairstyles, so that they develop their own individuality. At birthday and Christmas give them different presents, exactly as you would the other children. Try to develop personality characteristics, needs and interests in each that are singular to that child. For example, when one twin's pair of shoes wear out, replace them. This does not mean the other twin has to be provided likewise, until their need arises. There may well be an opportunity for one to join the Scouts, or take part in a Judo club and the other may not wish to do so, and this is much to be encouraged.

There are one or two balances that one must strike, however. For example, bicycles allow for a great deal of mobility for children to visit friends, in parks, and so forth. Hence, it probably makes sense for both twins to be given a bike at the same time. This enables them to move on to the next stage of developing independence.

Parents and schools need to be particularly sensitive with twins. I was talking to a ten-year-old boy who was at the same school as his twin brother, but in a different class. His brother had been invited to a party and he had not. He was heartbroken. Twins are usually much closer than normal siblings and this separation hurt. However, it is an essential part of life; they have to learn to be different and to have their own strengths and weaknesses, but on occasions like this, it is well worth contriving a treat for the twin who is not going to the birthday party, so that they feel that there is at least a fair balance. It is a mistake to contrive a second invitation, creating a climate of manipulation.

Quality time, spent individually with one or other parent is never easy in any family, and particularly difficult with twins, when mealtimes, bedtimes, and so forth, are identical. However, even 30 minutes per week with a parent, as a regular pattern can be immensely valuable in helping to develop individuality. Especially with twins, a father's role becomes extremely important, as it is a particular burden for a mother, who has little time and whose energies will, understandably, flag. Quite apart from helping in general, quality time with the twins can be worthwhile, and rewarding for the father.

So to the thorny issue of school. It is easy for the dominant twin to reign supreme if a classroom is shared. Certainly, they need to sit well apart, so possible invidious comparison does not take place. However, it is far better if they can be put in parallel classes. In this way, their education is separate, and individual, but they can still play together at lunchtimes.

It is important to start, from the very first day, treating twins as separate individuals, with their own characteristics and each with their own needs. This does not mean disregarding the originality of their rather special kinship, but allowing them to develop together when they wish to do so, while allowing for individuality where happily appropriate.

18

Drugs – Understanding and Management

I feel sure that if we were to pinpoint the issue that perplexes parents most with children between ten and eighteen years of age, it would be the problem of drugs. We know the damage addiction to hard drugs can cause: the gradual destruction of life, the violence, degradation, unhappiness, criminal implications for the whole family, lost hours of work, and education. Once our children have gained their social freedom by their mid-teens, parents fret they may be introduced to drugs and have their lives shortly reduced to tatters.

We can only help our children if our response is balanced and knowledgeable. Evidence also suggests that the happier relationships are at home, the greater the degree of understanding between children and their parents. The warmth and friendship that exists is the greatest possible protection against drug abuse. So often the use of drugs revolves around an amalgam of retreat and defiance. Anger, ignorance and hysterics get us nowhere, and simply expose the vulnerability of our argument all too quickly. Young people often know a great deal more about the subject than we do.

It is important to begin the discussion of drugs, their use and abuse, before children reach the end of their primary school years. Evidence suggests that the vast majority of children's first drug experiences come through a friend and not through a pusher or dealer at the school gate, as we all imagine.

However, this discussion cannot begin sensibly unless we understand our subject. We cannot talk about drugs without including nicotine and alcohol, both drugs with proven dangers. More working hours are lost per year through alcohol abuse than any other single substance. Alcohol is often in the background of motor accidents, domestic violence, sexual abuse and social inadequacy.

However, these are legal drugs and a part of our society, but it is vital that children are aware of the risks nevertheless. It is ludicrous to attempt to discuss the misuse of marijuana, for example, while embarking on our fourth pint of beer. 'Abuse' refers to the misuse of legal substances or any use whatever of illegal substances. This helps us differentiate between illegal drugs, and alcohol and tobacco.

By the time children are first exposed to possible drug abuse, they need to know exactly what their parents' attitude is, and what the response to abuse would be. There is no reason why families with teenage children should not have an instant home drug test kit available, and the circumstance in which it might be used made clear to all. Not only is this a useful way of assessing whether abuse has occurred, but several young people have commented to me that it helps them say no if there is a real chance of being caught when they return home. "Oh, my Dad's got one of those kits – he'll kill me." As is true of all criminal activity, the likelihood of being caught is the greatest possible deterrent.

DRUGS OF ABUSE

We are finding that many pre-teens have their first foray into the misuse of drugs via alcohol and nicotine. From there, it is a short step to other forms of substance abuse. This might take the form of inhalants, glue sniffing, puffing gasoline or even misusing items readily available in a supermarket. Some cold medications, over the counter diet aids, including ephedrine or suda ephedrine and some cough syrups, are alcohol based, and offer another source of abuse, especially when mixed with alcohol. There is a proven link between this type of substance abuse and possible brain damage, especially glue and inhalant sniffing.

Children need to be aware of these dangers before they face the threat. They will be confronted by challenges and need to be aware of the risks that they are taking. Not only are these serious issues in themselves, but evidence suggests that the earlier children are introduced to this type of abuse, especially if it also includes nicotine and alcohol, the more likely they are to become addicted later in their lives.

Much discussed social drugs are:

1. Marijuana

2. Crack Cocaine

3. Ecstasy

4. LSD

5. Heroin

6. Ketamine

7. Other forms of hallucinogens, including mushroom abuse

There is a major misconception to deal with, in terms of the difference between physical and psychological addiction. For example, many people believed that cocaine was not a dangerous drug because it was psychologically, but not physically addictive. This has lead to a cocaine epidemic in this country. It is now known that addictions are characterised by both physical and psychological changes.

'GATEWAY' DRUGS

Nicotine, alcohol and marijuana seem comparatively 'safe' drugs, which do not seem to lead to obvious clinical addiction, but may be a 'soft entry' into a dangerous and potentially addictive world. Children need to know exactly what the drugs are which they may be offered, what effects they may have and what the risks are. For example, there are good reasons for being angry if a fourteen year old is found using marijuana, but the anger has a different focus compared with heroin, for example.

Marijuana is mood altering; it lowers defences and inhibitions, and makes the management of motor vehicles and machinery dangerous. It makes people forgetful and confused, and may seriously undermine any attempt at a work ethic. This is certainly relevant on the day of taking the marijuana, but possibly for a day or two afterwards, especially if it is taken on a regular basis.

In many ways, our anger should be levelled in a similar way to alcohol abuse, bearing in mind that alcohol precipitates violence and addiction on a more regular basis.

The greatest pressure on our children will be from their peers, which can be a positive pressure, driving towards sporting excellence, academic performance, but it can equally be threatening when it involves drug abuse. We all want to identify with our groups and this is particularly true of the developing teenager. To be rejected, much less mocked by our peers is almost impossible to tolerate. The vast majority of youngsters will have their first exposure to drugs before their twelfth birthday. Training in drug awareness needs to begin remarkably young.

THOSE TELLTALE SIGNS

- *Dramatic changes in clothing style, hair, choice of music.* Is your youngster making an obvious effort to fit in with a peer group and dressing down to do so, beginning to use language to fit and even listening to music that they would not have tolerated only a couple of months earlier? This does not necessarily suggest drug or substance abuse, but it is certainly an indicator that peer group pressure is taking its toll.

- They are *beginning to skip school,* are becoming extremely dilatory about meeting their commitments around the house, homework is seldom completed. They seem to show little or no remorse for their tardiness. If you have any doubts, call the school and check the young person's attendance record. Remember how easy your signature is to forge on a sick note!

- *School reports are deteriorating rapidly,* their position in class is dwindling and aspirations for public examinations are beginning to drift. Interest and motivation in school as a whole is on the wane, and they wait restlessly for the school day to finish so that they can drift back to their friends again.

- *A feeling of isolation* from the rest of the family. Has an otherwise close child suddenly become distant, rather cold in their responses? If you ask about the matters of the day, are their answers misleadingly vague, eye contact avoided? Are they beginning to eat in their room, playing music in a solitary state?

- Most worrying of all, *dramatic changes in personality* often occur. Firmly held attitudes may suddenly reverse and become negative, critical and hostile. A warm personality suddenly becomes very unsettled. Erstwhile boyfriends and girlfriends are left in the lurch. Are they becoming increasingly oppositional and confrontational? Obviously, this may reflect normal vagaries of teenage, but it may not, especially if the onset is very sudden, and particularly if this includes violent mood swings, from buoyant, over active and manic, to depressed and lethargic.

- *Changes in sleep pattern.* Does your child stay up late or even all night and refuse to get up in the mornings at a decent time? Is it a nightmare trying to get them to go to school at all? Are they crashing out and sleeping at inappropriate times of the day? This may well be an indication of stimulant abuse. Equally, if they are sleeping far too much and for far too long, they may be abusing some form of depressant. As with so much of our behaviour, it is when it becomes excessive that it becomes diagnostically important. The normal, amenable child is suddenly given to excessive use of obscene language. "Where has she suddenly learnt this filthy language?" a mother asked me recently. It may be that this is the unfortunate jargon of their current peers, but they are clearly responding to peer group pressure and this may well also include the abuse of drugs.

- *Over or under eating.* This obvious sign of drug experimentation can easily be over looked as normal teenage behaviour. Does your child come home in the afternoon, after being with their peers and dive straight towards snacks in the fridge? Smoking Pot has a long reputation for giving a person a desire for 'munchies' and your refrigerator will be a ready source of snacks to satisfy this craving. Is your child skipping meals rather too often? Use of stimulants will suppress a person's appetite. An unusual loss of appetite, especially in a young girl who will want to look thin anyway, may be a sign that she is also using stimulants.

- *Paranoia* – Why is everyone always after me! Are you and most other authority figures becoming regarded as 'the enemy'? Do they have constant stories of friends, teachers and others plotting to undermine them and being deliberately unfair. If they really do seem rather paranoid, from an otherwise fairly normal beginning, this is not normal teenage behaviour and is one of the most common signs of drug abuse.

- *Dilated pupils* – red eyes, glazed eyes. If you think your child is experimenting with drugs, watch their eyes. Their pupils particularly respond very quickly to the influence of drugs.

- *Anger* – Anger and frustration is normal in all of us, and particularly during teenage, but the sudden onset of a violent side of a child's nature, particularly uncontrollable fits of anger, may be a further indicator of abuse. It will often take the form of yelling, verbally abusive threatening behaviour, rather than physical violence.

- You may be alarmed to find that you are *immersed in a welter of lies* all of a sudden. They are living a lie and are often having to maintain this lie to cover up their actions.

- *Excessive expenditure.* If the child's normal allowance never seems enough, and they are constantly coming to you with less and less credible reasons for needing more money, you have to ask exactly what they are buying with the extra cash. If they are particularly round sums, like five, ten or twenty pounds, this may be a further indicator, as drugs are often sold in precisely this type of easily moved amount, not requiring change.

- Finally, *speech is easily affected by drugs*. If a child is smoking marijuana, they will be inclined to speak slowly, or will often express ideas that are inappropriate, out of context, or appear to "have lost the plot". The misuse of stimulants tends to produce hyperactive behaviour and, as a result, fast, overactive and sometimes thoughtless speech patterns. A particular indicator would be normal speech patterns one day, followed by exaggerated, over fast, excitable speech and behaviour the following day.

Other precipitators that may lead to drug or alcohol abuse:

- *Loss and bereavement.* Loss of a parent, close friend, and never forget the much-adored family pet. A relationship breaking up, especially a first heart-felt teenage love affair; the culture shock of moving to a new city, particularly a new country, will produce uncertainties and place great pressure on the need for peer group interaction.

- *Abuse.* This may be physical, emotional or sexual.

- *Relationships.* A lonely, isolated child, who finds friendships very difficult to make will be particularly vulnerable.

- *Peer group pressure*

- *Family tensions*

- *Conflict between parents*

- *Bullying, teasing or school failure*

- *Teenage sexual development.* Worry about body image, especially in teenage girls, confused sexual feelings associated with guilt, sexual inadequacy, possible rejection, possible attraction to gay sex and anxiety about becoming homosexual, can all produce enormous pressure on a developing youngster. In general, almost everyone experiences a fear of failure at some time in their lives, but for some, this is almost insurmountable without the support which comes from drugs.

- *Academic pressure.* Youngsters from over-expecting families, who are in academic schools are particularly vulnerable to this type of pressure. It allows them to relax and feel safe but is likely to build a barrier between the youngster and their parents. Finding a sense of identity in teenage is never easy. The image expected by their families is radically different from their peer group, this, too, can be most unsettling.

Other warning signs

- *Groups.* If groups tend to be absenting themselves, on a regular basis, usually on the same day of the week. If the group is inclined to distance itself from other members of their year group and as far away from supervision points as possible. If rumours are beginning to float around that the group is involved in either taking or dispensing drugs, or they are found talking to strangers on or near the school premises. Shop lifting sprees or other forms of theft. Associating, often for a very brief period of time, with another teenager, often very much older than themselves, who is not a normal part of their group.

- *The drug culture.* The brick-a-brac of drug taking. Watch out for spoons that have become discoloured by heating, probably over a candle, foil containers or cup shapes made from silver foil, again discoloured; metal tins, pillboxes, metal foil wrappers, unexplained small plastic or glass phials or bottles; drinking straws with no apparent drink associated with them. Unexplained sugar lumps, syringes or needles; cigarette papers and lighters, but not packets of cigarettes, per se. Plastic bags and butane gas containers (possible solvent abuse); cardboard and other tubes (watch out for heroin abuse); shredded cigarettes, home rolled cigarettes and pipes (cannabis); paper (about two inches square) folded from an envelope. Look carefully for possible heroin abuse.

CONFRONTATION

We all hope that this confrontation with our children will never arise. It is important that the ground rules are laid down very early, so that children know exactly what to expect, and what symptoms will lead to your suspicions and possible action.

It is never helpful to confront a young person, or indeed an adult, while they are in any way intoxicated, as this will be met with lies, denial, and little real sense. Wait for a relatively placid moment and deal with the issue in privacy, away from other members of the family, involving only mother, father and the young person concerned.

Make it quite clear that you love the child and that you will do anything to protect and care for them, but that you have real reason for believing that they are seriously at risk.

At this point, outline the symptoms that you have observed. Allow the discussion to range honestly openly. The quiet, controlled approach to this type of dialogue works so much better than an irrational loss of control. Allow the young person to explain, if they can, why the symptoms may have occurred, or indeed to admit that experimentation with drugs or alcohol has taken place. You need to find out exactly what the abuse has been, how long it has been going on for, what the real threats are from the drug involved, and how seriously at risk, if at all, your child actually is. If they have shared a joint at a party, or consumed a couple of cans of lager, it may be sufficient for them to be aware that you care and that you have been aware and alerted at the very outset. You are not prepared to let them slide into serious abuse before showing your concern. Discuss the pros and cons, and make it absolutely clear that their social freedom at this age depends on mutual trust and respect. They have breached trust, and this must now be re-earned, possibly by restricting their social movement for a time until they have proved that they can be trusted, and that no further abuse has taken place.

If the symptoms have been severe, although the user is no longer under the influence, lies and denial may still follow. You must insist on outlining the telltale signs of which you have been aware and this may be the time to use the home testing kit. The young person needs to know that this will be as inevitable as the breathalyser to the alcohol abusing driver.

If matters seem more serious, and there is a danger of genuine addiction, physical or psychological, there are a number of useful contacts to which parents can apply:

CONTACTS

ALCOHOLICS ANONYMOUS AND NARCOTIC ANONYMOUS
Cntactable at 202 City Road London EC1V 2 PH. Tel: 020 7251 4007 Email: ukso@ukna.org
They also publish a wide range of pamphlets which this UK office will advise on. They provide news, possible meetings and support services.

DEPARTMENT FOR EDUCATION
Drug misuse and the young - Guide for the Education Service 1992

APPENDIX

MARIJUANA

Marijuana is a common name for the Hemp plant, Cannabis Sativa. Marijuana ('pot', 'grass', 'weed', etc.) does not contain just one chemical.

The marijuana is absorbed quickly into fatty tissue and is stored there for a long time. As a result, a single dose may take between three and four weeks to get out of the system completely.

However, while marijuana smoking may create a sense of well being and euphoria, it does tend to make mental or emotional problems even worse, and may well produce shakes, headaches and a feeling of lonely isolation. It also contains fifty percent more tar per ounce than ordinary tobacco and, therefore, the nicotine associated risks are worse. The feeling of well-being and, indeed, lethargy often serves to suppress sex drive and sexual performance, especially with prolonged use, and can even lead to impotence. Marijuana smoking during pregnancy is particularly risky. It goes without saying that manipulating motor vehicles or dangerous machinery while under the effect of marijuana is particularly dangerous.

Unfortunately, although some of the effects are pleasant and relaxing, they can also create false moods and lead to the user experiencing inappropriate, inaccurate feedback from the environment. The world around is 'lying' to the user. Research suggests that young people making regular use of marijuana do less well physically and are generally less capable, achieving significantly less in public examinations.

In essence, the occasional use of marijuana seems to have little or no ill effect, but its regular use can be more damaging than was at one time thought.

CANNABIS – HOW IS IT TAKEN?

Cannabis is most commonly smoked. Usually by mixing with tobacco, rolling it up in cigarette papers into a cannabis cigarette, often called a 'spliff', 'joint', 'reefer', or 'jay'. However, it can also be smoked with or without tobacco in various forms of pipes and smoking devices such as 'bongs' or 'water pipes'. Nowadays, the smoking of cannabis through pipes, often using water to cool the smoke, has become more prevalent due to its greater efficiency. This method is safer since it circumvents problems associated with tobacco smoking. Cannabis can also be taken orally, either eaten directly or mixed with food such as cakes, biscuits – 'hash cookies', or even hot drinks. However, the effect of taking cannabis in this way is less predictable. Cannabis acts slowly, and there is a great danger that the user will abuse, long before the effect hits them, where a smoker can stop as soon as they find they have reached the required level of intoxication. Smoking cannabis produces fairly instant intoxication, the effects lasting for one to four hours depending on the amount used. Fatalities from cannabis use are largely unknown, and the 'morning after the night before' effect is far less profound than that produced by alcohol. No headaches or nausea, more a slightly woolly headed abstract feeling.

The positive effects of cannabis as an effective reliever of the symptoms of multiple sclerosis, hyperglycaemia and, in certain instances the medication of the terminally ill, have become topical again. It is important to remember that cannabis has been used medically world wide for centuries, and in Britain it was legally prescribed up until 1928. In fact, Queen Victoria used it to alleviate period pains, although some women have found that heavy cannabis use makes their periods irregular. Cannabis smoked with tobacco during pregnancy produces the same risks to the mother and child as smoking cigarettes. I should also mention that although concerns have been expressed, there is as yet no conclusive evidence that long-term use of cannabis causes lasting damage to physical or mental health, other than the effect of the nicotine with which cannabis has been smoked.

ECSTASY

Ecstasy, or methylene-dioxymethyl amphetamine (MDMA), is a synthetic hallucinogenic stimulant, which usually comes in pill form. Unfortunately, ecstasy, or E as it is known, has dropped dramatically in price in recent years, especially if bought in bulk, which makes it all too easily available to the youngsters. Warn them that if they are confronted by 'E', brand logos with which they are often stamped can be a very misleading. Quality and purity are major issues. They are often mixed with other active substances, most commonly amphetamines (speed), caffeine and ephedrine (a natural amphetamine-like substance). It is worth recording at this point that the implication that pills can often contain a cocktail of heroin, cocaine or LSD has not been substantiated in laboratory tests. Ecstasy is a potentially dangerous drug, regarded alongside heroin and cocaine. The Law takes a very stringent view on the use and especially dealing in Ecstasy..

LSD

LSD (lysergic acid diethylamide) is one of the major drugs making up the hallucinogen class. LSD was discovered in 1938 and is one of the most potent, mood-changing chemicals. It is manufactured from lysergic acid, which is found in ergot, a fungus that grows on rye and other grains.

LSD, is commonly referred to as 'acid' and is sold on the streets in tablets, capsules and, occasionally, liquid form. It is odourless, colourless and has a slightly bitter taste and is usually taken by mouth. Often LSD is added to absorbent paper, such a blotting paper, and divided into small decorated squares, with each square representing one dose.

The effects of LSD are remarkably unpredictable. They depend on the amount taken, and the user's personality, mood at the time of taking, what they expect from it, and the surroundings of which they are part when the drug is used. Normally, the user feels the first effects of LSD between 30 to 90 minutes after taking it. The danger in the naive user is that they assume it is not going to affect them at all, and may be involved in driving a motorcar or dangerous machinery by the time it begins to take its effect. Physical effects include dilated pupils, higher body temperature, increased heart rate and blood pressure, sweating, loss of appetite, sleeplessness, dry mouth and tremors. The user may also feel several different emotions all at once and swing rapidly from one emotion to another, which can be extremely alarming. If taken in large enough doses, the drug induces delusions and visual hallucination. The user's sense of time and self changes. Sensations may seem to 'cross over', giving the user the feeling of hearing colours and seeing sounds. These changes can be frightening and cause panic. Users refer to their experience with LSD as a 'trip' and to acute adverse reactions as a ' bad trip' which can flashback hours later, or even weeks or months after the initial taking of the drug. LSD is not considered an addictive drug and most users abandon it voluntarily over time. However, it does tend to produce tolerance which means that users have to take increased doses to achieve the same effect. This is clearly an extremely dangerous practice, as the results become more and more unpredictable.

Interestingly, in the early days, the effects of LSD were likened to those associated with psychosis and it was even used experimentally in psychiatry to simulate psychotic disorders.

E'S AND WHIZ

In the 1960s teenagers and more specifically 'Mods' enjoyed Dexedrine (dexies/dexy's midnight runners), Durophet (blackbombers) and Drinamyl (Purple Hearts after their blue and triangular shape). These tablets combined amphetamine and barbiturate in one handy pill. Rather absurdly in the mid 1960's it became illegal to possess or import amphetamines, but its manufacture and prescription were still regarded as appropriate. The Drinamyl Purple Heart was reshaped and renamed French Blues and continued to sell.

By the early 1990s the demand for E was high but the quality was low. Many 'clubbers' switched to Speed. It suited them perfectly. The more you took E, the speedier it became. A few grams of Speed could replace 10 E's for those who craved the buzz and the energy.

There is a clear danger of becoming dependant on these drugs, both chemically and culturally. It becomes increasingly difficult to cope with this type of social situation, without the drug boost. This can obviously have a damaging effect on a young person's life, as staying up partying all night till the early hours of the morning will hardly be conducive to effective schoolwork. Dehydration is a serious problem in the club environment, and lives have been lost as a result of failure to understand the effect of these drugs, they fail to take time off from the dance floor to drink appropriate amounts of water.

KETAMINE

Ketamine is a fast-acting 'dissociative anaesthetic'. It works by shutting down the body's nerve paths, leaving respiratory and circulatory functions intact.

Since 1970, it has been a popular medicine in the UK and the United States and all over the world as a safe anaesthetic for children and the elderly. Ketamine comes in three main forms. The most common form is a white powder which is snorted.

TABLET

Often masquerading as a brand of Ecstasy, usually very diluted, and cut with a stimulant like Ephedrine, which produces a mildly trippy, speedy effect.

LIQUID – KETAMINE HYDROCHLORIDE

Is intended for use as a hospital anaesthetic. It is occasionally injected by recreational users, which can be extremely dangerous. Some users have passed out immediately. It is particularly dangerous mixed with alcohol. Far too many people have 'drowned' in their own vomit as it may provoke violent vomiting. At low doses, K is a mild, if rather weird stimulant. However, at medium to high doses, it becomes a very powerful paralysing psychedelic. Its effects are like a combination of cocaine, cannabis, opium, nitrous oxide, and alcohol. The onset of K is very rapid. In 10–20 minutes, you may find yourself hardly able to move and, at higher doses, even approaching out-of-body and near-death experience, dazzling insights, hallucinations, the apparent ability to communicate with external forces, and falling into a deep trance state, are not unusual. The user's eyes may move sightlessly from side to side, and their bodies assume bizarre postures. Any attempt to explain these sensations leave the user mumbling often non-sensical inanities. The effect lasts for 45 to 90 minutes, and leave an after effect very like recovering unhappily from a hospital anaesthetic. Over-use can leave the user feeling achy, confused, disorientated and virtually shell-shocked. Long term users have become so involved in the drug and its effects, that they find it very difficult not to retreat back into the K world, to escape from the real one.

COCAINE

Cocaine is a fast-acting nervous system stimulant, extracted from the leaves of a coca bush, a high altitude plant which grows in the Andes of Bolivia, Peru and Colombia.

It usually comes as a fine white powder, which is snorted in lines and is rapidly absorbed through the nasal membranes. Many users also dab it on their teeth and gums.

Cocaine is diluted vastly in its journey to the street, and may well be bulked up with corn starch, talcum powder, or even Italian baby milk powder. The rumour that Coke is regularly cut with anthrax, bleach or strychnine has no foundation in fact.

CRACK COCAINE

Cocaine mixed with baking powder (sodium bicarbonate), a smokeable version of cocaine with a shorter but more intense hit is called 'crack' after the sound it makes when you light it. It often very quickly induces a state of psychological dependency. Cocaine is, of course, a class A substance, hence there are very serious legal implications for its possession. The variability of its response, and, particularly, the serious uncertainty about purity levels, which can range from 20 to 65% of actual cocaine, render the user extremely vulnerable.

HEROIN

Heroin is an opiate – a very powerful painkiller. The body and the brain are packed with opiate receptors, meant for endorphins, the body's own natural pain-killing substances produced in emergency moments of shock or injury.

Heroin is a powerful, addictive painkilling drug. It is the most used, most rapidly acting, most addictive of the opiate family, which includes opium, morphine and codeine. All the opiates are derived from opium, and naturally occur in juice extracted from the seed pod of certain varieties of poppy. Heroin is, in fact, heavily refined opium.

Heroin is a white powder with a bitter taste, although on the street it often comes as granules, powder, solution or in pill form. The colour varies from white to dark brown, largely due to the additives that are often included.

Most users inject heroin either intravenously, where the response is extremely rapid – a matter of seconds, or intra-muscularly where the effect may take some six to eight minutes. In each case, the heroin powder is diluted in a little water. The brown heroin that dominates the UK and Dutch markets is insoluble in water and has to be dissolved in acid, usually citric acid from lemons. However, an increasing number of people are choosing to smoke or snort lines of heroin, rather than injecting it. When smoked, heroin is heated on foil and the vapour inhaled through a tube or rolled-up bank note. This is what is commonly called 'chasing the dragon'.

Not only do first time, irregular users, often experience nausea and violent vomiting, but the overall effect may take many hours to wear off, rendering the user into a protracted sleep-like state, able to contribute very little to the environment around them.

Heroin is an extremely addictive drug – never be fooled by users who smoke or snort it and appear not to be becoming addicted – give them time and they will. The injection of heroin, especially intravenously, can lead to addiction extremely quickly. It is only a short time before any sense of stability in life depends on a further 'fix' and the impact of withdrawal can be devastating. An individual's entire life becomes geared to their next injection. The world of work is often completely forgotten, marriages tumble, and social relationships dwell almost entirely within the drug culture.

Other drugs have their implicit risks and dangers, but none to compare with the opiates. It is vital that wherever our youngsters choose to experiment, it is never in this market place, from which retreat can be difficult and extremely painful.

CONTACTS

ADDICTION COUNSELLING TRUST
Tel: 01494 461361

PAGODA
Parental action and guidance on drug abuse
Tel: 01494 727787

NATIONAL DRUGS HELPLINE
24-hour helpline for drug users and solvent abusers, their families, friends and carers. Can send out free literature and refer callers to local agencies.
Tel: 0800 776600 (Helpline 24 hours)

NARCOTICS ANONYMOUS
A self-help group of recovering addicts who meet regularly to help each other stay clean.
Tel: 020 7730 0009

TURNING POINT
Over 45 projects offer residential rehabilitation, day care and street level advice to people with drink, drug and mental health problems.
Tel: 020 7702 2300

19

Pop Idols and their Influence

What harm may be caused by more violent lyrics in modern music?

Tom

I received a letter from rather alarmed parents of fifteen-year-old Tom, who had become secretive, physically aggressive, and verbally abusive. They felt that this had been a dramatic personality change, could not understand why Tom treated them this way and seemed resentful of all they stood for. He was staying out late, coming home the worse for alcohol, and was worrying less and less about his personal hygiene. His mother wandered into Tom's room to find him lying on his bed listening to rap music, with his eyes closed. She stood for a moment or two listening and was stunned as the character in the song drove in depressed desperation off a bridge, with his girlfriend tied up in the boot of the car. She listened on to the foul language, the aggression, the urge to defy authority.

Tom's mother and I worked together towards understanding the nature of this type of cult behaviour. The same singer was described by a major newspaper as "having a gift for comic timing and impersonations, wilfully offensive etc, etc…..". Hence, we must accept that this particular pop star was regarded as having talent and was approved of by the musical authorities and could not, therefore, simply be dismissed.

I spoke to Ben, Tom's brother, who was nineteen, to ask him his views. "He is a good singer - I only listen to the rhythm, but my brother takes the words more seriously". The combination of professional production, talented rhythm and singing, and a violent and anti-social message, is a tricky one. As parents, we find little to admire in the music, and are understandably alarmed by the cult that begins to develop around these young singers. The alarm is heightened by our obvious exclusion from it. We are left with an uneasy feeling that forces beyond our control are now having a profound influence on our youngsters. Tom's mother was finding that she could not discuss even minor matters with him, without risking abuse or Tom walking out. Thankfully, it was an emotional storm that passed after a few months, but both parents needed support in the meanwhile. On more mature reflection, Tom was apologetic and joined a counselling group.

This type of behaviour has been generated by many examples in history – James Dean, Jimmy Hendrix, Sid Vicious. Each generation tends to adopt its own idols. This, in itself, need do no harm, but do not expect to feel included. The clothes, hairstyles, and the general manner are the first stages of involvement. Anger, resentment and rebellion against society tends to follow rapidly. The brighter, more intelligent youngsters, often regard this as a 'quirky' part of the singer and his songs, and are not moved. It is the 'vulnerable' youngster, who is already at odds with the world who may be particularly affected.

Above all, do not over-react to a cult. It may be partly our own resentment at being excluded that is driving this reaction. Watch out for the early symbols of dress and general manner, etc., and then wait for the next stage to develop. We must then ask the fundamental question, 'Why does anybody produce provocative behaviour?' Surely it is to 'provoke'. Rebellion needs something to rebel against if it is to be successful. The cult and its leader will achieve its greatest 'result' if, by virtue of his songs, he can actually create cross generation friction, and an effective challenge of authority. Remember, a 'row' with a teenager proves that the cult is being effective. It is often fathers who are most vulnerable, seeing this type of defiant, oppositional behaviour as a direct assault on themselves and all they stand for.

You are entitled not to like a variety of types of music – that's a personal choice. Hence, asking for certain types of music to be played elsewhere is a perfectly legitimate request. If the youngster plays it in his own bedroom, then ignore it. Remember, it is the noise that you do not particularly like and to which you are objecting, not the singer and the cult. Do not attempt to ban or confiscate the music. This will only romanticise the whole issue. It is vital to remember that as parents, we are being tested, albeit sub-consciously, to see if we will respond to the challenges. Any head on collision will simply reinforce the conflict and make matters worse.

Do not be panicked into over or even under reaction and being defensive. Remember that there will always be some behaviour which you find unacceptable and this will remain the case. The young person must know that certain types of language, behaviour, provocation, and so forth, are not acceptable, because they are outside the 'norms' for your family. It is the behaviour that you are criticising, not the child, or the music. Do not give the cult guru this pleasure and success.

20
Pets are Not Just for Fun

Yet another anguished plea from the RSPCA – "Don't buy pets for Christmas just because something furry seems to be in the Christmas spirit". Once again, as with every Christmas, dogs and cats will be left along the motorways.

Anthea

> In a tantrum, Anthea kicked a kitten downstairs simply because her mother had insisted that she look after it. This caused a small animal a great deal of pain. Pets are not just for fun, they are living creatures, but even more importantly, they form a fascinating part of the development of a sense of responsibility.

Fundamentally, our role as parents is to bring our children to adulthood as successful and independent adults, able to strike out and make a life for themselves. It is a subtle, ever-changing role, part of which involves building an increasing awareness of the needs of others and how other people often depend on our support and kindness. As babies, our children need a massive amount of support and nurturing in order to survive, and so do small animals. Pets offer a marvellous opportunity for youngsters to learn how to care for initially helpless creatures. They also learn about the need for a disciplined, regular approach in the meeting of their needs. It is often irksome at first. A favourite television programme has just begun, but the time has come to feed the gerbil and clean out its cage. Life is like that – as they will find when they have children of their own to care for! Sometimes, other responsibilities must take precedence.

The difference between fantasy and reality is vital to establish before a pet is even bought. It is easy for children and adults to see a lovely cuddly puppy, full of play, who then piddles all over the house and eventually grows to be a long, rangy mutt, who sweeps everything off the side-tables with its tail. A staggering number of men buy pets for their wives or their children, on a whim, shortly before Christmas. If only that puppy could be clean, self-feeding, self-walking, and not grow old!

If a pet is to be acquired, there should be a family discussion involving both parents and the children, to decide exactly what will be involved in having this animal as part of the family. It must be seen as a 'family member' – not simply a creature that is left upstairs to be forgotten.

David

David was in constant conflict with his father over many issues, but the family Alsatian had become a particular focus. David had never wanted the dog in the first place, and had made his feelings quite clear. His father had forced the issue and insisted that an Alsatian was something that he had always wanted and why should he not have the dog. However, no commitment was ever entered into with any other family member, and it was, therefore, perceived as 'Dad's dog'. Having bought the animal, David's father now tried to insist that every family member should share equally in its care and management. He worked very late, was seldom home in time to walk the animal, and was often far too tired to bother feeding it.

A poor example to set David.

Let's assume that a family meeting has taken place and that they have agreed that a dog should be bought and each member now has an established role, with a rota posted quite clearly on the side of the fridge, for instance. It is then up to every family member to fulfil their role. It is a good exercise in joint management within a family, and it demonstrates quite clearly to the children that it is not just they who have responsibility for this new pet. Neither are you, as a parent, going to allow the children to abdicate their roles.

Children often respond very well to a contract drawn up within the family, in which the various roles and responsibilities of all concerned are clearly delineated. Each member signs the contract and this, too, is posted for all to see. This impresses on the minds of young children that they are entering into an important responsibility for the life of a living creature, which cannot be taken lightly.

John

John, who at twelve years of age, should certainly have known better, failed to feed his gerbils, and as a result their three babies starved to death. He was stunned, tearful and very upset. Fortunately, the adult gerbils did survive and I hope that John has learnt a lesson from the suffering that he inflicted. A family contract could have involved support and supervision and the baby gerbils would have survived.

No hearts on sleeves, please! Establish where the pet will live; whether there is proper accommodation for them; who will be responsible for them and precisely what that individual's role will be. Remember, that the care of an animal is not something that comes naturally to children, and they may need to be instructed clearly on exactly how to manage the life of the animal. Your local vet will be only too happy to help with advice.

Finally, what do we do if a child simply refuses to cooperate? The parents should not take over the child's role, on the apparently honest ground that the animal is suffering. Suddenly, as a parent, you inherit a hamster and a pair of goldfish! The contract should make it clear that after a pre-established number of failures to cooperate, the pet is returned to the pet shop or a new home has to be found for it. Very few children, or, indeed, adults, want to face the ignominy of having to admit that they have cared so poorly for a pet that it has had to be found a new home. Abdication of care makes the pet a negative experience, and a cop-out if parents simply take over. Young people must not learn that if care becomes inconvenient, it can be abandoned without sanction.

HOW TO COPE WHEN THE PET DIES

Daisy

A parent telephoned about her fourteen year old daughter's emotional state. Daisy had just heard that their elderly dog had cancer and might not last for more than a few months. The mother was worried about how Daisy would handle this loss. We met in a family group, and helped Daisy to come to terms with the reality of this loss.

Charlie

I remember eleven-year-old Charlie, who had a pet cockerel called 'Tony', who had adopted Charlie as his parent. Tony, the cockerel, coped quietly and happily in the back yard until he heard Charlie come back from school, at which point there was a pandemonium of crowing and flapping up at the glass windows of the kitchen door. Tony would then follow Charlie up to his bedroom and wander happily round the bedroom while Charlie completed his homework.

Charlie came to see me because he was dyslexic, was finding his work in school very difficult and was a rather lonely, isolated little boy. His parents were busy professional people, who were largely unaware of Charlie's isolation. Tony meant a great deal to him – he gave unquestioning love – he never talked back, he was never cross. Tony was only content when Charlie was with him.

One hideous afternoon, Charlie arrived back just in time to see the neighbours Alsatian clear the garden fence, dive through the yard door which had been left ajar, and destroy Tony in a flurry of feathers.

The loss of Tony would have been dreadful enough, but to actually see the destruction was heart breaking. His parents had been slightly irritated by the cockerel, and were not altogether sorry to see him go. As a result, they completely misunderstood Charlie's sadness, and his desperate need to be understood and to 'grieve' for his lost pet. It was only on the third meeting with Charlie that he mentioned this loss and quickly dissolved into inconsolable tears. Our counsellor worked with Charlie, and subsequently with his parents. Charlie gradually dealt with his grief and his parents were horrified to appreciate how much they had misunderstood their son. It was the boy's first confrontation with death, and the loss of a crucial pillar of his identity.

As parents, we need to remember that many animals may bond closely with their owners. This is a bond that needs to be fully understood and also that its loss will cause considerable upset and unhappiness.

Daniel

Daniel, who is twelve, had a pet rabbit called Smoky. He was another quiet, solitary, almost depressed little boy. Smoky was found dead on the kitchen floor one day. Daniel's father's attitude was "Don't be silly - it is only a rabbit – we will get another one!" Daniel couldn't tell his father, but he told me "How can I get another Smoky?" Daniel had invested an immense amount of love in his rabbit, and was now fretting about life and death, and wanted to know where Smoky was. As the weeks passed, Daniel became increasingly depressed and found it difficult to leave his room. After his father's comment, even parental love was now being questioned.

It was at this point that he was referred to me. It is difficult for us as parents to accept that three or four months down the line, a child can still be 'grieving' for the loss of a pet. In Daniel's case, matters were made worse by the refusal of his parents to accept his grief. We worked together as a family group and I am delighted to say that the local Rabbi was also extremely supportive. The 'team' gradually came together and realised that only when Daniel was able to deal with his loss, would he move on to the next stage of his life. They built a little grave at the bottom of the garden and Daniel now feels that he has 'honoured' his lost pet and said his goodbyes.

Malcolm

Malcolm, who was fifteen, presented a curious problem. He and his father loved walking in the country with their golden retriever, Max. On the way back from a walk, Max was hit by a Landrover and killed. Both Malcolm and his father were very upset, but while Malcolm grieved, his Dad would not admit what he saw as a weakness. He became increasingly grumpy and difficult and was unreasonably angry if Malcolm showed any signs of frailty.

There was an enormous row over dinner on one occasion because Malcolm actually shed a tear. His school work fell away, his concentration in class drifted, and he dropped from third in his group to fourteenth in the summer exams. By now, Malcolm was actually experiencing a reactive depression which he found very difficult to deal with. His father became angry if he mentioned his unhappiness, and his mother was bewildered by their joint anger.

Once again, through counselling, we dealt with the bereavement. The family had a joint funeral at which their local Vicar assisted. At long last, Dad allowed himself to cry. He and Malcolm hugged each other, dealt with their grief, and have now moved on to a new pet. Indeed, I rather suspect that this 'sharing' of grief has created a significant bond between father and son. Why on earth do we fathers often see grief as a weakness?

CONTACT

PETSEARCH
This is a centre which runs voluntary free help lines to aid people in finding missing pets. They also operate a National Database Register of lost or found creatures. To aid people who have lost a pet or whose pet has died, they run a counselling service. The telephone number is: The Rev Rus Green, 01452 830571 (http://www.ukpetsearch.freeuk.com/psabout.htm)

21

Bereavement – And How It Affects Us All

Death is the one certainty in this world, and yet, one of the most difficult subjects to discuss honestly and openly. We hide from explaining the cycle of life to our children because; "It might upset them". It might, but then you will be there to deal with the tears and help them construct the realities.

At sometime in almost every child's life, they will have to face the loss of a grandparent, uncle, aunt or even their mother or father. The closer the relationship, and the more the individual is a fundamental pillar of the child's identity, the more shattering the loss will be. The child's whole world may seem to implode and fall apart with a panicky feeling of there being nowhere to run for shelter. It is an important time to be honest with our children, and to be prepared to share our own grief and tears. They are real emotions of a real and tragic loss. The last thing we would wish to communicate is that for some reason we do not seem to care. It can often be a time of colossal emotional bonding between surviving family members, from which they each derive immense support. It is a time when you begin to remember the value of the person you have lost. This, in itself, can be a negative, rather depressing reflection, but as grieving passes, it is important to reconstruct the happy, positive memories of the family member who has been lost, and be comforted by the fact that their memory and the strength that they had in the family, goes on beyond death.

PRE-PLANNING FOR DEATH

This sounds a remarkable heading, but it is, in fact, a valuable avenue to explore. We know that the eventual loss of someone close and dear is virtually inevitable, and the more shattering and inexplicable the shock, the longer it will take the child to recover and reach that vital stage of healing.

From a very early age, look at the life cycle of the seasons around, the way seeds develop,

77

grow and the leaves eventually fall; the life cycle of wild animals and birds, even the vicious work of predators. The loss of a family pet can be devastating, but is, nevertheless, a useful model around which to build a real understanding of the grieving process.

People in some cultures are much better than others at recognising and dealing with the need to say goodbye, and allow themselves to move on to the next phase of their existence. Allow children to talk about the possible loss of a grandparent, even the loss of their mother or father, and avoid burying this possibility in patronising reassurance. You may find that when a child does first experience a critical loss of a fundamental part of their identity, that they have a period of panic during which they worry about further, more possibly fundamental losses, and even their own death. Allow them to talk through this and deal with it honestly and openly – it will pass. It is part of their grieving process, and their way of dealing with the loss. Remember, we all have to rebuild that pillar of identity that has been so cruelly swept away. This, of course, is why even after a long illness, with inevitable death at its end, the final parting often comes as a desperate shock. That pillar, however vulnerable, was at least there.

THE FUNERAL

The funeral is a sad, cold affair in most cases, but need not necessarily be so. Often these days, churches and crematoria are willing to play lively, happy music that would have been favourites of the person who has been lost. A funeral is a time to say goodbye, to honour the person who has died and to celebrate their life and how much they brought to the lives of others. Hence, the happier a funeral the better. This is no loss of respect to the individual who has died.

FINANCIAL SECURITY

There is enough to worry about at the time of bereavement, in terms of mutual support and attempting to hold the family together, without worrying about the possible loss of income or even the family home. It is sensible to make appropriate financial arrangements in terms of insurances, to be sure that if either parent is lost, the family will remain totally financially secure. At least then, during bereavement, the family can move from a solid, predictable base, without the anxiety of possible further losses and a dramatic change to their lifestyle.

Avoid repressing the possibility of preparing a Will. As the family pass through the grieving process, after the loss, the last thing they need is to find that their security is rocked by disputes, arguments and even court proceedings created by the absence of a Will.

THE GRIEVING PROCESS

Bereavement, and the grief that follows it, is inevitable and follows a relatively predictable pattern. Clearly, the length of time that any individual spends in each of the various phases of grieving will depend on the person concerned, the background from which they come, the support they receive, and their own psychological strength.

It is a vital time for support, and the extended family suddenly becomes hugely important. Never worry about calling on an uncle, aunt, grandparent or close friend to come and spend time with you and the children, to help with the grieving process. Most of us like to feel needed, that we are contributing and helping in some way, and yet at a time of family loss, we are often shy and inhibited about making that phone call.

It is therapeutic to understand that grieving is a process, people will go through certain stages, but that there is a light at the end of the tunnel. Healing will occur, they will accept, they will rebuild their identities and will move on. Above all, it does not mean that the love that they felt is in any way diminished. It has now taken the form of loving, supportive memories, and not an artificial state of denial and anger.

SHOCK

The shock at the death of a close family member is inevitable, even if it was in many ways anticipated. It is a shattering, numb, cold phase, but it does have a curious value in itself. It has a numbing, almost anaesthetising effect that allows the bereaved family members to carry on and see themselves through the funeral and all the organisational paraphernalia associated with this early stage of bereavement. It is often many weeks later when the 'anaesthetic' wears off, that the real lonely sadness is felt. It is at this time that people, especially those on their own particularly need support. During this shock phase, be sure to include the children and make them part of the experience. Do not marginalise and isolate them under some curious pretext that you are protecting them. All you are doing is protecting yourself from having to witness their anguish. Help them with their tears and share them.

DENIAL

Denial often follows the shock phase. The loss of a child is especially devastating and may even take the form of leaving the child's room exactly as it was and never changing it, with a curious deep-seated feeling that if nothing is changed, nothing has happened, no one has died, and that the person may soon return.

ANGER

It is hardly surprising, once we have dealt with our shock and denial, and the fuss and commotion of the funeral is over, family members have departed and returned to their own homes, that we begin to feel anger and resentment, almost a sense of rejection. "How could he go and die, if he really loved me!" "How could Dad do this – just before my A Levels!" "If only the doctors had done their jobs properly, this would never have happened – I'll sue them". All very familiar. This is a phase; it will pass. The lesson to be learnt is not to over react to this anger, or make decisions which are based on the anger, not the realities.

BARGAINING

Small children, particularly, will often go through an apparently pointless phase of suggesting that if only they could be really good, "Daddy would come back". "I promise I will never be naughty again, if only you don't let this happen". This is the time for an understanding cuddle, possibly a shared tear, but resist entering into the bargaining game. Particularly true when young people first become aware that someone close to them is entering a terminal stage of an illness.

DEPRESSION

Often, several months down the line, a reactive depression is only too understandable, especially after many years of marriage, facing the realities of having to rebuild life, with a major pillar of our identity shattered and gone. Keep going, keep moving. This is a time when other family members will be so important. Be prepared to ask for help from associations like CRUSE. It is their business to know how to help and support you through these difficult, depressing times. You may feel that this is not the time to share your agony with children who are dealing with their own bereavement.

ACCEPTANCE AND HEALING

Eventually, one morning, bereaved people wake up with a sense of acceptance. It takes time, often many months, or even years to truly accept. Only at this point does healing begin, rebuilding identity. If the person that has been lost really loved us, they would want us to be happy, successful and get back on our feet. They would not like to see us broken and defence-less. We need to fight back towards healing in honour of our deceased loved one, and not let their death pull us down into depths of despair. From now on, life begins to move on, new jobs emerge, children take their exams, new relationships develop, and even new marriages take place.

THE EFFECT OF BEREAVEMENT ON DIFFERENT AGE GROUPS

The under six year old

This age group frequently do not see death as real at all, simply a drama that the family seems to be going through, focused on a particular individual. This is often confirmed by cartoon characters and computer games. Children of this age are constantly asking apparently tactless questions about death – how it occurs, why it happens, and "Mum, will you be next?" It is part of their learning to understand the process of death and grieving. In this age group, there is no reason why the child should not be part of the grieving process, including the funeral and the rituals associated with it. However, the general advice is that it is unwise to actually allow children of this age to see the deceased, let alone attempt to kiss them goodbye. Whilst this is an honest response, it often lends itself to unresolved nightmares and fears which may continue for many years in various guises.

At this age, children normally move on, albeit still talking about the individual that has been lost from time to time, but still not profoundly overpowered by grief. If after three or four months, they have still not come to terms with it, then this is the time to seek professional counselling.

Six to twelve year olds

In this age group, it is important to be honest and discuss the cause of death, what will now follow in terms of funeral arrangements, and to involve them in a simple, gentle way with the entire process. There is a curious tendency for some children to believe that in a bizarre way, they actually caused the death. They blame themselves, almost in an attempt to gain control over the situation. Only total honesty will allow them to see that they are, in fact, in no way to blame and, indeed, need to be part of the grieving process as a member of the family.

The teen years

The more fundamental the deceased has been, the longer the grieving process will last. They will experience most of the same emotions as the adults concerned, including anger, helplessness, loneliness, denial and guilt. Unless they have experienced death before, they will have an instinctive feeling that death will never happen to them or anyone they know. It only happens to those outside the family. They are, nevertheless, aware of the phenomenon. When it does occur, it may be shattering and may lead to a great deal of unhealthy introspection about their own mortality. You need to judge some five or six months down the line, whether this needs counselling support. Above all, you need to be alerted to the signals that may suggest the need for proper professional help:

- Spending an increasing amount of time alone and seldom smiling. Finding little, if anything, funny around them. Even a dramatic change in the music they choose to play during this time.

- Increasing pallor and lack of appetite. Inability to settle to a family meal.

- Lack of sleep, constant fatigue, falling asleep at the wrong times of day. The school may even comment that they are nodding off in class.

- Increasing fears of being left alone. Constantly phoning parents when they are out of the house to check that they are all right. An increasing sense of vulnerability and potential loss, which is perfectly normal in the early stages, but half a year after the event, should be coming under some degree of control.

- A sharp drop in school performance, difficulty with study, incomplete homework, revision that is never complete, and deteriorating exam performance. Do remember that as a parent, you too will be passing through the grieving process. Avoid over-reacting to the behaviour of those around you, but if you do feel concerned that these behaviours are not diminishing or are unnaturally severe, then go for counselling yourself to discuss the problem, to get your own mind in order, before suggesting that the family member should go themselves for counselling. You may simply be over-reacting.

REMEMBER

Remember the bereavement and loss are affecting every family member and try to look outside yourself at the needs of those around you. Parents and children need to be aware of the process in which they are involved and that healing will eventually emerge. It may be hard to believe at the time when the loss is agonising, but it will eventually come and it is, perhaps, encouraging to be aware of this.

Talk about your feelings, and ask your children how they are feeling. They do not need to explain all their emotions to you in detail, but the fact that you have opened yourself to questions, discussion and anxieties, is very supportive. An angry adolescent may be encouraged to find a game of squash a useful outlet! Accept the anger and use it. Do not be driven by it.

Offer your opinion only when it is asked for by the child, usually the opportunity to talk is what is needed. Do not imply that you can fix it and make it all right – "Don't worry dear, it will be all right". How often do we tell people 'not to worry' in absurd circumstances, when, of course, they are worrying. Rather too often, we are trying to keep our own worry at bay, and do not want the anguish of dealing with somebody else's unhappiness, whilst struggling with our own.

Look after yourself and the family physically. It is easy to withdraw into a shell and not bother as much about personal hygiene, clothing and diet. Snacking and "Oh, I can't be bothered at the moment" is all so easy. If an individual becomes rundown and undernourished, they become less and less able to cope with the stress involved in bereavement. Not only are they vulnerable, but their very vulnerability worries those around them.

Patience

Take your time. Try to come through the experience as a family, possibly learning, maybe for the first time, that you are a part of a vital team whose mutual support is of benefit to all its members.

22

The Emerging Young Adult

As we try to steer our children through the minefield of adolescent development, the problem is not made any easier by the multiple 'hats' that we often have to wear if there are several children of differing ages in the family.

• During these adolescent years physical growth, puberty and the alarming impact of overactive hormones is only too apparent. In many ways, these youngsters are driven by forces quite beyond their comprehension.

• Sexuality rears its head, quite properly, during these years – how many teenage boys think of much else!

• Communication skills often prove a serious stumbling block for the adolescent, who feels misunderstood and unable to make effective relationships. This is particularly true when attempting to relate effectively to the opposite sex.

• There is an unconscious awareness that leaving the security of the family is not far over the horizon.

• Friendships assume exaggerated importance. Loyalty to these relationships is often of paramount importance in an adolescent's life. It is practice for coping later without family support.

• A parent who makes a teenager lose face in front of friends may be hard to forgive.

• Educational pressures are notorious. Families build expectations around a young person's performance.

• Moodiness can have so many causes, and can so easily be projected onto the unwitting parent. However, how many people can youngsters actually trust with their moodiness? Most people will not tolerate it and will quickly become rejecting. Equally, it is important that the adolescent learns that there is no reason why other people should suffer unfairly because of their moods.

- They should be encouraged to retreat to the bedroom and read, play records, ring a friend, but, above all, withdraw their 'grumpiness' from the family before it causes unnecessary upset.

COPING WITH ADOLESCENTS

Families benefit greatly from having a pattern of mutual trust established long before a child reaches adolescence. Remember the tremendous value of personal freedom. A serious infringement at 12 years of age, for example, might lead to the child being 'grounded' on the following Friday night. Earning and providing trust is vital in these early stages before fully-fledged adolescence is reached.

An allowance becomes increasingly important in the social and personal life of young people. Controlling money and appreciating its importance and that "it does not grow on trees" is part of the process. By 18 years of age most young people are either in a job or moving firmly in this direction and becoming responsible for their own financial resources. By now they have moved away from 'pocket money' as a source of sweets and toys, to an allowance being essential for their social and personal lives.

By middle teens children should be responsible for buying at least some of their clothes, make-up, bus fares, computer games and financing their social lives. Hence, curtailing an allowance has an obvious impact. The money is not a 'right'. It is a part of a developmental programme and, as such, can be legitimately increased and decreased, where appropriate.

In our search for viable behavioural sanctions, remember the value of television and computers. Most children invest a remarkable amount of time every week in this electronic world and its restriction can make the point very firmly. It is often at its most effective if the restriction is for a matter of minutes, rather than hours. Sanctions are about controlling a breach of established boundaries, not inflicting pain and punishment, per se.

In the middle adolescent years the control of personal freedom becomes an increasingly necessary part of social development and equally a sanction for a parent, but to be used sparingly. Control of this and allowances are the key areas in which sanctions can be imposed. But remember the tremendous pressures that adolescents are under. It is a world full of self-doubt and stress, socially and academically. Family values are being questioned. Peer group loyalties are immensely powerful influences. Trust and respect, built up in the earlier years, will now be particularly valuable in helping both sides understand the pressures with which they feel inflicted.

At the Sixth Form stage two key sanctions are appropriate. Firstly, withdrawal back to an earlier level of social freedom. The young person then has to re-establish 'trust' to earn back the appropriate Sixth Form level of freedom. However, for a relatively minor breach, a single evening of being 'grounded' may well prove perfectly adequate. This is irritating for the youngster but there is also a loss of face within their peer group if they have to explain why they are not able to attend a party.

Do not forget that trust goes in both directions. It is impossible to maintain credibility while insisting on one rule for children that is openly abused by the parents. Are we prepared to reciprocate with a sense of trust? It is easy to panic, as a youngster, if parents have said that they would be back well before midnight and at 3 a.m. they have still not returned.

23

The First Time Children Holiday Unaccompanied

I remember so clearly that feeling of unreasonable panic the first time my oldest daughter suggested that she should be allowed to go away on holiday without the family, albeit only to Cornwall. She was proposing a trip with five other girls from her school and they planned to go for a week or ten days. "Don't you realise I'm grown up now?"

I had the inevitable fantasy of a convoy of slightly older, teenage boys also making their way down to precisely the same point in Cornwall – "Oh, but I had no idea they were coming, Dad!" Young people easily forget that their parents were young once.

In essence, most parents of teenage children will have to face this particular trauma at some time. What exactly are we so afraid of? We are living with the quiet assumption that our children are part of our family, part of our team. They need the team, our leadership and guidance. For the first time, they are suggesting that this may not be the case. "Could they survive even one evening without me?"

Having dealt with the challenge to our control, or even our right to the control, we then need to look at the realities of what truly concerns us. With our daughters, let us be absolutely honest with ourselves, we are terrified that the entire ten days will be one long, protracted, exhausting and possibly damaging sexual orgy! We have worrying images flashing before our minds of the huge emotional and even physical changes that will overtake our daughters following this experience. Will they ever be the same? Will they really be our daughters any more!?

A sideways glance at a teenager's social life will make it quite clear that a myriad of opportunities for sexual mischief exist in their lives in any event. There is, after all, safety in numbers. The reality of my particular experience was that in a group of giggling teenagers, there was great mutual protection. No one girl wanted to step outside the framework established by the group. In fact, in this single sex group, they had tremendous fun, and my fears of a sexual orgy never materialised.

We alkso live with the fear that our sons may degenerate into 'laddish' disgrace.

I have enjoyed examining the fundamental role that we play in preparing children for adult life. They pass through so many fascinating stages. However, the teenage years are particularly unpredictable. Children prior to puberty are still open to change. They are malleable and subject to our influences and parental pressures. However, in middle adolescence, by fourteen or fifteen, these days will have passed. The teenage girl who had been so open with her mother for many years, may now have become quiet, secretive and less communicative. It is the time of challenge. It is the phase of a child's life when they look back over all they have learnt. They begin to put together their own standards and their own criteria by which they will later live their lives which can be infuriating for a parent.

By eighteen a child is supposed to be independent, and even at sixteen may have left school and taken up a job. They are able to make their own decisions about where they will go, with whom they will live and where they will go on holiday. They may even disappear to Ibiza with a group of hooligans in the summer and, indeed, have the sexual orgy that so terrified us earlier in their lives. We have little to say any more at this point in their development.

Our role as parents is to prepare our children for their departure from the nest at eighteen. It is courting disaster for a young man or woman to leave on their first, major unsupervised trip following their eighteenth birthday with no experience of how to cope on their own.

The decision about unaccompanied holidays without parents will rest, at least in part, on the age, maturity and previous experience of the child concerned.

As parents we should develop a programme towards independence that seems appropriate for each of our children. In this way we can be reassured that they were able to make decisions for themselves and protect their own safety and health by the time they are eighteen.

As young as eight there is no reason why children should not begin to have overnight stays with friends, go on Cub or Brownie camps, go away on school trips which involve one or two nights away. In general terms, the child is learning to cope without a parent, albeit with surrogate parents available throughout the experience.

Roughly, between the ages of ten and fourteen one would hope to see a child involved in Summer camps, holidays away from home with friends' families, rather more adventurous school trips and on to more structured young people's holidays, but all with management and supervision in the background.

There should then be some degree of supervision, especially of the behaviour of those around them. Drugs and alcohol are the second major threat – our children may be introduced to drugs and will not know what they are becoming involved in. Proper drug education is vital and is, at last, becoming a regular part of their education. We know this threat hangs over them in their everyday social life. Have they the maturity to cope away from the familiar background, perhaps in a foreign city? Have we been able to offer sufficient advice?

By seventeen or eighteen the point has been reached where a group of youngsters going off together, when each may be involved in a reasonably close relationship, actually makes very sound sense. If they have decided for themselves that their relationship should be sexual, then we may be quite sure that this has been initiated long before they go on holiday.

The most important facet of this part of the exercise is that the youngsters should be fully conversant with the use of contraception. It may well be that as a couple they could usefully visit their family doctor for a private and confidential discussion.

It is to be hoped that by the end of this process, at eighteen plus, young people are able to take part in major trips abroad, often during a gap-year. They may be adventuring into parts of the world with inadequate sanitation and little or no medical care. It is vital that young people discuss their plans with their parents. That they are aware of the need for medical cover and have some first aid knowledge. They also need to do their research and know exactly how they will travel and the sorts of places they will stay. The 'backpackers' path is well trod in many corners of the world these days. It is ridiculous for a youngster, barely out of school at eighteen to set off across the world, only to find themselves becoming ill in the foothills of Tibet, with no transport, no medical support, and little notion of how to handle the crisis!

It seems only fair that youngsters should acknowledge a 'deal' in the world of travelling. They need to recognise that love and care are a part of our parental role. We have nurtured them through to this tender age. It is appropriate that we will be anxious about the risks which they are about to take. Adolescent development depends on taking calculated, carefully planned risks – not poorly equipped, quixotic forays into the unknown.

- Worried anxious parents can easily be difficult stroppy parents.

- Expect young people to discuss their plans in a mature adult/adult fashion.

- They should show you a map which they leave with you to explain exactly where they are going and what their route will be, where they will be staying and with whom.

- Ask them to explain exactly what their travel plans are.

- They should check whether or not they will need vaccinations with the family doctor, and the possibility of a basic medical kit to take with them on their travels, if they expect to be in countries with little or no medical facilities.

- Share with them that parents fantasies often run wild and that they easily imagine their children dead on one of the highways of the world, or totally destroyed by drugs or that they have even been hustled into the white slave trade!

Young people need to be aware that this sharing and planning is not only sensible but demonstrates their care and love for you. They are helping to diffuse your anxieties.

CONTACT

THE FOREIGN AND COMMONWEALTH OFFICE (FCO)
Provides consular assistance and advice. Runs a 'Know Beffre You Go' campaign, which issues sound travel advice for world travellers. This covers health, jabs, travellers' tips, checklists and information on what to do if it all goes wrong, plus how Consuls can help.
www.fco.gov.uk/knowbeforeyougo

TRAVEL HEALTH – BBC HEALTH
Warnings and information on the danger of a growing number of exotic maladies.
www.bbc.co.uk/health/travel/index.html

BBC LIFESTYLE WATCHDOG
Useful and up-to-date information under their travel section
www.bbc.co.uk/watchdog/reports/health/index2

Part 3

Common Issues
and What You Can Do

24
Attention Seeking

INTRODUCTION

It becomes increasingly apparent that in all of us, the drive for attention and recognition is fundamental to our well-being. We all need it, big and small, powerful and weak, and some find it far easier to attract than others.

Eric Byrne in his clever book Games People Play, describes our immense need for a 'stroke', as he calls it, which we would regard as a unit of attention. He describes at one point a janitor in an office block who grows or 'shrivels', depending on whether he had been recognised and acknowledged. A quick "Oh, hello John. How is your wife?" from one of the executives is enough. Bothering about people's names is so vital. It is an obvious way of making someone feel that you care, recognise, and acknowledge them.

Let's imagine that an individual requires, notionally, ten units of attention in any one day, to feel complete and satisfied and not to 'shrivel' as Eric Byrne would have said. We can speculate about the individual's reaction if these units are not fulfilled. Never underestimate the drive to complete the quota. For children, a row and a clout may actually be fulfilling. Some battered wives have returned time and time again to their brutal husbands, and, in counselling, it has emerged that for them, this is a perverse form of attention seeking.

Why is it that some shops and restaurants are so successful? Could it be that they are only too aware of how much we value our 'strokes'? They make us feel special. The local pub, with a friendly landlord, often fulfils exactly this need in his 'regulars'.

Is it naïve and immature to "want to be loved"? Surely, we should be beyond this. Absolutely not! Most people have this need and if they deny it, they are being dishonest to themselves. Children depend very heavily on love, recognition of worth, on being wanted and even needed. You can give a child immense attention by making it clear that without them you would be incomplete. However, some people are shy, private individuals, who build barriers against the very 'strokes' that they so badly need. How often have you heard, "Oh, he's tough! You can't hurt him – he doesn't care!" Deep inside, he is churning and feeling desperate. Not everyone is an open book who finds sharing worries easy. Many people do not know how to describe their anxieties, and, in any event, are terrified that their friends will find them silly or immature, or, they may simply not have the language skills to cope in the first place. But they often care profoundly.

The question must then be asked – if the drive is so great, what will happen if I cannot attract attention because no one has noticed my need? What if my worries are poorly understood even by myself? How can I cope if I am afraid of retribution, punishment, or even hurting someone else by expressing my concerns? Those units of attention have got to be found somehow. Shortly we will discuss several of the mechanisms which lead to exactly this. We must also bear in mind, on the other hand, the proud individual who denies the right to seek attention when they desperately need it. Stress is buried, unmanaged, only to explode in due course.

Sean

I will never forget Sean, a mildly dyspraxic boy of twelve. We should all have noticed his pallor, lassitude, and the increasingly hunted look during his first term in secondary schooling the previous year. His tiny middle school had beaten a larger school in a football match. In the dressing room, one of the opposing teams players reckoned, "You wait till we get you at secondary school in September – we'll sort you!" When Sean began secondary school, these same boys picked on him mercilessly, day upon day, thumping and pushing him in the playground and on the way home. They threw his books into the river, stole his cap and ripped it. They even pursued him around the supermarket where he was shopping with his Mother. The poor lad became depressed, but his pride would not let him tell me, his psychologist, or his teacher, let alone his busy parents. As his depression worsened, one afternoon he borrowed his father's .22 air rifle, levelled it at his temple and fired. Fortunately, this was an awkward operation, physically, for Sean, and the pellet simply traversed his scalp and emerged on the other side. He was rendered unconscious, but no brain damage was caused and all was well.

However, his gesture terrified his parents and shattered the professionals working with him. Sean had neither sought help nor, until then, made any subconscious effort to seek it, with almost disastrous results. The mechanisms for care were insufficient. Fortunately, he and his parents learnt from the experience that sharing and loving one another allowed for the admission of anxiety, frailty and tears, if need be.

As parents, we must be aware of the warning signs of stress, and make it our business to be supportive, before matters bubble over and get out of hand. Pallor and dark ringed eyes are typical, as is loss of appetite and poor sleep rhythm. Showing little joy in anything and abandoning favourite activities are also worrying signs. If, suddenly, friendships have been dropped, clubs are no longer attended and there is a tendency towards school refusal, we need to beware. However, there are a number of less direct and less obvious routes towards attention seeking. Remember those pillars of identity. If they wobble or are seriously threatened, stress is almost inevitable. It may require work and effort, often with the help of a skilled counsellor, to restore the balance. In the world of attention seeking, 'things are seldom what they seem'.

STEALING

Stealing is such a complex subject, which seems easy and obvious on the surface. People steal because they want what belongs to other people – it is for personal gain, maybe even generated by a sense of envy and even malice. So where does attention seeking come into this story? Even at the simplest level, we all know the story of the old lag who gets caught stealing, yet again, so that he can return to the comfort and security of the familiar world of prison.

An enormous number of children, and even adults, steal because they feel a sense of personal lack and inadequacy, and hope that what they steal will be some compensation. Often true, in the very short term. Some children feel that their pillars of identity are vulnerable and that theft gives them temporary respite. But what has been stolen disappears all too rapidly, leaving a sense of emptiness and guilt.

Can it ever be fair to say that a child actually wants to be caught? I have seldom met a child who would admit that this was the case, and yet so often there is a broad trail leading to the offence. We must never forget the enormous, almost primitive drive to seek attention, to fulfil our daily quota. As parents, we need to be particularly aware of the adolescent child's early struggle towards establishing their own identity, while still depending heavily on us as primary pillars. It is a time of great insecurity, when marital uncertainties can cause the pillars of a child's identity to rock almost uncontrollably. The arrival of a new baby, for instance, forces a youngster to share what may well have been a pillar that was, until then, a private reserve. I am not suggesting that we can condone theft, but must accept that the trail needs to be followed, the shaky identity dealt with at its source, and the child's pillars firmly re-established.

Clare

Twelve-year-old Clare was caught stealing from her Mother's handbag. The child left an enormous trail that led to her being discovered. Questions were asked. In floods of tears, the truth came out. At a psychological level, Clare needed to be caught. If you catch your child stealing, look for the trail – there will often be one, and then examine the pressures that have led to your child behaving this way.

In Clare's case there were fundamental issues to deal with. She was miserable at school, failing and the butt of the jokes among her classmates. As it turned out, she was profoundly dyslexic. It was a disgrace that her primary school had never drawn attention to her disability. Fortunately, diagnosis was completed, the secondary school proved supportive and remedial help was put in place. This has done wonders for Clare's morale.

Another issue revolved around her Mother's drinking. Her Mother at last accepted that she was alcoholic and went to Alcoholics Anonymous for help. Claire's father joined Alanon (the family support group), and the whole family backed the tremendous effort that Clare's Mother was making to deal with her difficulties. Clare felt that she was no longer isolated and matters quickly resolved themselves.

What would have happened if Clare had not responded, and had allowed her Mother to find that she had rifled her handbag again? This would have been a subtle form of psychological attention seeking. Why did she "want to be caught?"

- Clare was experiencing stress and we needed to begin to look at her reasons for seeking attention in this way.

- There was no point in asking Clare outright what the problem was – children seldom know on the surface.

- Her parents had to begin 'listening' more carefully to Clare, her moods, her life and her needs.

- Were they giving her enough time? Did she feel she could use them as confidants?

- Was there specific conflict with her Mother or Father, or conflict between her parents that she was anxious about?

- When marital upset or divorce hit a family the adults involved are often so wrapped up in their own problems that they completely miss the signs of the, often silent, emotional upset and confusion which their children are suffering.

- Were her parents working so hard or were they so socially involved that they were impatient with her?

- Were her friends or other children in the family giving her a bad time? Was she being bullied?

- Was school proving a pressurised, stressful environment?

Theft is frequently a great deal more complicated than sheer 'mischief'.

Managing stealing when it occurs

- This type of stealing is not uncommon. It is however, not excusable and must be dealt with promptly.

- Being angry and upset is a perfectly normal human response.

- When the anger has subsided, sit down with the child and discuss the issue in an adult fashion.

- Make it quite clear that the first offence may be regarded as part of growing up but the second most certainly will not. The world is full of 'winners' and 'losers'. The losers are those who fail to learn by experience.

- One 'statutory' warning, no further punishment, but it must not happen again.

For the vast majority of youngsters this is enough.

Summary

In essence, petty thieving in our youngsters is not unusual, and not normally a life shattering event. However, each instance must be treated seriously, and there are two classical patterns to watch for. The adrenaline rush 'fun brigade' who must learn a major lesson from their first experience, and the other, more worrying group, who are leaving a trail which needs gentle and sensitive investigation. Fortunately, the psychopathic 'thief' is a rare animal.

CASE STUDIES

MICHAEL

Eleven-year-old Michael found himself with a number of household chores, each of which earned him a modest amount of pocket money. Then he was caught stealing money from the housekeeping tin in the family kitchen, to buy computer games in an effort to keep up with his friends. He had no excuse. He was succeeding academically in school and at sports. He was earning money but had to replace what he had stolen, and would be allowed to maintain his jobs after the debt had been repaid. In counselling sessions, it became quite apparent that he was far from happy about his stealing. It had made him feel dirty and deceitful. He felt very close to his parents, but acknowledged that the stealing had caused a gulf which had made him feel miserable. Despite the cynical way in which he had begun stealing, he was now relieved that he had been caught and was being given a realistic vehicle with which to make good the damage. He was soon performing his tasks competently, and was delighted to feel that he would have a "wage" each week to buy the things he needed. Michael now had an appropriate way of attracting all the attention he needs.

JEREMY

Some years ago I worked with Jeremy, who was experiencing classical kleptomania. He had a locked drawer in his bedroom in which he had hidden a heap of trinkets, gadgets, toys and books that had been stolen from shops and friends over two years or more. He was using none of them – he did not even enjoy having them – he did not want them in the first place – he had plenty of pocket money and could buy all that he needed. A compulsive wave would descend upon him as he found himself moving towards the shop counter. His hand would reach out and take something, almost beyond his control. It had become a neurotic pattern and this needed a great deal of sensitive counselling from a psychologist or a child psychiatrist. Jeremy had to work for a long time on understanding the nature of compulsion and how to manage it. Even now, years later, he still feels tempted, but on the two occasions that he has slipped, his Counsellor has helped him to develop the courage to return to the shop and give back the stolen goods. Jeremy had a great deal to compensate for – an absent Father and the birth of a much adored baby sister who 'stole' most of Jeremy's attention from his Mother. His compulsive stealing kept his pillars of identity artificially stable until he was caught.

DAMIAN

A father was very angry that the school were taking a firm line with his son, Damian, who had been caught petty pilfering in Woolworth's with two of his school pals. "Surely boys will be boys?" said Damian's father, "We all nicked when we were kids – he's done no harm!"

Petty pilfering in pre-adolescent youngsters is far from unusual, but this does not make it any more acceptable. It emerged that 11-year-old Damian had been 'scrumping' fruit from a neighbouring orchard, and he and his friends had graduated to theft of fruit from local market stalls. Markets were only once a week, so Woolworth's became a substitute. Each boy set a target for the other to steal. The adrenaline rushed. They all emerged sparkling eyed with their trophies, often of no real use to them. However, this is stealing, and when it comes to light, must be taken seriously. Once caught, the "game" is over. It is important to emphasise to youngsters that 'winners' learn from experience; losers get caught over and over again. Should it occur a second time, it is worth involving the local policeman to offer a caution. The youngster has no further excuses.

MICK

Thirteen-year-old Mick had been caught for the fourth time stealing from the changing rooms in school, this time a scout knife.

Mick has now been held to account and, to his counsellor's alarm, implied that what was available was his by rights. He wanted the scout knife, so he took it. The cell phone was left available, so it became his. Not only did we have to deal with this rather psychopathic young man, with only the barest shreds of a conscience, but we also needed to be aware of the danger of leaving temptation lying in a child's way.

Following court proceedings, Mick started in therapy, gradually learning to appreciate the rules of the 'social game'. He began to realise that now that he had been caught, he would never be dealt with lightly again, and that there were, therefore, pros and cons to the advisability of his behaviour. He will never have a conscience, but a psychopath can be taught what rules apply, and what 'seems to work best', but not the development of conscience, per se.

HANK

I have known Hank since I diagnosed his dyslexia over eight years ago. He was never an easy personality. He had an air of arrogance which hid his enormous self-doubt. He was difficult to deal with at home and was rude and aggressive with his special needs teacher. Support for his dyslexia was terminated very early in his schooling and he rapidly began to find other ways of compensating for his somewhat damaged ego.

Shortly after his first shoplifting offence fifteen months ago, I agreed to see him again on a regular basis aimed at developing a degree of insight into his behaviour and what motivated it. Sadly, the pull of his peer group was far greater! They became damaging and almost irreversible new pillars of his identity.

Some weeks ago, after a third pint of beer, he was persuaded to break into a flat owned by an elderly lady, thought to be away on holiday. She was not away. She was terrified. Hank is now in a Young Offenders Institution. It is this picture that haunts the minds of parents dealing with children who have been caught stealing.

LYING

Lies are usually told as a form of problem avoidance, to divert attention and blame or sometimes as a strategy to pass the blame to others. Children must understand that trust, mutual respect and love are closely intermingled. If we cannot believe one another, we cannot rely on each other's support, either. It is worth reminding children that they are as much fundamental pillars of our identities as we are of theirs. If they rock our security, it has a profound effect on us and our happiness.

However, we must never lose sight of the 'games playing' so often implicit in lying. Why would a child sometimes tell a blatant lie and persist, in the face of solid evidence to the contrary – with a stupid lie, from which there is no retreat? Lengthy, unpleasant attention is worth more to the child than the few seconds that would have followed telling the truth! We need to look within ourselves. Why does our child have such a maladaptive and painful need to seek this type of attention? Why is his daily quota of attention not being satisfied?

Parents under pressure can be volatile, even explosive, and very unpredictable. This often brings with it an instinctive need for the child to lie, sensing that if only they can contain the problem and divert attention, a major explosion will be controlled. They know the truth will eventually come to light, by which time parental tempers might have settled. Is the lie simply to keep parents' volatile behaviour at bay?

Daniel

I worked with a mother, dealing largely with the 'dyslexic' difficulties of her son, Daniel, aged 12. However, the issue that really worried her reminded me of Hans in his Alpine village, all those centuries ago. He teased the villagers so often that a wolf was on the prowl, that they eventually took no notice of his cries, with a very sad outcome for Hans!

We looked at why Daniel constantly lied about his lack of homework but, more particularly, about the brutal way that he said his teacher dealt with him, and how his friends had begun to bully him in school. Yet, on investigation, there was seldom a shred of truth in his allegations. A germ of truth perhaps, but this was being totally exaggerated and distorted to create an image of a harassed and misunderstood boy. Very much the 'cry for help' type of lying, a search for excuses, clutching for an alibi to explain failure.

Daniel was assessed and dyslexia diagnosed. He had coped with seven years of academic failure. However, he now had a strategy for the immediate future and remedial teaching which helped to resolve his difficulties.

I also spent time talking to him about the 'cry wolf syndrome' and he began to see that he was often his own worst enemy. However, there had been very good reasons for feeling inadequate, depressed, and that he was failing both himself and the family. Hopefully, as improvement gained momentum, he no longer needed to search for alibis.

What should we categorise as a lie in the first place? It seems obvious – not telling the truth, claiming something to be the case which it frankly is not, denial of responsibility when one is flagrantly guilty.

Then there is the subtler world of half-truths, the clever use of language which allows the creation of an impression which is quite clearly not so.

Janice

I had a 16-year-old in the practice who had been told that she must not go to nightclubs because of the risk of drugs. There was a local club called the Adam and Eve. On returning home, long after her 11 o'clock curfew, she denied having been at the Adam and Eve and said that she was with two of her friends. The implication was that she had been at their homes. In fact, she had been in a neighbouring town, visiting a nightclub there! When the truth eventually emerged, she said "Oh, but I told you I wasn't at the Adam and Eve. I didn't tell you a lie." But this half-truth caused a major family row which, in a perverse way, the girl found rewarding, fulfilling a neurotic need to attention seek. We then searched for the real underlying pressure that was causing this provocative behaviour. A major pillar of her identity, her father, had threatened to leave home after an affair had come to light in which her mother had become embroiled. Even her mother could not be relied upon as a pillar. How could her father even consider just abandoning his daughter?

As parents we have responsibilities too. How often do we talk about 'white lies' that we tell our children. Be careful that these do not catch you out in the final analysis. If you are having to answer your child, it is no good saying, "Ah, yes, but that was a white lie." This happens occasionally in my practice when parents assure anxious children that they will be sitting upstairs waiting for them, and then go shopping for half an hour. We are careful to intercept them on these occasions, rather than allow a panicky child to find that their parents have deceived them. It is not meant as a real deception but this is certainly what it becomes in the child's mind.

Why Tell Lies?

- The primary intention must be to avoid punishment, reprisals, or criticism. It simply deflects the blame elsewhere and leaves us unhindered. Ninety-five percent of us have at some time in our lives told a lie. Sit down with the child, explain that a lack of trust is a serious state of affairs. From now on lies will be treated as very serious offences, regardless of what they have been about. The first incident is a learning experience to which the child is expected to respond, and there will be no further punishment. Further lies will be regarded as extremely serious, with unpleasant sanctions to follow.

- Perpetual, rather silly, meaningless lies, which are almost always discovered, need a little closer investigation. What signals are the children giving? We need to look carefully at how we are actually managing our family. Are we less than consistent in the way we respond to our children? If we lose our temper rather too easily, the child's instinct may be to deny and lie simply to divert the explosion. Ironically, by the time the 'dust has settled' and the lie has come to light, parents have often cooled down and the explosion does not occur. This simply teaches the child that if they can keep parents at bay for a couple of hours, they will be easier to deal with. The child needs to know that lies are not acceptable, but, equally, as parents, we may well need to be very much more consistent.

- Very rarely do we meet the pathological liar, often with a psychopathic personality, who does not know the difference between truth and falsehood. They will respond as suits them best, often on a perverse whim. Management is likely to involve the lengthy input of a child psychiatrist and a great deal of patience from the family. This is a rare condition and other explanations are far more likely, even in the persistent liar.

In essence, look carefully at what you are told, especially at the underlying intent. Are there dynamics within your family which need adjusting of which the lies are a subconscious expression?

COMFORT EATING

Comfort eating is a familiar phenomenon. "If only I could have a bar of chocolate, I'd feel better!" "I'm feeling depressed. I'll nip down town and grab a hamburger!" To some extent, a self-inflicted wound, as we know it will spoil our appetite for an appropriate meal and may put on unnecessary weight. Almost as we eat it, we sense the inadequacy and failure implicit in the behaviour.

However, there is some biological validity in this behaviour. If blood sugar levels run down, a boost does restore spirits, helps concentration and gives us energy. It is a question of control and moderation. If your child is inclined to comfort eat, then regular meals, with properly balanced nutrition, become extremely important. Be careful not to allow blood sugar levels to run down too far. There is nothing wrong with a boost to our 'joie de vivre', but it is when it becomes excessive, compulsive, potentially damaging and distorts our nutritional balance that problems begin to arise.

Chloe

Chloe, who was 9, was always making slabs of richly buttered toast until her Mother began nagging her about her weight. Chloe retreated to her bed and became a 'secret' comfort eater. The crumbs in her bed and the butter stains on the sheets told their own story, but her Mother took matters no further until she found the residue of ten individual fruit pies stored in Chloe's wardrobe! At this point, she and I met to discuss Chloe and her rather compulsive over-eating.

Chloe's father had begun travelling overseas on a regular basis, and was frequently away for three or four weeks at a stretch. He was extremely busy, and Chloe had little or no contact with him during these times. Chloe, who was a middle child, was struggling for a position in the family, close to her father and felt his absence painfully. "I feel better about Daddy if I have a couple of slices of toast!"

When this came to light during counselling, her father decided to buy a range of post cards which he pre addressed and on which he wrote brief messages to Chloe in his hotel most nights. He also dealt with his business e-mails each evening and always included one for Chloe. This allowed them virtual nightly contact. For Chloe, it was not so much what her father said, but the very fact that he loved her enough to make the contact. Chloe never found her pillars of identity easy to establish and her absent father made this even less secure. As a middle child, so much had to be shared and even fought for.

This special relationship between father and daughter has helped to resolve the 'middle child' syndrome, as she now feels that she has her special place in the family. Fortunately, the other two children do not feel in any way left out of this process. We also discovered that she was being teased in class for being "porky". Obviously, this was not being helped by her over-eating. It is extraordinary how self-destructive people can sometimes be. However, her self-image has much improved, and she has become more confident about herself. She is beginning to take more exercise and the pounds are falling away.

Colum

Colum, who was at boarding school, saw me because he was dyslexic and might need extra time in his GCSE examinations. He was becoming hugely overweight and marginally depressed. I had a session with the boy and both his parents. It became apparent that it was always Colum who grabbed the second portion of any meal, and, indeed, had often eaten it before others had managed their first! Matters came to a head when he was caught, yet again, in school, slipping out to the village chip shop and returning to his room with a large helping of chips. The stench of cold, stale chips was unmistakable.

We first had to deal with Colum's depression. He was referred to a child psychiatrist and spent a short period on medication. He soon felt better and his dyslexic difficulties were being addressed. He felt at last that his life was under control. Chip shop visits stopped, but I suggested to his parents that they all became pro-active in managing his over weight problem. He began counselling, and the counsellor referred him to a dietician and to Weight Watchers where he was treated as a young adult. It was now a 'cause celebre' within the family that Colum was trying to lose weight and was actually achieving his targets on a weekly basis. The family were 'applauding' appropriately and he was beginning to feel special and in charge of his own life at long last.

Davina

Ten-year-old Davina brings us on to a rather more serious facet of over and under eating. Food can easily become an attention-seeking vehicle, as we described earlier. However, its absence or food refusal can be even more sinister. Davina had an increasing number of foods that she was refusing and constantly wanted to know "Is this going to be fattening?" She would begin to comfort eat 'safe foods', especially fresh fruit, between meals, to the point where she had destroyed her appetite at mealtime.

Davina was becoming torn between that awful empty, lonely feeling and the sense of well being if she ate appropriately. She was far from under weight, but her body image and its apparent lack of appropriateness was in her own mind.

With Davina, the family struggled to avoid the desperate 'Catch 22' of attention seeking. With food refusal we often nag and pester and by doing so we actually increase the chances of further food refusal. The neurotic behaviour is being reinforced by the very attention that is supposed to stop it. But when we stand firm and say nothing, the child starves to the point where we have to take action. It is vital, with this type of eating pattern, that the response is swift and positive, and taken very early on in the process.. Above all, 'do not feed a neurosis'.

Give attractive food, in sensibly small portions, and do not comment. Clean away the plates when the family have finished, making no comment at all as to whether the particular child's plate has been cleaned. Produce the pudding and do not become involved in a verbal battle. If, after two or three months, there is evidence that weight loss is becoming a problem, and that despite being careful about feeding and not paying it attention, the issue is still not improving, see your family doctor and discuss referral to an appropriately qualified child psychiatrist. It is very important that we avoid the early onset of anorexia nervosa or bulimia, two severe forms of eating disorder requiring sensitive treatment. Do not let food dominate your family.

Remember that when we are empty, the hunger pangs can be very uncomfortable, particularly if they are fuelled by adrenaline caused by anxiety and stress. A sudden input of food can be very relaxing. It boosts the blood sugar level and creates a benign sense of contentment. However, taking it at a neurotic level, Freud would have regarded it as a search for oral satisfaction and it often implies a lack of perceived love, especially physical contact.

We do not need to worry about occasional comfort eating or even the odd period of gluttony at Christmas time, for example. It is more of a concern when it becomes a perpetual habit, and even more if it is secretive and furtive. Avoid over reacting, but do ask the question: "What is causing the stress and pressure that is leading to this neurotic behaviour?" If there is no immediate answer apparent, do not be afraid to seek help from a psychologist, counsellor or via your family doctor, a psychiatrist, especially if you suspect anorexia nervosa which requires very skilled, qualified management.

CHILDREN WHO ARE CONSTANTLY FEIGNING ILLNESS

In most families, illness tends to attract attention, and quite rightly so. It is a time when children feel vulnerable, often in pain and need family help and support. There is also the process of recuperation and preparing for the return to school. We are conditioned from a very early age to see those around us attracting apparently undue attention because they are ill. Despite the unpleasantness of an illness, the warm, cosy feeling of attention is very pleasant. Is it any wonder when children are unhappy, feeling that the pillars of their identity are threatened, they resort to a well-tried pattern of attention seeking? However, for the 'illness' to be credible, appropriate symptoms may have to be invented. Headaches, backaches, and tummy aches are classic, because it is difficult to check whether they really exist.

Beware, however, the psychosomatic illness which may be caused by stress, may be painful and the individual is genuinely 'ill'. This is not a form of malingering. It is important, with attention seeking faked illness, that it is spotted quickly and the family doctor involved to provide legitimacy to further illnesses, which may genuinely necessitate time in bed. Nevertheless, with faked illness, we must always ask why the individual needed this comfort and attention. Why was there not an easier and more appropriate forum within which this attention could be sought?

Thomas

> I was asked how to deal with a son who was constantly faking illness to avoid going to school. His Mother recently came in behind Thomas, who was in the bathroom, in time to see him pushing a toothbrush down his throat to make himself sick. Thomas had complained of violent tummy aches from the moment he awoke each morning. He was white and seemed quite unable to eat his breakfast. His Mother now felt that he was lying to her and falsifying his illness as he was obviously making himself physically sick.

We need to be careful that everything is not dismissed as 'malingering'. Thomas's Mother should have visited her family doctor to confirm that there was no organic reason for the tummy aches. It is possible that these were real, and the toothbrush episode was a desperate struggle to produce 'evidence' that would be taken seriously. In fact, Thomas was developing an ulcer, but his father had often commented; "Oh, you great git, you make far too much fuss!" The toothbrush was his only mechanism for attracting positive attention. No one could gainsay 'real vomit', could they?

There is a fundamental ground rule. A child only stays at home if it is a weekend, a holiday or they are genuinely ill. For Thomas, an agreement was reached with the family doctor. If he felt unable to go to school, he should automatically go down to see the GP. It was important to break the cycle of being 'homebound'. Let the doctor judge whether the boy is sick enough to stay off school, and abide by this decision. In these circumstances, if the lad is declared too ill for school, the attitude must be "sick children should be in bed until they begin to convalesce".

Feigned illness may well be a 'cry for help' which we should not ignore. These situations are often more complex than they appear, and it may be wise to seek the advice of a psychologist, qualified counsellor or your family doctor.

CASE STUDIES

JUSTINE

Justine's parents were separating, and were going through an extremely unhappy emotional time. Justine felt that if only she could stay at home, she could in some way control what happened. So she began inventing 'blinding headaches'. The family eventually became involved as a family group in therapy. Justine began to understand the worrying nature of her parent's problems. The family was helped to deal with them and Justine returned to normal school attendance again. If you know that a child's pillars of identity are likely to be threatened, take care, and make plans to reinforce the wobbling edifice of their identity.

KATIE

I remember Katie, who produced temperatures of 104 or more, every week. She really was ill and needed to stay in bed. There was no doubting the genuineness of her condition, and yet by early afternoon she was always much better and able to take part in the family meals and activities in the evening. There was absolutely no question of Katie 'malingering'. But how was it possibe to explain a real "illness" that seemed to occur on the same morning every week. We kept a diary of days, times and circumstances. Fascinatingly, it emerged that she had a piano lesson on the days the temperatures occurred, and it was these that she was, subconsciously, desperate to avoid. The piano teacher was abrasive, shouted and pinched her cheek violently if she played a bad note. Stress can produce remarkable physical symptoms. Once the source of stress was removed, the temperatures no longer occurred.

BEN

Ben was the more typical school malingerer. He had a mild dose of flu and was thoroughly enjoying the luxury of being at home, the regular meals on a tray, TV, and, above all, no schoolwork. His father caught him trying to shake the thermometer up to create a 'high temperature'.

His parents decided that lying and cheating of this kind was unacceptable. He had broken the thermometer and had to pay for a replacement out of his pocket money. We also instituted a star chart in school, related to the maturity that he displayed in class, and this was linked to pocket money at home. Ben began performing more steadily, and was rewarded for his efforts. He was also told the story of "cry wolf – don't fake illness – people may not take you seriously when it really matters". Don't seek attention for inappropriate reasons.

JASON

Jason was very pale and often violently sick shortly before needing to leave for school. The family doctor suggested that he might be suffering from migraine. However, long after the attack had petered out, he still insisted that he should not go to school. His parents soon found that if they forced him to return to school, this rapidly provoked a further attack.

I sent him to a Paediatrician who made a clear diagnosis of his Attention Deficit with Hyperactivity Disorder, and treatment was put in place. We dealt with the root of Jason's stress and he no longer needed to 'use' his migraines, albeit subconsciously, as a vehicle for work avoidance. Since his treatment on medication he has been more able to remain on task in class.

DAMIAN

Damian became increasingly miserable, developing classic tummy aches, and frequently being sent home ill from school. He was a jealous little boy, responding to the arrival of his baby brother. He had enjoyed his role as "only child" for six years. His world was falling apart. Great efforts were made to give him special responsibilities, helping with the baby. His father began allocating a deliberate hour of quality time to Damian, every Saturday. The pillars of Damian's identity, once vulnerable, were secure again.

25

Bullying

Bullying is pernicious damaging behaviour, which, at its very least, causes unhappiness to the victim, a sense of power and control in the bully, and a vicarious, malevolent thrill to the hangers on. There can never be any excuse for persistent bullying, whether physical or verbal abuse. Indeed constant verbal persecution can be even more tainting and damaging, as it so often attacks the family, and parents in particular. The aim is to rock the very foundations of the individual to the point where the pillars of his or her identity are so insecure that they collapse and the individual becomes an over-ready victim. Unfortunately, the old world advice to stand up to a bully because "they are always cowards – fight back", is ill conceived. The bully is often bigger, older and almost always surrounded by cronies. Fortunately, bullying is now a high profile issue in all our schools and strategies are firmly in place for its management and eradication. Children need to be aware of a system from which they can expect an efficient response, if the need arises.

Jonathan

Jonathan taught me a salutary lesson about the effect of bullying and how inept we, as parents and professionals, often are in spotting those crucial signals before a tragedy occurs. Jonathan was eventually found, half starved, frozen and terrified, hiding under a canal bridge. It was evident that he had tried to hang himself. His neck was raw and bleeding, he was panting and desperately afraid.

Jonathan had arrived in his new school to be told that there were initiation rituals through which he and other new boys must pass. The boy principally involved in orchestrating this systematic, ritualised bullying, extorted money from Jonathan for every day that he refused to comply. The pressure mounted, his locker was ransacked, his new watch smashed, and he came home with a cut lip and badly bruised ribs. When a cursory enquiry was made by his mother, he simply muttered about rough football matches. Increasing pallor, the out of character tears, bruises to the back, ribs and upper arms should all have been signals that were sadly missed. This went on for weeks and weeks, driving Jonathan further and further into an emotional corner. He was hide-bound by the schoolboy code

– "I must never sneak". His parents knew that all was not well, but had no idea what the problem was and Jonathan was unwilling to tell them.

I was asked to see him because his otherwise excellent school reports were beginning to deteriorate, and he was becoming withdrawn and distractible in class. He was a delightful young man, with a high IQ, and much to offer. None of us spotted the truth.

With the benefit of hindsight, what were the vital signs we could have recognised?

- Inadequately explained bruising to back and upper arms.

- Jonathan was becoming increasingly withdrawn, which, for an extroverted child, was a worrying symptom in itself. He was often close to tears. Some children even become clinically depressed.

- A placid, amiable boy suddenly developed a very short fuse, snapping rudely at his parents, and even at his favourite teacher on one occasion. People became less sympathetic with what they interpreted as teenage moodiness.

- His concentration and performance in class were deteriorating steadily as the term advanced.

- He was constantly 'losing' things. His parents were becoming angry at having to replace endless sports equipment, textbooks, and even having to have his blazer repaired on five separate occasions.

- Apparently neurotically, he was no longer prepared to go to several parts of his hometown which had been favourite haunts.

- His beloved football, for which he had shown considerable talent, was dropped, and he dodged games lessons whenever possible.

We are increasingly aware of the pressure that bullying forces upon both adults and children. The National Association of Head Teachers has issued new guidelines suggesting, "All Heads have a legal duty to prevent all forms of bullying in their school". Indeed, schools can now be held legally liable for failure to address bullying for the distress and damage which this failure may cause, especially if it is allowed to continue after being reported. The bullying may include not only physical pain and stress, but a significant reduction in school performance, for which the school may be found liable if the bullying is not being appropriately managed.

A "What to watch for" list now exists. There is a developing mechanism for dealing with bullying, should parents feel that the symptoms exist in their child. It is vital that all incidents are looked into very carefully, to see exactly what the dynamics of the circumstances are. I am not excusing bullying in any way, but simply suggesting that circumstances need to be investigated thoroughly. There are occasions when behaviours are invited, or a rude approach is met with a robust response, or a failure to comply is interpreted as a form of abuse.

Jason

Jason was an interesting case in point. He was a heavy handed fifteen year old himself, who was used to getting his own way and was almost always able to achieve his ends, often leaving his victims hurt and unhappy. He was included in the school under sixteen rugby side, but forgot his new bootlaces. He tried to insist that one of the other boys should part with theirs, only to find that the bulk of the team rounded on him and suggested that he sorted out his own problems for himself. He pleaded persecution and bullying. As two or three of the other boys had spare pairs of laces, his pleas were, initially, listened to with sympathy. However, once matters were investigated in detail it became clear that Jason was, in fact, being given his just deserts and with infinitely less pain than he himself would have inflicted.

I remember sitting in a Head's office observing a thirteen year old, who had been referred to me, cruise his lonely way across the playground. He noticed a group of older boys to his left, and walked very close to the group muttering something as he passed. They took little or no notice. He wandered back towards the school, and this time, barged straight through the middle of this older group and clearly said something provocative over his shoulder. Still no response from the group. He returned moments later and this time was chased and thumped for his pain. The aggressive behaviour was not to be tolerated but I had to help this lad look at his body language and at the way in which he was actually inviting trouble. He was almost enjoying the attention seeking involved in his victim behaviour. He had been referred to me because he seemed to find himself being bullied in every school to which he was moved. The dynamics were now becoming much clearer. A period of counselling taught this lad how to play the 'game of life' more efficiently and he found other, happier vehicles for attention seeking. His unhappy homelife proved a big issue.

There are two sides to every story.

What to do?

Mechanisms need to be established which not only work but can be seen to work, for the comfort of the parents, teachers, but, particularly, for the child who is being bullied.

- The establishment of a Parents/School Bullying Council within your child's school. This should be easy for the child to approach, without any fear of recrimination, and should involve an initial assessment of all the circumstances in discussion between the parents, the Head Teacher of the school and a specifically designated member of staff.

- If either party feels the issue should be taken further, then interviews should take place with both the youngsters concerned, but separately. Both sets of parents should be involved in the discussions. It is vital that the story is made absolutely clear so that the dynamics can be understood, fairly and in their entirety.

- If bullying is proven beyond reasonable doubt, then the bully should be suspended, pending the parent's signing of the new government pledge undertaking that their child will bully no longer. A recurrence of bullying should involve further, lengthier suspension, and the involvement of the School Psychological Services.

- Weekly counselling should take place with both children involved. It is vital that we monitor any possible return of the behaviour.

- It is important that the bullied youngster receives counselling in the management of this type of behaviour, including Assertiveness Training. Body language can be extremely important in the management of bullying, as can learning to control your temper. Insight can bring considerable protection on a future occasion. Group work and role-playing can prove a great help in appreciating the signals that our body language are conveying, often unwittingly. Is a child reflecting an animal readiness for conflict or defiance? Are they looking so vulnerable and defeated that they become an easy target? Is the child concerned rising to the bait of teasing like an over eager trout, and encouraging an increasing number of 'fishermen'? Above all, the schoolboy ethic of not "telling tales" simply cannot be allowed to apply to this kind of damaging behaviour.

- The bullies themselves need help. Bullying often comes from a considerable degree of insecurity and vulnerability. The child or adult needs to understand what is pushing them to over-assert themselves to recoup a fragile ego. Once again, role-play will encourage the growth of insight.

Fundamentally, the management of this scourge in our schools must be dealt with honestly, and robustly. All concerned must feel that they have easy and ready access to support and will receive a fair and honest hearing – and that action, if necessary, will be taken. Safeguards against recrimination are crucial if the bullied child is to feel safe enough to report the problem in the first instance.

DON'T TELL TALES

I have been confronted several times, by parents and school teachers, worried about bullying, with the 'mixed messages' of "Don't tell tales". We were all brought up with this ethic, and pride ourselves in our strength of character and the way we are prepared to protect our friends.

Sharon

Sharon, 11, characterised the dilemma beautifully for us. Her parents had been grateful to be told that her brother had been stealing from his mother's handbag, and dealt with it accordingly. Sharon basked in reflected glory, but subsequently many of her tales were not even true. I discussed with her parents her tendency to curry favour by telling tales on her older brother. He only had to step out of line in any way and she ran to her father, to explain exactly what had been going on. She was jealous of her bright, successful brother and saw this as a way of manipulating her parents.

We discussed Sharon's insecurities at some length, and discovered that a mild learning difficulty was at the root of much of them. She felt that she was failing and falling even further behind the high standards her brother had set. This problem diagnosed, she received additional support in class, and began to see the world as a more positive place. Her parents encouraged her to join a young people's drama group, and she was thrilled to be involved in their latest production. Sharon no longer needs to undermine her brother. Her brother, David, has been encouraged to take an interest in his sister's drama and Sharon has actually been to watch her brother play rugby. The contact between them is much more positive. Point scoring is no longer necessary.

However, matters can become much more serious …

Miranda

I remember well the anguish of twelve-year-old Miranda's parents who I had come to know well over six months of counselling. They rang up to say that she had failed to return home from school, and it was now 10.30 at night. What should they do? I advised calling the Police. Miranda was eventually found, cold and miserable, crouched in a barn in the countryside. Her parents were called and they arrived, with the family doctor, to find their daughter in a state of shock. With the help of a sedative, she slept through the day and was at last able to describe the pressures that she was under.

The target for the bullying had been her early physical development. She was developing breasts. She was over-sensitive and before she knew it a small group of her classmates were deriving increasing enjoyment from reducing her to tears in the playground, pursuing her home, ringing on the home telephone, and leaving vulgar messages on the answerphone. She had tried to mention it to her parents, who felt it was "just part of growing up".

If only they had listened. Frequently, the beginnings of teasing and this type of persecution are remarkably simple and apparently rather silly. She had several friends in her class who knew exactly how miserable she was but were "not prepared to tell tales". She had even suggested killing herself. With her friends unwilling to support her, she began to feel that the whole world had turned against her. This was inexcusably cruel behaviour and a gutless response from her so called friends.

The family and Miranda were involved in regular counselling for several months and gradually Miranda became a more confident teenager.

Asif

The case of Asif was far more desperate. An Asian boy, Asif was beaten half to death, requiring forty-eight stitches and six weeks in hospital. He was beaten by three white youths while a number of others looked on. There were several people not directly involved who knew the truth of this attack. One must question whether the "don't grass" ethic is what it seems, or is it simply fear of retribution? 'Don't tell tales' in Asif's context renders the onlooker guilty of being party to the attack – there can be no defence for this type of cowardice.

Unfortunately, months have now passed, and the Police have no leads. It is certain that a number of people could put matters to rights, rapidly, if they only had the courage to do so. Meanwhile, Asif is beginning to respond to counselling, but the nightmares have not yet passed.

John

John, now 15, arrived home in tears. Despite the fact that he was shaking almost uncontrollably for more than an hour, his parents were unable to draw the story from him, as he felt that he could not 'grass' on his friends. It eventually emerged that three boys in his class had tortured a cat to death, ostensibly because the daughter of the household concerned was not prepared to accept a date.

We sat down together and decided that we needed to be quite precise in our definitions. There needed to be a list of 'zero tolerance' activities which must transcend the tale telling ethic. No one should accept this brutal behaviour. There should be nowhere to hide for these boys.

Diana

It took a great deal of work, over many hours, to persuade Diana, who is now fourteen, that emotional and sexual abuse by an uncle should be discussed. Her life has been materially changed and may never be the same again. The uncle had absolutely no right to have so inappropriate and permanent an impact on another human being. He had given up his right to the protection of secrecy. However, Diana needed support and counselling in the early stages when her family, especially her older brother, turned on her in disbelief. At long last, all concerned came to terms with what had happened – it was not simply an invention by Diana. Her Uncle is now in prison.

Darren

Bullying in and out of school is a current issue, discussed often in my office. A worried parent said just the other day, "We know Darren is being bullied in school, but he simply won't tell us who is responsible". He was found crying in bed at night. He refused to go to school without a great deal of cajoling, was losing sleep and eating far too little. This boy had been made ill and terrified by the behaviour of three boys and a girl in his class. He was afraid that they would retaliate and he would be beaten even more, if he breathed a word.

I persuaded Darren's parents that these youngsters have no right to persecute anyone in this way. They were to try to persuade the school that they need a forum in which these 'zero tolerance' behaviours can be safely discussed without retribution. This forum would need to meet on a regular basis to consider any current cases. The forum is now convinced that any form of retaliation against Darren or anyone else, should be seen as an extremely serious offence, which would automatically involve the Police. It is difficult for a youngster to seek out a suitable teacher to talk to by themselves, and far too often we, as adults, simply respond, "It will do you good to cope with your own problems, and don't come here telling tales!" We need to see bullying, both physical, emotional and verbal, as a 'zero tolerance' activity.

In essence, as a community, we need to see any behaviour which materially changes the life and stability of another person as being quite unacceptable. The victim's protection must become of paramount importance and we must take pride in the establishment of this new ethical code.

David

David, who is now sixteen, provided us with a subtle example of our new code at work. He lit a fire in his comprehensive school, which injured no one but put a number of people at risk and caused a certain amount of damage. This was dangerous behaviour and caused criminal damage. The potential risk to his schoolmates fits our 'zero tolerance' criterion. David, however, blamed a friend for what had happened, and the friend was arrested by the Police. He pleaded innocence but would not 'grass' on David. He faced Court proceedings with the possibility of custody. The life of this perfectly innocent teenage boy was likely to be dramatically affected. David boasted about his behaviour in the safety of his own home. David's parents eventually convinced him that he had, therefore, abdicated any right to the silence of his friend. Ironically, he had just plucked up the courage to accept responsibility and clear his mate, when the friend decided that David was no longer entitled to his loyalty and told the Police the whole story.

Even at the very last, David has been given no credit for his belated honesty!

CONTACTS

CHILDLINE
Tel: 0800 1111 (24 hours)

NATIONAL SOCIETY FOR THE PREVENTION OF CRUELTY TO CHILDREN
Tel: 0800 800500

THE SAMARITANS
Tel: 0345 909090 (or your local number will be in your phone book)

ANTI-BULLYING CAMPAIGN
Room 37, 10 Borough High Street, London SE1
Counselling Advice Line: 020 7378 1146/7/8/9

BULLYING ONLINE
Also Email bullying; mobile phone bullying and keeping safe in cyberspace. Useful advice and assistance.
http://www.bullying.co.uk/

KIDSCAPE
Bullying, safety – advice and parent counselling
Tel: 020 7730 3300

26
Conflict Between Our Children

Many years ago I sat alongside my stunned classmates and stared open-mouthed at our English teacher, Spider Kelly, as he sat cross-legged on the top of a bar stool stroking his Bernard Shaw beard, declaring quietly: "Do you know, the only person I have truly hated is my sister." We suddenly began to realise how naive we sounded as we struggled to claim that you must love your Mum, your Dad, your brothers and sisters. In his languid way, Spider simply said: "Why?"

There is a fundamental blood bond between Mother and child and, to a lesser extent, Father. However, children are only loosely genetically related to one another, of different genders, often separated by age or, more problematic, very close in age, or they may even be twins. As long ago as Cain and Abel, siblings have killed each other for personal gain, jealousy or because they could not tolerate the opposition. Animals are born with an instinct to survive and to push those who might hinder this survival out of the way. We have now become so sophisticated that we hardly recognise this primal urge in ourselves.

As children growing up in the same family, indifference is the least likely response to one another – jealousy and rivalry are quite likely but there is also the possibility of an immensely strong bond. No one is likely to know you better than your brother or sister. If an affection exists and mutual interests are shared, a tremendous, mutually supportive relationship may well develop.

Colin

Within most families the primary reward for which children struggle is the approval of their parents, the gaining of their attention and time. Life is often easier if the two or three children concerned are reasonably separated in age, all of equable temperament and all performing adequately, with no need to challenge one another. This is seldom the case. I worked with a family where the daughter was six, bright, alert, with a very 'sparkly' personality, but the 12-year old boy, Colin, was hyperactive, marginally dyslexic, failing in school and finding it difficult to make friends. Colin said to me: "Why am I always the one in the wrong? She never gets blamed!" The sad truth is, he was entirely right. He was not easy to deal with. He found it extremely difficult to sit still for more than a few minutes and was very jealous of his little sister. Much poking, prodding and taking of his sister's property went on. His parents found him extremely irritating and were very relieved when he went to bed. We had to work steadily at managing his distractibility and working on his dyslexic vulnerabilities in the hope that we could rekindle his battered self esteem. His school was prepared to become involved in helping him and his parents realised that he needed his own reward system to build up a sense of their approval. Furthermore, he was the older child and this created a 'window of time' in the evenings. His sister began going to bed 45 minutes earlier, and his father started using this slot to rekindle his relationship with his son.

Charlie

We can undoubtedly ease the way and understand some of the dynamics under-lying sibling conflict. Before the arrival of his sister, Charlie had been an only child for twelve years, a comparatively late arrival in the marriage, much adored and still rather spoilt. His little sister, Sarah, was now nearly three months old. Charlie complained endlessly, his motivation in school had dwindled and he was refusing to go to guitar lessons. His parents, understandably, felt that he was being unnecessarily difficult and their approach was rather punitive and authori-tarian. The more they insisted that he finished his homework, and threatened to stop his allowance, the more he began to make himself ill so that he could legiti-mately refuse to go to school. They eventually came to me when Charlie tried to push his little sister out of her pram.

We looked at Charlie's need for a notional ten units of attention in any one day, all of which were being satisfied and more, before the arrival of his little sister. Obviously, love now had to be shared, but, importantly, the more of a nuisance he became, the more unpleasant was the attention he attracted. His parents agreed to adjust their management strategies. He was given tasks to do which made him feel essential to the welfare of the family, and his father cut a deliberate 'window of time' each evening to spend with Charlie. This became a deliberately structured routine to which Charlie looked forward.

Charlie was allowed to help feed his little sister and while the baby was having her bath, he ensured that all the relevant clothes were brought in and organised for his mother. She made it quite clear that she could not have coped without his assistance. Once he was in bed, his mother came in, sat and chatted to him. He began to see helpfulness and sharing as a way of attracting the missing units of attention. Curiously, he became the most critical if others failed to do their share!

Luke

Luke, who was now seventeen, came to see me to discuss the possibility of extra time in his A level exams because he was dyslexic. We discussed study skills and he complained bitterly that his two younger siblings were allowed ready access to his room, to play with his computer, and he was punished for being selfish if he made them go away. He also complained that when anything went wrong, as the oldest, he was always blamed. Luke, as an older adolescent with important study to consider, needed space. He also needed the sanctuary of his own personal area. The family began to insist that the others respected Luke's space and the situation calmed considerably.

The middle child syndrome is well documented – Claire was a prime example.

Claire

Claire had an older and a younger brother. By the time thirteen year old Claire's younger brother started school, she was beginning to feel like the 'meat in the sandwich'. She became increasingly infantile, behaving more like an eight year old, and even returned to bed-wetting. We must remember that the youngest child attracts attention because of their youth and their understandable needs, and the eldest child has a natural position of seniority. The ten units of attention needed each day are difficult to achieve for the middle child. It is easy to be forced into a great deal of maladaptive attention seeking.

It is vital that we find a particular area of interest that we make special for the middle child, and carve out deliberate 'windows of time' when they are given the undivided attention of one or other parent. In Claire's case she was showing a flair for tennis and her father began to take her to tennis lessons at the weekend, watched her play and planned to take her to Wimbledon the next year. We all seek our 'place in the sun', to feel special, but as parents we often need deliberately to create a vehicle which will allow this to happen.

Squabbling between children in a family is normal. If you interfere in children's squabblings, you will seldom know the real truth of what has been going on.

Let them get on with it is the primary message. However, we should be allowed peace and quiet in our own homes. It is best to blame both children for the uncivilised noise that they are making and despatch them to their separate rooms for a brief period to cool off. They can then return provided they are prepared to be civilised and terminate the conflict.

If physical injury is being caused or there is a deliberate attempt to damage the property of another then obviously intervention is necessary. The dynamics of why this has occurred may be all too apparent, but it could equally well be that their anger and hostility needs greater intervention via a Counsellor or Psychologist.

REDUCTION OF CONFLICT

- Stand back and look at the actual dynamics within your family. Remember that your approval and the time you spend with individuals is of fundamental importance. Why might one member of the family feel insecure, angry or jealous? Are you being even handed in the way you deal with your children? Are you avoiding having favourites?

- Remember that your children, especially those separated by a significant age gap, are not truly experiencing the same family. The older child may remember the rocky, turbulent time your marriage went through before the birth of your second child - for example. Is your older child resentful? The water has been calmer for the second child.

- A child of, say, eleven who suddenly finds a new baby arriving will inevitably feel that your time and love must now be shared. Involve the child wherever possible in the arrival of the new baby. In the evenings when the baby is asleep, make a 'window of time' quite deliberately available for the older child. They must go on feeling special and valued.

- Where a child has particular vulnerabilities, build on their strengths. One or other parent needs to find a platform which is a special contact between themselves and the child. A child with no academic or sporting ability may still have a fascination for football, and a trip with his Father to watch his 'star team' play may prove immensely rewarding.

- Being even handed does not mean that everybody gets the same thing on the same day. Each in his own turn.

- A degree of jostling for attention, noisy squabbling, loud complaining to parents about the abuse of an older sister, for example, are all perfectly normal.

27

Tweenies – Is Your Daughter a 'Tweeny'?

Celia

Celia, who is 11, has had a number of 15 and 16 year old boys showing a considerable interest in her. She has been wearing make-up for some months now, and looks at least 14. Her mother discovered Celia and her boyfriend kissing in her bedroom. The boy was sent packing. Her parents were furious and Celia was extremely upset. However, she had been allowed to make-up and dress as she did with no objections from her parents. Indeed, her father had admired how pretty she looked. In Celia's mind, she now had a boyfriend of whom she was extremely fond, and what harm had they done?

Her parents were beginning to see the dilemma. In an effort to please their daughter and even be proud of her good looks, they had colluded in producing a 14 year old lookalike who had neither the wisdom nor sexual experience to cope with the demands made upon her. Her parents began a protracted period of counselling. They struggled to reassert their control and to decide how best to deal with their daughter, whose behaviour would have been perfectly normal had she, indeed, been 14.

It has to be accepted that most positive and well-balanced children will want to 'grow up'. The demand for earrings, make-up, smart clothes, and so forth, are a natural part of any girl's aspirations. It is our role as parents to contain and monitor the whole process of growing up through these vulnerable, early teenage years. Desperately wanting something, does not mean that they should necessarily have it.

With Celia's parents, we looked at the whole 'tweeny' issue and, the body language that it implies. Why do children wish to 'ape' teenagers? Undoubtedly, it makes the tweenies look older and prettier, but they also look sexually mature. It is important for families to establish standards and not to allow any manipulation. The cry that "all my friends use make-up, have the clothes they want and are going to "raves" must not become pressure on parents. It is up to us to have the confidence in our own child rearing ability, to control the stages of our children's development.

We went on to look at the consequences of allowing this exaggerated, artificial teenage development. It is expensive and the costs need to be balanced against the child's other needs and the needs of the rest of the family. If you look attractive and give the appearance of being 14 years of age, your body language may well communicate exactly this to older boys. It is a time of rampant sexual development in young people, and we must anticipate that our daughters will become sex objects to teenage boys. At 11, girls are too young to take this type of social and psychosexual pressure. Why, as a family, are we prepared to be party to a lie? Be 11, and enjoy it. Life passes too quickly. Don't be forever searching for another age to be.

We then looked at the type of social environment that we are implicitly accepting if we make our child an artificial fourteen-year-old. The parties, Saturday night raves, the discos, have all got to be taken on board and, once again, at this pre-teen age children are simply not mature enough to handle this level of social experience.

Jerry

Jerry, now 12, had been fighting her parents for 'tweeny' gear for some months. It was beginning to disrupt her education and family life. Her parents and I sat down to look very carefully at what to allow, and when. We accepted that Jerry was perfectly entitled to have attractive clothing but it should be age appropriate. We also accepted that most parents will allow pierced ears and sleepers at this age, and this was agreed with Jerry.

We also conceded that if Jerry was going out to a party, a little light lipstick would be perfectly reasonable, and at this pre puberty stage of Jerry's development, it was not inappropriate that she should begin to become aware of her physical appeal.

Puberty, a girl starting to have her periods, is clearly a major developmental watershed. The onset of early adulthood will be the beginning of more sexual body language. Once again, social signals were looked at very carefully, and discussed with Jerry. Given half a chance, she would have left the house unwittingly advertising that she would be 'easy' for any boy who cared to make an offer. She was horrified when this was explained to her. We spent considerable time looking at image building and the range of non-verbal communication that would become increasingly important to her as she developed into an adolescent. Once puberty was firmly under way, we felt that there would be no harm in subtly applied make-up, to encourage Jerry to begin to explore gender differences and the early stages of inter-personal, psychosexual experience. We would expect her to become increasingly careful with regard to personal hygiene, the state of her hair, and the care with which she applied what little make-up she used.

Once again, appropriate behaviour and appropriate social signals and body language were areas that needed careful thought.

We felt that for Jerry, the first serious boyfriend would also have implications for dress and make-up. Carefully chosen, attractive clothing, well applied make-up, jewellery, and so forth, are all part of the psychosexual arena.

In my view, by the time a girl reaches the 6th form, at the end of her secondary education, or has actually left school her appearance should be entirely in her own hands. All we can do as parents at this point is act as 'counsellors', but only when asked to do so. The offer of make-up lessons with a beautician or colour stylist can be a much appreciated birthday present.

In essence, encourage your daughters to enjoy each age and stage of their development. Discourage them from pretending to be something that they are not. Deception has its price.

28
Bolshie Teenagers

One of a parent's toughest jobs is trying to keep the channels of communication open with their teenage offspring, particularly when slammed doors, moody sulks and arguing have become the norm. So how are we to tell whether the behaviour is normal for a typical teenager undergoing confused and worrying hormonal changes, or a serious cry for help.

Insisting that a youngster sit down and discuss their problems seldom if ever, actually works. You will find it difficult to encourage your child to open up, share their problems and deal with their anxieties, if there is no available time in a busy week for this to happen. It is at times like these that a regular family forum becomes helpful. A family get together at least once a week, where everyone is encouraged to talk honestly and openly about their lives – parents included, at least allows for a forum of communication. However, deliberately establishing these forums in somewhat of a vacuum seldom survives for more than a week. Meal times have to arise and there is no reason why Sunday lunch and at least one other weekly meal could not be shared by the entire family, with no excuses accepted from any family member. It allows the various 'team members' to chat about events of the day in an easy and relaxed fashion. Individuals can learn to understand each other and the pressures that we all live with. The 'communication forum' will make it easier to spot emerging anxieties. It even allows us, as parents, to express some of our concerns, so that our children feel that they are a supportive part of the team, and not simply parasites who need an occasional lecture! We have to face it, if we have no regular family forum, little sharing will take place and many of the more subtle symptoms that need our support and investigation will simply be missed.

It is also a time for being honest and consistent in your own parental attitudes, whether it be about sex, drugs or crime. Consistency, credibility and honesty are so important, especially to teenagers. If you rave about the evils of marijuana whilst smoking the last of twenty cigarettes and finishing your third glass of Scotch, you can hardly expect to be taken seriously by your teenage children!

One of the main signals that all may not be well is a marked increase in moodiness and a wish to be solitary. Is the young person cutting off contact with their family and friends? If they usually spend their evenings with the phone glued to their ear, have you noticed that it does not ring nearly as often now? Are they bursting into tears? These are all quite difficult signals to pick up because, of course, they are all associated with 'normal' teenage behaviour. However, I would say that cutting themselves off from friends is particularly unnatural. All you can do is watch for changes in their patterns of behaviour and be alert.

Similarly, if they are going off their food and suddenly refusing to eat things they have always liked, there could be something wrong. Yes, we all do it – and teenagers more than most – but if it is a dramatic change in pattern, beware.

Interrupted sleep is another give-away. If you hear them up and about at night, getting glasses of water and rummaging in the fridge – why can't they sleep? A rise in the number of minor illnesses, such as tummy aches, vomiting and rashes are other symptoms, especially when the child uses them as a reason for not going to school. These are often psychosomatic and stress-related conditions, but still genuine, so give the child sympathy and find out what is behind it. Likewise – and this applies especially to younger teenagers – look out for unexplained bumps and bruises, especially on the upper arm, side and back which could indicate bullying.

Are clothes, books and school gear going missing more often?

All these signals may have perfectly rational explanations – but at least you should ask.

Of course, in order to sense a change in the patterns of behaviour, you need to know the normal patterns in the first place. You cannot relate effectively if you simply pass 'like ships in the night'. Children can sense when a parent does not have time, or even worse, seems unwilling to share it.

So, if something does not seem right, what do you do? Start by saying you love them and want to offer to help. Avoid any hint of accusation which can sometimes be difficult if they are throwing rude comments back in your face. Emphasise that you are a team and must work together. Do not forget that children can be depressed just as adults can, and often cannot just "snap out of it". Do not be afraid to ask for your family doctor's support, assuming the youngster is in agreement.

Talk to them when emotions are not running high. Do not start discussions late at night; things always look worse at 1am than they do the next morning. Likewise, do not start a discussion when you have lost your cool - or they have. Get them on their own, so that they do not have to embarrass themselves by revealing their problems in front of other siblings or friends, particularly if broken relationships or sexual difficulties are involved.

29

How to Teach Your Children to Listen

I remember hearing my old Scottish grandfather, a local GP, muttering to my parents, "Peter hears but he dinna heed!" Disobedient, but Grandad was also pointing out the fascinating difference between hearing and processing.

Gemma

Gemma, 11, an attractive child, with an easy manner, had learnt the trick of seeming to listen, then going happily her own way. Infuriatingly, she would later argue, "That's not what you said – you are always changing it". As an only child, she had become spoilt and over-indulged. She simply would not listen. During counselling, it was remarkable how quickly Gemma and her parents began to see that life needed rules for its 'games'. They began to develop a consistency of management where mutual respect was vital for the team's successful functioning. For example, Gemma worried terribly if her parents promised to be back at eleven o'clock and then arrived at two. Her parents were equally upset that Gemma seemed to be so successful in school, so popular with adults and children, yet constantly a source of friction within the family.

We went on to look at 'hearing' and 'processing'. Surely if the language underlying a concept is clear and we have been at pains to explain exactly what we mean, there is no excuse for failing to 'understand'? We then reflected on a traffic direction which Gemma's father had sought the previous day. The traffic moved on and, to her amazement, her father stopped and needed to ask for the directions all over again! This time he went through the directions very carefully with his informant before moving on. By repeating what was expected of him, he was forcing the information firmly into the left hemisphere of his brain where he processed it thoroughly. He was now able to make his way from A to B without any further interruption. This made them realise that if there was an important instruction for Gemma to grasp, they must ask her to come close, gain eye contact, keep it brief and ask her to repeat exactly what was required, in her own words, before embarking on the task.

Kevin

Ten-year-old Kevin was struggling with his mathematics. What frustrated him, almost to the point of tears, was that his teachers and parents assumed that he was not trying. A maths concept was explained to him and he would nod in apparent understanding. However, he then sat frozen, unable to cope. From then on, when new tasks were explained or an old one revised, as soon as Kevin appeared to understand, he was told, 'now, you be teacher'. He then had to explain the task for himself. In this way, we ensured that he had understood and above all, he was made to process the information more thoroughly which enhanced his understanding. This 'you be teacher' technique has many practical applications.

David

There are some children whose problems are specific which make listening much more difficult. David is 10, and has an attention deficit with hyperactivity disorder (ADHD). He is constantly on the fidget and his mind wanders like a restless butterfly. Inability to concentrate and listen is a fundamental part of his diagnosis. David's condition is relatively severe and has only just been diagnosed.

It is hoped that with the management of David's ADHD, he will begin to find listening skills far easier to acquire. I am hoping that the family will become involved with the specialist staff in the school. We looked at the management and development of David's listening skills.

James

James is 14, dyslexic, and as is the case with over 40% of dyslexics, found complex language difficult to process, but to hear him chatter socially, no one would have anticipated any difficulty at all. It was no surprise that his parents and teachers became irritated with him. The incoming language, especially when it was complex, confused him. When questions were long and complex, he quickly became muddled, his brow furrowed and either he was unable to reply or his answers were inappropriate. The processing of complex language was a therapeutic need for James. His parents began to understand exactly how his learning disability affected him. They worked with a speech and language therapist to help him and to understand the nature of his disability.

30

My Child's Unfortunate Friends

I doubt if there is a parent who has not, at some time, had grave doubts about their child's choice of friends. It can easily cause stress and anxiety, and lead to conflict and deceit in families.

If you have concerns, you first need to look carefully at the reasons for your doubts and realise that you cannot orchestrate the behaviour of the friends your child will meet. Remember too that if you make your displeasure known without having the full facts, you will drive the child further towards the very people you want them to avoid.

A friend of mine came to see me because he was disturbed about the young man their fifteen-year-old daughter had met. He had long hair, an earring and wore torn jeans. Had their daughter become involved in totally inappropriate company? How could they control it?

I horrified them by suggesting that he and his wife ask him to tea.

Two days later my friend returned to express his immense surprise. They had not realised that the young man was in the sixth form of the local grammar school and was hoping to become a probation officer. He was already working with young people in their hometown and was a founder member of a new youth club. He is now seeing their daughter regularly and even plans to go on the family holiday this month. The couple are dismayed to think back on the hasty judgement they made on so little evidence. Such a cliché – don't judge a book by its cover.

We all have an image of our children and what we would like them to be – often a projection of what we wish we had been. There is nothing wrong in wanting standards for our children, but do not judge too quickly.

It is when an association provokes worrying changes in our child's behaviour that friendships come in for the greatest investigation. It is often in the rather secretive teenage years that friendships develop with youngsters from totally different backgrounds. Suddenly we find our family code of conduct on acceptable behaviour being defiantly flouted. How often is the teenager's explanation – "Jane's parents don't make her come in at this ridiculous time!"

Jason

Consider the child who is vulnerable, impressionable, who often finds it difficult to make relationships in school, and who can easily be led and even used by powerful peers. There may come a time, quite objectively, when the child is seriously 'at risk' and a relationship is rapidly becoming the key focus of their lives. Thirteen-year-old Jason was at a boarding school. He was about to be expelled for frequently leaving the school grounds and had been caught stealing for the third time. Fortunately, the school had the sensitivity to see that this was 'out of character'.

It emerged that at school there was a group of three other boys, led by a very powerful personality, who had 'allowed' young Jason to join this group provided he produced cigarettes, booze and even cash, to justify his 'membership'. The pressures became immense as he took increasing risks to pay his dues. Fortunately, this came to light. He had the courage to discuss it confidentially with me in considerable detail. He was happy to allow his parents to join the discussion in due course. This 'freed' him from his tie to this group. With the support of the school, he was moved to another House, with a different House Master. Association with the gang was broken and the school alerted to their methods. Jason learned that friendship cannot be bought.

Sandra

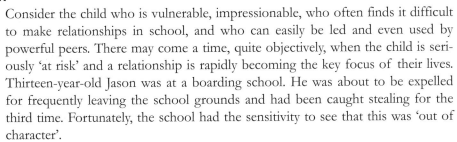

Sandra, 15, began coming home very late, did not phone and was often the worse for drink. Her parents wanted to stop her seeing her friends, especially her boyfriend, in the hope that her behaviour would improve. I suggested that they talk to her about her behaviour and the risks involved, rather than attack individuals. I emphasised to them that it was not the boy they disliked, but the behaviour to which Sandra was exposed.

All sides struggled to maintain an adult/adult discussion, but her parents managed to outline their concerns, saying they were worried she was in danger and although they did not want to intervene in her friendships, they would have to unless she modified her behaviour.

Once the situation had cooled down, Sandra was sensible enough to see that her parents were right to be concerned and if she did not want to put her friendships at risk, changes had to be made. Enlightened self-interest can be a great source of insight.

She learned to phone her parents if there was a chance of being seriously late and so far, has not returned home drunk again. Her parents now accept that it is important to allow the youngster the opportunity to change her behaviour before becoming too draconian. Sandra has kept her boyfriend.

Karen

Sadly, it does not always work out like this. Karen, 14, seldom came home on time and on several occasions did not come home at all. She had become very defiant, abusive and had begun to steal from her mother's handbag. She was also resentful and unwilling to make any changes. There was a clear need to sever the link with her friends.

Her parents discussed this situation with the school, who offered to move her to another class in her year, but it was felt she would carry on seeing her "friends". So a new school was found in a different part of town and after a very difficult term, she began to make new friends. However, anger and resentment remained. The problem should have been tackled earlier. Karen would have benefited from a period of counselling but remained hostile to the idea.

In deciding how to manage undesirable friendships, we need to consider: are the children in school together? It is difficult to allow a child to associate in class, in the playground and at lunchtime, and then deny access to the friendship after school.

A head-on collision with a child at any age will almost inevitably be explosive. Avoid conflict if you can. Friendships are a fundamental part of our identity. You are asking the individual to give up a 'pillar' of their identity. This is particularly true in teenage, when the young are struggling to establish an identity of their own. An attack on friendships is readily seen as a direct attack on your child and what they stand for. Our parental dilemma is that we see one of our own 'pillars' being threatened and possibly alienated from us.

If hard evidence of potential damage, or harm being done to your child exists, then a direct confrontation may be inevitable, but be sure you know the facts and are not just reacting to adolescent moodiness and identity struggle.

Worrying associations almost certainly need to be broken.

However, the issue will be traumatic for all concerned. The problem is often best dealt with via a third party, a psychologist or counsellor, with whom the feelings of all concerned can be expressed without undue emotional heat. The details need to be brought into sharp relief so that they are fully understood. The traditional family 'games playing' needs to be extinguished – "Oh, you never did like my friends!" The reality of any real threat should become apparent to all concerned.

A change of school may well be necessary to create an entirely new peer group and in these circumstances an embargo on contact, while extremely unfortunate, may be necessary. It is usually important that the school are also supportive. Forbidding contact with other youngsters in the same year, in the same school, is ridiculously untenable.

If you do have to come down hard on your teenager, do it by degrees – do not suddenly snap and ban them from everything they enjoy doing. Stipulate that they have to come home straight from school every night for a month and if they do that, allow them to go out for a couple of evenings as a reward. Encourage them to join new clubs or groups to make new friendships, which may lead them away from bad influences and give them new pillars of their identity. Sometimes kids are as keen as you are to change their lives. They do not know how to go about it. Keep discussion as adult/adult as you can.

Factors to watch for:

- Is your child becoming a major factor in a group of bullies?

- Is your child beginning to lie and steal?

- Is your child absconding from school on a regular basis?

- Do you have evidence of alcohol, drug or substance abuse?

- Are they pleading illness far more than usual?

- Are they constantly rude and defiant without any real cause?

- Do they defy curfews and time control understandings?

- Are you worried that they may be becoming depressed?

How to react:

- Do not simply react to your prejudices.

- Be sure your criticisms are truly objective.

- You may need to create alternative environments in which new friendships can develop.

- Only engage in head-on conflict if no other route proves possible.

31

Does My Child Have to Be Competitive?

We spend our lives trying to encourage our children to perform and succeed and yet we seldom ask if such competitiveness is necessary in our modern society.

Jack

Jack's mother wrote to me, describing a rather sad nine year old, who was already feeling a thorough failure. On closer examination, Jack was neurotically competitive. If he could not come first and win at chess, the board got kicked over. He refused to take part in cricket any more, and he had even abandoned the Cubs. Jack was rapidly becoming unrealistic about his own abilities. He lived in a world of fantasy where he always imagined himself as the leader and the winner. Jack could not see that preparatory steps were necessary.

We worked on two separate targets. Jack's father was high achieving, had played county cricket, and was a first class squash player. There were problems within the marriage. His father expected far too much, not only of Jack, but of his wife, who he found irritating. For him, only excellence was satisfactory. He was still neurotic about being dropped by the county side over ten years ago and from then on had only played with the second eleven. This burning frustration in Jack's father resulted in him pushing his son quite unrealistically. Jack was bright, athletically able, and could one day excel, but not if the whole process remained unrealistic.

Our first target was to work with Jack, looking, in this instance, at joining a judo club, but also helping him to achieve a more realistic appreciation of what would be involved and the disciplines that would be vital. We established a series of steps through which he had to go, with targets at the end of each, rather than rushing straight towards competitive excellence. He seemed excited by what appeared to be far more attainable targets. Expertise had to be earned and worked for – then he really could enjoy it!

With this in mind, we looked back at why he had abandoned the Cubs. He had been furious that one of his classmates had been made a 'sixer' and demanded equal promotion for himself. He completely failed to appreciate that his friend had been a member for eighteen months and that he had only joined three weeks earlier. He began to see that if he re-joined he would have to work through the developmental stages.

Secondly, we moved on to help Jack establish the criterion of a 'personal best'. He was running in the school sports that summer and had established a personal best for the 50 metres. He and his father agreed that this would be their year's target, and Jack would be allowed to go out for a hamburger with his father if he could beat this on sports day. Crucially, the outing would take place whatever position he achieved in the race. Jack was to look at his own performance and what was attainable, and not to be forever comparing himself with others. Fortunately, so much of modern athletics is geared to the very positive criterion of a 'personal best' – no one can do more.

Sarah

Competitiveness in children has many shades. I worked with a very gifted young lady, Sarah, in the January before her A Levels. She typically worked for four or five hours every night after school, and her essays had been at a first class academic level. However, essays that were meant to take an hour were taking Sarah three hours; she was aiming for perfection. She found the mock exams frustrating because she was never able to achieve anything like this level of perfection because of the sheer nature of time-limited exams. She abandoned her A Levels, and refused to go to school.

Sarah and I worked together and reoriented the criterion of 'success' in exam conditions. Sarah began to realise that exams needed an entirely different type of information processing. It was a matter of refining data, being very accurate in the answering of questions, and establishing the best that could possibly be achieved within a given timeframe. She began to see her responses as sophisticated 'exploded notes', which should never be compared with essays written with the freedom of time. We also set limits on her essay work, which had from then on to be completed within the timeframe prescribed by her teacher. She had to learn to work within these constraints. Sarah returned to school having dealt with her neurotic anxiety and went on to complete a degree at Cambridge.

Mark

Mark was sixteen when his mother wrote to ask me why he was never prepared to compete, either academically or in sport. She was devastated during the schools sports, to see him winning comfortably in the 100 metres only to deliberately slack off and allow two other boys to pass him. Once again, Mark's parents accepted that they had perhaps looked for too much from Mark in his early years. Every time he achieved, whether in class or in football, they wanted him to push one notch further. Subconsciously, Mark began to realise that success would inevitably bring additional pressure. He was beginning to feel that he must win.

He simply could not stand the strain. It was his way of fighting against the pressure.

We worked as a family group, establishing that secreting adrenaline is a vital ingredient in motivation and performance. Our bodies use adrenaline to prepare us for performance. Mark's challenges would inevitably provoke these responses. He looked carefully at what he needed to achieve, and established that he wanted to go to university to study history. In an academic grammar school one could make certain assumptions about his intellectual capacity. He ultimately performed with considerable success in the GCSE's. Mark was unmotivated at the beginning of his A Levels. He was not allowing himself to perform appropriately – once again, terrified of peer group comparison. He sensed that 'Mark could do better if he tried' was preferable to having to accept ineptitude.

We worked on 'Mark' competing against 'Mark'. We posted three of his history essays on the wall in the kitchen and established these as a criterion level. It was also apparent that they were not sophisticated enough to achieve the A grades that he was looking for. Mark forgot about struggling to compete with his classmates but worked towards improving against his own standards on the kitchen wall. As a new essay demonstrating increasing maturity appeared, the weaker of the examples on the wall was removed, to be replaced by the new one. By Christmas, Mark was beginning to see the level to which he must move if he was to succeed when he came to mock exams and timed essay work.

Mark was given a great deal of help by his school on revision strategies, note taking, and preparing himself for examinations. They also helped him look at exam technique. He began to pick and choose the questions that he would answer, analyse exactly what his response should be, and then prepare his essays in an increasingly sophisticated way, but always against the pressure of time. He needed to come to terms with working against this type of pressure. 'Mark' is now competing against 'Mark' with considerable success and, almost incidentally, his performance is now near the top of his group, but this comparison seems much less important now.

32

Information and Communication Technology: A Curse or a Blessing?

Mobile phones have become an increasingly sophisticated, lightweight and adaptable part of our everyday life. The vast majority of youngsters, over the age of ten, have a mobile phone, often rather too much in evidence! Teenagers travel extensively, have hectic social lives and may experience understandable delays. Mobile phones make it easier to keep their parents and friends informed. There is much less excuse these days to leave parents in anguish late at night because a teenage daughter is late coming home. If only youngsters could realise that anxious parents make angry parents! The mobile phone has become a regular part of society but social rules for its use have still to be established. In the excitement of a new 'toy' that allows instant, albeit expensive access, it is easy for a mobile phone to cause more problems than it cures. Information and Communication Technology (ICT) can be compulsive, addictive and expensive, as well as educational, entertaining and informative.

IS YOUR CHILD BEING PERSECUTED BY A MOBILE PHONE?

Henrietta

Henrietta, who is now sixteen, visited me because her dyslexia was likely to entitle her to extra time in her GCSE's. However, our first meeting became almost totally absorbed with the serious problem she was having with her mobile phone. I wondered why, when she came through my office door, she looked so distracted. When she had received her first obscene text message she had taken it as a joke. Indeed, the caller's number was included in the message, and she replied. The game was on! She received messages thick and fast. The caller, a boy, was becoming increasingly obsessed with Henrietta, who was no longer replying, except in distress to ask him to stop. From this point on, the boy's obsession took a very unpleasant, threatening tone. He had become angered by her rejection. Clearly he knew which school she attended and was watching the school gates morning and evening. On several occasions he commented on the colour of her clothing and even named the friends she was with. Because she felt in some ways responsible for encouraging these calls at the outset, she was loath to discuss them with her parents. By the time she plucked up courage, attempts to track the sender were blocked, as she had made no previous note of his number.

I asked her parents to join our consultation and we decided on a positive strategy. First, she was to ring her service provider and ask for a new number. Secondly, she was to discuss with them the nature of the calls that she had been receiving and give them as much detail as she possibly could. When she did this, they promised to liaise with the police. The evidence is that in these circumstances it is sometimes possible to track the caller and, indeed, a number of prosecutions have already followed. This behaviour is never a 'joke'. It is unfair and emotionally damaging - have no sympathy with it. If you can track a caller, prosecute.

There is a vital rule for all of us to remember in these circumstances. The caller's behaviour was neurotic as well as malicious. The fundamental maxim says; "Don't feed a neurosis". Never reply in any way to a call of this nature. Nine times out of ten the caller rapidly loses interest.

Danielle

Thirteen-year-old Danielle was being bullied by other people's telephones! Her father had decided that there was no place for a mobile phone in the life of a thirteen year old and had been confronted by a furious Danielle who insisted that it was a vital fashion accessory; "How can I expect to meet my friends if I haven't got one!" It seemed to her father that many of her friends wandered the streets with phones clamped to their ears, whether or not they were making calls! He felt that this behaviour was both ridiculous and expensive. We discussed this together. It was decided that initially Danielle would not be given a telephone because she had asked in quite the wrong manner, and had been rude and unpleasant in the process. This type of behaviour should not be rewarded on any account, whether a mobile phone is at issue or not.

However, Danielle made a great effort to be co-operative and it was agreed that she would be given a mobile phone for her fourteenth birthday. It was accepted that increased social contact was becoming a part of her life. She was being allowed out on Friday and Saturday nights, sometimes until ten or eleven o'clock at night, and a phone was great security in these circumstances. From a parental point of view, if a child is delayed, for whatever reason, and has access to a mobile phone, there is no excuse for not letting their parents know. Equally, if two young people are in a car late at night and it breaks down, it is extremely valuable to have a mobile phone to call for help, rather than expecting them to wander the streets looking for assistance.

Danielle's father has agreed to allow her one £20 phonecard per month – no question of running up bills! The phone has been given on the clear understanding that she must budget its use within this allowance. Her father has also made it clear that he will not allow himself to be blackmailed by his daughter if she no longer has airtime available and may, therefore, be unsafe. If this situation occurs, she would lose her telephone and not be allowed to put herself at risk. This would curtail her social life until she had earned sufficient funds to be able to use the phone again. Without this undertaking, it was quite clear that Danielle would have used the entire £20 allowance long before the end of the first week, let alone a month.

Monitoring phone usage

Mobile 'phones can easily be monitored by a check on the charges or, in the case of pre-paid, the rate at which the pre-payment vouchers are used. In addition, most phones record the last ten numbers dialled, which can be checked against chat-line and sex-line numbers (the famous 0898 numbers advertised in the tabloid press). It should be stressed that most 'chat lines' cost up to £1 or even more per minute! When a child is given a mobile phone, an agreed contract of use must be established and adhered to. The 'phone should always be considered a privilege that may be withdrawn on breach of that contract. One of the first rules should be for it to be handed back to the parent or guardian on a regular basis. It should then be checked, in private, for numbers accessed and costs accrued. A brief hand back prior to issuing the new monthly card makes good sense.

THE DANGER OF CHAT ROOMS AND CHAT LINES ON THE INTERNET OR MOBILE PHONE

Chat lines have become a recent and potentially expensive feature of electronic communication. They are readily available and much advertised on television. All it takes is a phone call, after which you are asked to give a summary of your life, your interests and aspirations, and these are circulated to other members of the chat room who decide whether or not they want to call you back. Chat lines on the Internet are even easier to access. What harm is there in communicating with somebody on the other side of the world? For years, penfriends, for example, have been a regular part of life. It has increased understanding of other cultures and, at times, penfriends have shared holidays together, often with considerable mutual benefit. However, the level of psychological involvement and the depth of commitment involved in the intimacy of a telephone call, in a silent room, is very different from a letter which had to be penned, posted, and with a long time delay before a response.

Celia

Celia, spoke to me about her forthcoming marriage in the United States, to a man she had known for some eight or nine months. It emerged that she had never met her fiancé, Damon but had become profoundly enchanted with him via a 'chat line'. She clearly felt emotionally committed, and her heart missed a beat when her fiancé came on the line. She felt that she wanted to live with no one else in the world, and yet had become painfully aware that this relationship was based on words. These might have been real and honest, but could have been largely fantasy, with Damon attempting to create an image which might have been far from the truth. She had decided to set back the date of her marriage and to visit Damon. They planned to discuss their engagement, the marriage date, and expectations for the future.

Celia spoke to me at great length about this approach to making a relationship. She was socially shy, had great difficulty in making friends, but found that no such difficulty arose on the Internet. She no longer had to be afraid of the way she looked, dressed, moved, or that other people might find her boring. She commented. "I couldn't believe it was really me talking!" She began to realise that the Internet sessions were almost therapeutic. They allowed her to release pent up feelings, thoughts and emotions, but, she admitted, sometimes she pretended that she was something other than she was. "I think I was painting a picture of what I would like to be!" She found it much easier to talk about her personal problems, her conflict with her parents and her anguish at being dropped by her first boyfriend. Once she became involved with Damon, she found it easier to discuss sexuality in an uninhibited fashion, and they shared their sexual fantasies. Indeed, in many ways, by the time her American trip was planned, they had shared more than some married couples ever do!

We discussed this at a clinical meeting, and the various levels of motivation and involvement that exist in these chat rooms. For some, it is simply sharing day-to-day experiences, in a naïve and simple fashion. However, verbal 'games playing' comes to the fore, very rapidly. From an early stage, boys particularly try to make themselves as interesting and attractive as they can.

James

James admitted that he wanted to use chat lines as a deliberate seduction tool. He felt that if he could encourage a girl to laugh, talk about sex and begin to fantasize, he could then spend time attempting to create an attractive image of himself. If the girl was prepared to settle for no more than sexual fantasising, no harm would be done.

However, in ninety percent of cases, the boys encourage the girls to meet, feeling that a sexual bridgehead has already been built.

Life and relationships are more than carefully woven verbal spells. I am not suggesting for a moment that language does not have a significant place in our lives and our friendships, but think of the cues that are missing. Communication is much more than words, and this is especially true of body language. We can tell much by the way people are sitting, and, more particularly, from their faces, and especially their eyes. The stature and physical attractiveness of another human being plays a major part in our psychosexual lives and yet all this is largely unavailable in a chat room.

Matters worsen if we begin to think of irritating mannerisms, the way a person moves, dresses and even the social environment of which they are a part. If a relationship is to be forged, these are all issues that must be borne in mind.

Danny

Our most dramatic case in recent times, must be Danny, a shy fifteen year old, who was shattered to lose his first girlfriend and resorted that same evening to a chat line. To his happy amazement, he very quickly found new friends who were eager to listen to his problems, and with whom he shared a great deal – at a cost that shattered his father three weeks later! Unfortunately, Danny became obsessed with two of these friendships and could not rest if he had been unable to make his nightly contact with each of them. He hardly ever left his room. He began to refuse to take normal phone calls and would not even see his school friends at the door. School attendance was becoming increasingly difficult and it was at this point that his mother referred him to me.

It took several sessions for Danny to be honest about the emotional trap into which he had fallen, and to accept that he wanted to be free and to move back into the real, three-dimensional world. Fortunately, his summer holiday gave him a three week break to kill off the neurotic 'cycle'. It was a struggle for the boy to drag himself away from the security of those two dimensional friendships into the world of the unknown and uncertain. He returned for further counselling after his holiday, joined a local drama club in the autumn, and began to make genuine friendships.

Receding into a Virtual World

In most cases, working or playing on a computer is a one-person operation. The great attraction of computer games and many sites on the Internet is that they offer activities in the cyber world that would be too expensive or impossible to achieve in the real-time world. These could include access to pornography, violence or friendships. It must be remembered that, while these are virtual images, contacts can form the basis for compulsive obsessions – the young are particularly vulnerable. Beware the 'nerd-syndrome'! Given the chance, some people will become increasingly drawn into the cyber world and will begin rejecting the real world, real friends and their families. They begin to identify with the personalities portrayed on the screen, and 'the game' can quickly assume too great an importance in their lives. Problems in a virtual world can always be 'worked out' or, as a last resort, solved by the 'off' switch! Asperger sufferers, for example, who tend to find real relationships very difficult, are particularly prone to these temptations as the cyber world does not ask for personal relationships and seldom requires the need to understand others feelings or emotions.

Protection from Unsuitable Internet Sites

A responsible parent would not allow a 12-year-old to watch an 18-rated film on the TV or video but far worse is available through the Internet, including sites run by and for paedophiles. The ability to hide behind the technology enables paedophiles, and the like, to build up 'real' and close relationships. These are, however, 'virtual' relationships where the image and personality of the person is only what they want to portray and that may be far from the truth. In a chat-room, or on a chat-line, it is perfectly possible for a paedophile to be anyone he/she may wish to be, and thus to deliberately mislead those on whom they wish to prey.

There are programs that will bar unsuitable sites from access by young people (most based on a password system) but these programs have limitations, can be circumvented and frequently bar perfectly acceptable sites that may well be needed for schoolwork research. For example, a National Art Gallery site may be barred because it contains masterpieces that include nudes – the Birth of Venus (et al).

Thames Valley Police have launched 'Childsafe', an initiative aimed at warning young people of the dangers of using Internet Chat-rooms and being targeted by paedophiles. The package contains video, posters, leaflets, mouse-mats and teacher's notes and lesson plans. Information is also available on the following web sites:

www.childnet-int.org

www.nspcc.org.uk

www.chatdanger.com

COMPUTER GAMES

The success of a computer game is judged purely on its 'addictive qualities'. Most have a series of levels that require ever-greater skills to complete. The designers deliberately build this into their games to increase popularity and thus sales. It works in a similar way to the addiction to gaming-machines manifest in many teenagers. There is a compulsion to try and 'beat the system'. Although this 'addiction' may be relatively short lived, players will inevitably progress from one game to the next, valuable hours 'wasted' in the process.

DO COMPUTERS ALREADY RUN OUR CHILDREN'S LIVES?

In a recent public lecture in London on computer technology, the specialist alarmed many of his listeners with his laptop dream. He saw the disappearance of school, as we know it, with the replacement of books by laptops – solitary children, tied to their flickering screens. The vision of 'geeks' or 'nerds' who were becoming increasingly socially incompetent, with no need of peers, parents or teachers, was the nightmare scenario with which he left many of his listeners.

We are moving increasingly into an information technology world, which we need to learn to control and manage.

- In the majority of cases, children have a far greater understanding of modern technology than their parents. How many adults rely on their ten year olds to programme the video recorder? It is strongly recommended that parents attend evening classes to become familiar with ICT for both their own use and to enable them to monitor use by the young people in their families.

- Access to ICT is often available in private and without parental supervision through computers and mobile phones, for example, in use in the child's bedroom. Computers can easily be housed in family rooms, where, if necessary, covert monitoring can take place and a degree of social interaction is also available. A parent showing a genuine interest in what the child is doing may not be interpreted as monitoring. If a parent shows interest in ICT by attending a short course of evening classes, children will delight in showing how much more they know. 'Pupil' suddenly becomes 'teacher'. If the computer has to be in a bedroom, the door should be left open so that the screen can be checked easily, when passing, and even greater 'interest' needs to be shown by the parent. The youngster needs to be aware of the risks and threats that ICT can still pose. As parents, we have a monitoring role which children must accept.

Jon

Jon was infuriating his parents by refusing to turn up at family meals in the evening – "Oh, but I haven't finished my work yet." This new found academic motivation needed to be encouraged, but at what cost? Jon was extremely knowledgeable about the myriad of uses that he made of his computer. However, the family felt that meal times should be a forum for getting together and chatting. Jon's procrastination would bring with it the risk of being banned from his computer for 30–60 minutes if he failed to meet his family mealtime commitment.

Insist on 'quality time', especially family meal times and, above all, ban meals being taken to the bedroom so that the youngster can continue on the computer. I would also suggest 'screen free' times of the day, especially the weekend when children can develop other interests and activities, but be sure the rule is the same for the whole household. Credibility is lost if you are staring at your computer screen, while forbidding the child to access theirs.

At the same time we must not lose sight of the immense value to be derived from computers, which, properly controlled, extend the horizons and quality of education significantly. Already relatively young children are coping remarkably well with their computers and are at ease with both the hardware and the software.

Jenny

I was recently looking at Jenny's project for school. Some of the information was derived from a school visit to a Roman site, part from the Internet and part from an encyclopaedia programme. The result was a beautifully constructed project from which the child had learnt a great deal. The piece of work was in itself a marvellous vehicle for communication. Certainly, for the older student, Internet access is proving invaluable, allowing for contacts with a variety of worldwide resources.

Sarah

Sarah, who was mildly dyslexic, was a particularly able girl of seventeen, but was struggling to cope with English, Economics and Biology at A-level. More than modest grades were proving unlikely. She had been producing some of her work using a keyboard and we suggested that she should increase her typing skills to about thirty-five-words-per-minute and we would ask for a concession from the exam boards to allow her to use her word processor in the A-levels. She would then be able to produce significantly more material and always with total legibility. Her hand would no longer tire after twenty to thirty minutes, causing her concentration to wander. Her grades improved dramatically. Learning to read and write are a vital part of the educational process, but why do we have to be hidebound by a pen or pencil?

We have much to gain from computers, provided we do not let them run riot in our lives. One must also be aware that second hand violence can indeed be a genuine concern.

Research papers often describe the increased incidence of violence resulting from television programmes and violent computer games. I have no problem at all with competition, either in sport or in computerised games, but I do have severe reservations about gratuitous violence; the primary aim of which seems to be to maim and hurt, with no penalties attached, no recriminations and no remorse. "Oh, it's only a game!" How many times do any of us need to be exposed to the cheapening of life before it becomes a worrying part of the way we view the world around us?

Aim to encourage your children to pursue healthier activities outdoors, instead of staying in playing on their computers all the time

Pat

Pat provided us with a fascinating example of the need to broaden horizons. He was, at twelve, a delightful little boy, with heavy horn rimmed, absent-minded professor spectacles. His friends described him as an 'IT fiend'. A gifted boy, with considerable quiet charm, he never ventured into the open air if he could possibly avoid it. Indeed, he seldom left his own room where he was equipped with all his IT hardware. He hated physical activity, and frequently reported sick on games afternoons in school. He only survived one night on a recent school camp and came home pleading a tummy ache.

At twelve years of age, he was moving into a phase of his school life, when there would be an increasing obligation to become involved in sport. He hated the cold, the mud and being hurt, and was becoming increasingly distressed and angry at being forced to take part in activities that he loathed. Pat's parents came to see me on their own, to discuss his increasing anxieties which were beginning to lead to the early stages of school refusal.

Our starting point was to respect Pat's individuality – to make no attempt to force upon him rough games, on cold, wet days or make any attempt to 'bully' him into any involvement that he dreaded.

We decided that the first step was to establish an activity which moved him out of the house and integrated him with other children, in an environment that Pat felt would be fun. He had already shown some flair and interest in drama. His parents found a local youth drama group which Pat joined. He was immediately involved, in a small part, in a new production. He was swept along by this new activity. Pat was now leaving the home, several evenings per week, and finding other children interesting company.

He was never a team player on the games field, but in other senses, adequately co-ordinated. The family decided to try badminton during the winter and went to the local sports centre together with another family. Pat coped much better with this individual sport, enjoyed the company of his parents, and began to show some signs of reasonable hand/eye co-ordination. This led to the possibility of tennis during the following summer. He has now joined a children's coaching group where the essence is 'having fun', as well as learning essential tennis skills.

Pat responded extraordinarily well to this gradual widening of his horizons. Having failed at the previous year's summer camp, I was delighted that Pat accepted a week at camp the following summer, bearing in mind that its principal orientation would be Information and Communication Technology. With a particular talent in this area, he would immediately shine among his peers. He would be allowed to follow his greatest obsession, and yet be involved, necessarily, in a camping environment. This was an ideal compromise for Pat.

Later that summer, the family went to Crete, and Pat and his father decided to look at two different ancient Greek sites on the island. Pat was bought a new camera and his father had a Polaroid. They worked on Pat's historical interest, much of which he could research on the Internet and it would also encourage his developing talent as a photographer. This first excursion into archaeology opened Pat's eyes to this fascinating world and encouraged both Pat and his father to pursue a similar interest in Roman sites in Britain.

33

Teenage Crush

A 'crush' can be wildly exciting or devastatingly depressing, and is almost always at the level of a fantasy which, by definition, can never be made real. Much hero worship is involved. In this instance, we are discussing the pre adolescent and early adolescent youngster, although adults are perfectly capable of 'falling in love' with a totally impossible love object. The object of teenage crushes range from pop stars, sports personalities; older, rather charismatic sixth formers; and, quite often, teachers and clergymen. Crushes are a normal part of adolescent development. The buzz of excitement, flushing to the roots of the hair and being left mumbling and inarticulate in the presence of the individual concerned are familiar symptoms. Hence, in essence, there is absolutely nothing wrong or inappropriate about a crush in itself. Its very normality is important to bear in mind if the issue eventually needs to be discussed. Teenage hormones are finding their first target.

Denise

Denise's parents were becoming increasingly aware that she was less and less willing to join family meals, had no appetite, was looking grey and distracted, losing sleep and finding her homework almost impossible to manage. Her mother visited her room and found her staring into the middle distance. At this point, as parents, it is right to become concerned. Denise's mother spent several sessions sitting in the child's bedroom discussing her day-to-day life, her friendships at school and yet nothing seemed to emerge. However, her drama teacher began to appear more and more often in her stories about school and it became increasingly clear that she was of fundamental importance to Denise. Her mother found herself intruding into an extremely private, vulnerable world which needed tremendous sensitivity, and a great deal of patience. It is easy to humiliate a young person in these circumstances.

Finally, Denise broke down and admitted that she 'loved' Mrs Thompson, could not get her out of her mind and felt almost faint when Mrs Thompson walked past her in the school corridor. Denise was also devastated by the possibility that she might, therefore, be 'gay'. The reality is that an enormous number of boys and girls have crushes, often on people of the same sex and it is usually no indicator of later sexuality. It is a curious amalgam of love, hero worship, identifying with the love object, wanting to be like them and, of course, this may include a desire for physical contact. It was important for Denise's mother to remind her that it had nothing to do with her later sexuality. It was perfectly normal for her body and mind to want to find another human onto whom she could project the sudden rush of emotion.

It was Denise's first experience of feeling an overpowering emotion for another human being. It became increasingly clear to her that this was a passage of time through which she must pass, and that before long her over-active hormones would begin to find more appropriate targets. Her mother's skill lay in being very gentle over several hours and thus allowing Denise to find this out for herself. She did not simply advise her to 'grow up', or comment; 'Oh, it's just a stage you are going through'.

Two years have now passed and Denise has a steady boyfriend. She commented the other day, when I met her again, that bringing this complicated issue to the surface and being allowed to talk about it had helped enormously. It put the episode into perspective.

John

John made precisely the same comment to me about his intense 'love' for a younger boy, David. He was sixteen at the time when David (13) had arrived in school. He had developed an enormous crush on this younger boy. He had never mentioned it to David nor had he attempted to do anything about it, he struggled for several months to rid himself of the image of David everywhere he went. It so happened that in English class, love and infatuation were being discussed in the context of Romeo and Juliet and a skilful teacher was able to discuss how other people can become meaningful in our lives.

This allowed John to discuss how he felt in a sympathetic and supportive group.

Once the issue was out in the open, John was able to cope with the situation and it never became a major issue. Again, it was vital that the problem was taken seriously, and discussed without criticism or condemnation. John settled, relatively happily, with his gay partner and remembered his crush on David with warmth and affection. He was relieved that it never developed into a sexual relationship that might have compromised the younger boy.

Parents are walking on eggshells if a crush has developed to the point where it is causing disruption in the life of their child. You will need patience, gentle tolerance and skilful negotiation to guide the discussion, but only as and when the young person feels able to become verbally involved. If crushes are not within your experience, you may be told details that worry you. You may feel that your child could be sexually compromised or in a state of worrying gender confusion. Above all, do not be critical or judgmental. It will simply drive the problem underground. Remember how easy it is to humiliate – especially when you are dealing with a fantasy love. You may feel that a few counselling sessions would help you cope with your child's dilemma.

I was talking to a family recently who had decided that the way forward was to tell the 'love object' of their daughter's crush and arrange for him to come round one Saturday afternoon so that the two could meet and the issue be discussed. An apparently worthy idea which, in reality, heaped colossal humiliation on the child. It is a fantasy world we are dealing with. A true crush does not and cannot become real and the last thing the child needs is to be humiliated in front of the love object by being told of its impossibility. It simply makes them feel extremely stupid, embarrassed and even depressed.

Stuart

Stuart's crush on a female pop star began normally, and was typical of thousands of young people. He had posters all over his room, bought every record that she had ever made, but was now beginning to borrow money to go to concerts that she was in. However, his girlfriend was becoming increasingly jealous, and Stuart angry and frustrated. His other friends regarded him as stupid and thoroughly over the top, which made Stuart even more angry. Girlfriend after girlfriend dropped him, and he was now losing sleep. His parents became punitive and made him take his posters down – "Stop being so silly – it is time you grew up!" Stuart then began writing to the pop star and once in a while, her Fan Club Secretary wrote back on her behalf which was sufficient to fuel his obsession. At one point, he went missing over night, and was found haunting the stage door of a theatre in which the pop star was working. He had reached the first stages of 'stalking' behaviour and needed considerable counselling to remove the 'secret veneer' from his obsession and to begin to see that this was not love but psycho neurotic obsessional behaviour.

His parents were drawn into the counselling and, in time, became sympathetic to the hurt and anger which Stuart was still feeling. Interestingly, their acceptance and the return of his posters brought the entire issue into a sensible, rational framework. Stuart is now sleeping properly!

Dee

Dee, who was sixteen, a fine sports woman and a talented tennis player, targeted her teenage affection at a well-known tennis star. She became hugely depressed if he lost a match and impossibly over-excited on the occasions when he won. Her parents became frustrated and irritated when she would talk of nothing else and became hyperactive for days. It was her depression, lack of motivation and the dramatic change, in an otherwise lovely, bubbly personality, that followed the tennis star's marriage that really worried her parents. Dee felt betrayed. She was referred to the school's counsellor because of her deteriorating performance in class. Fortunately, the counsellor had immense sensitivity, and looked further than simply setting academic and attitude change targets.

They worked together on the mainspring of these circumstances and her affection for this young man had to be put into perspective. Dee is now a fan, who has come to appreciate that the tennis star is a normal man, with a normal life that he must lead. There is no reason why she should not admire his talent and his personal style. There may be much of this young man that she will look for in the young men with whom she falls in love in due course. She has learnt to admire, yes, and even love, but from 'afar', and has learnt that this type of affection has its own rules and once these are understood, the relationship becomes perfectly manageable.

As parents, we must remember how painful and all consuming these crushes can be. They are certainly not a joke, neither must they be a target for anger or recrimination. If a youngster is allowed to bring a crush to the surface, discuss it rationally and openly, and have it accepted with sympathy, not only will the crush pass, but it will do so more quickly for the breaking of the 'secretiveness' shield.

WHAT DO YOU DO IF YOU FIND YOU ARE THE OBJECT OF A CRUSH?

It is, of course, understandably flattering to discover that someone has "fallen in love" with you. 'Transference', where a client or patient becomes obsessed with their therapist, is a common enough phenomenon in therapy. It also occurs in a number of other professions where trust, dependence and a need for emotional support are an essential ingredient. Clergymen, doctors and, of course, teachers, are classic examples.

There are one or two basic ground rules that apply to this situation, demanding a proper level of 'professionalism' from the individual concerned:

- Remember it is the role you play and the position you occupy with which the individual has become obsessed, rather than you as a human being. While the responses of the person with the crush may seem to be stereotypical, infatuated love, they actually know very little about you as a person, your likes, dislikes, or even the domestic environment of which you are a part. Step out from behind your professional 'uniform' and you rapidly become an ordinary mortal. Keep what is happening in perspective and at arms length.

- Be gentle and understanding, but never even consider the possibility of taking advantage of the situation, however attractive the individual concerned may be. You could do them immense emotional damage and compromise yourself professionally, or even find yourself behaving unlawfully. Never let it happen.

- If necessary, allow the individual concerned to discuss their feelings and take them seriously. Make it clear that you are flattered and that the feelings are not reciprocated. This does not mean that a friendship does not exist or that your support will be withdrawn. It is vital that the young person does not feel fundamentally rejected. It may even be helpful to discuss the whole phenomenon of the crush and how normal crushes are. Do not, in any sense, downgrade the individual's emotions or feelings – they are very real. They are unlikely to believe you, but the feelings will pass.

- Be particularly careful where any further meetings are held. If they are to take place in an office, ensure that a secretary or some supervising authority is close by, outside the door. Meet in a coffee bar or canteen environment where privacy can be achieved but where there are other people moving around in the background so that it is quite impossible to be compromised. If you find yourself totally in private and in no way chaperoned, you are likely to make yourself extremely vulnerable, particularly at the highly charged stage of a crush.

- Avoid physical contact of any kind – a hand on a knee, upper arm, a comforting arm around a shoulder, a gentle social kiss – all can be easily misinterpreted by the recipient who may, in their emotional state, completely misread your body language. Remember if a feeling of rejection does develop, anger and frustration will be inevitable and misinterpreted body language can be dangerously misreported.

In essence, be sympathetic, kind, and allow the individual to talk through their feelings if they must, but do not allow yourself to be compromised. Do not give sexual encouragement, either by word or body language. It is wise not to discuss this issue with anyone else, unless at a professional, counselling or supervisory level.

34

Teenage Sexuality

It is curious that the more we look at the sexual world of the adolescent, the more we find that our own adult fears are born of the generation of which we are a part, with all those attendant prejudices. Prior to the advent of the pill and the sexual anxieties that preceded its arrival, the terror of becoming pregnant was the greatest possible contraceptive! This has not been the case since the mid 1960s. Sexuality is now a freer, more honest, more open expression of our humanity. However, it can be misunderstood and many old taboos remain in place. How many children, for example, used to be told that masturbation was bad for them, could tire them, make them go blind, deaf, give them hairs on the palms of their hand, and so forth? It is also a myth that girls never masturbate and are not interested in that side of sexuality. This is so palpably untrue, leaving many girls feeling guilty and furtive. In reality, masturbation is an appropriate way of exploring our sexual functioning.

Sexuality in adolescence also coincides with a drift away from parental control, that vital stage of self-realisation, and the early phase of beginning to develop an independent identity. Privacy, a degree of withdrawal from the family and parental interaction is normal and, indeed, appropriate, and yet sexuality is often caught in a web of unnecessary guilt. First and foremost, we must clear our minds of these old vestiges and understand our subject. What is true about our bodies and how they function? What is pleasant and exciting and perfectly acceptable? What is truly dangerous and unnecessary risk taking? Are we trying to throw up a 'scare' smoke screen to keep our children virginal?

The act that leads to procreation is fundamental, animal and basic. This does not imply that an individual has any real understanding of the complex part that sex plays in our society. "The great subject about which nobody talks"! Everybody sees it daily on the television! Even the most intimate married couples fail to discuss simple physical details and preferences that would make an enormous difference to their sex lives.

Early adolescence

In the early years of adolescent development, there is an increasing awareness of the opposite sex, and the beginnings of physical and hormonal changes in children of both sexes. They may want to touch and play with each other's bodies and explore its excitements and, indeed, such shared gentle interactions in these years are perfectly normal. From the very earliest stages, it is important that youngsters know about procreation, the physiology concerned, and the risks involved. These are the years of 'penis' orientation in boys, who often think of little else for seventy percent of their waking day. For girls, there is often a mixture of fear and excitement as they have to face the onset of their periods and the early fears associated with childbirth and sexuality as a whole.

It is a time for honesty within families. Indeed, even for the very young, it is vital that questions are answered simply. It is important to have suitable literature around the house, to which parents can refer. Sit down with the youngster and, if necessary on a nightly basis, work through the chapters of the book, allowing plenty of time for discussion. By the tail end of primary school, sexuality would have dealt with in the classroom. Experience has suggested that youngsters at this age can be extremely sensible and rational about the subject and ask very interesting and worthwhile questions that they expect to have answered. By the time they reach their teen years they need to know the essential framework of sexuality and procreation, the basic rudiments of contraception and the realistic appraisal of the health risks associated with unprotected sex. For example, undue sexual activity in early adolescent girls has clear medical implications. Honesty, and a forthright approach to the subject is vital. It is important, as in our discussion of drugs, that children do not begin to sense that we are trying to cause 'panic' to keep them pure.

Teenage sexual development

Matters in the world of sexuality become serious once children enter their teenage years. An increasing number of young people have had some sexual experience, including intercourse, by their fourteenth birthday, and there is no good pretending otherwise. If this is to happen, they should be protected and need to know as much as possible about the world in which they are becoming involved, rather than being forced and badgered into sex by a partner. Hence, the health facets of safe sex, Aids, and so forth, are particularly important, as is a detailed understanding of contraception. It is also important to engender an attitude and atmosphere of mutual responsibility. If you like somebody enough to have sex with them, you should respect them enough to protect them and see that they are kept safe. Boys, particularly, need to be aware of contraception, but it is wise for girls to take suitable precautions such as carrying a couple of condoms in their handbags, once they are over sixteen and have become sexually active. Rather than take a risk or cause a quite unnecessary row, it is wise to be properly provided.

This is also the stage in life when youngsters need to become aware of the differences between the genders, in terms of the physicality of sex. Boys' gratification tends to be more instantaneous, whereas girls usually need to be in the mood and dealt with gently and sensitively to a point of arousal. Boys need to be aware of this as soon as serious sexuality appears on the horizon. We must also bear in mind that there are huge differences in attitude, particularly within different racial and religious backgrounds. The same is true of gay sex. Young people need to be fully aware. Ignorance is not innocence.

Before sexual intercourse becomes a regular part of a young person's experience, they need to be fully *au fait* with contraception, its use and to have easy access to it. A young person, about to embark on a sexual relationship built on love and mutual respect, who has the courage to go and discuss it, together with their partner, with the family doctor, is to be admired! However, the knowledge that this meeting has to be arranged through their parents, or that their parents will find out, may well inhibit the contact. We need to respect the young person's privacy and realise that sexuality will be a part of their lives for many years to come. It is important that they learn to manage it sensitively, intelligently, and yet still with a great deal of fun and excitement, as part of a caring relationship. Parents should make it clear to their doctor that they are perfectly happy for any such confidential advice to be given.

Sixth form level

Especially in the upper sixth form of schools, we should regard youngsters as young adults and not as children any more. Most of them will, by now, have had some degree of sexual contact, whether or not it has actually involved sexual intercourse. They are a relatively sophisticated group, usually with language skills, interested in themselves, their own development and the lives that stretch before them. They should be treated with respect, honesty and intelligence.

We seldom read a book and almost never see an adult film in which sex does not play a part. Sexual gratification, excitement and fulfilment is a clear aim of our society. We all acknowledge that in any relationship that we develop, sex may eventually play a part, possibly an extremely important one. It is quite remarkable that such an important subject is seldom discussed between two people who have an intimate relationship. Why the shyness and the reticence about something so vital? Mutual discussion is not only helpful, but it can be an exciting part of foreplay. Why can the girl simply not explain that her partner has missed the target a little, and help him to find exactly where he should be caressing her? Why can she not explain that he needs to go on for longer and that penile penetration is not always sufficient to satisfy her? Of all the subjects that causes most angst, unhappiness and frustration in relationships, sexual incompetence is probably the greatest.

I feel that part of the sixth form training should include discussion of orgasms, erogenous zones, the need for patience in both partners, and an attitude of working together towards finding sexual satisfaction, which almost never comes instinctively at a first attempt. It is easy for youngsters, particularly young women, to become alienated from sex early on because it has been such an unsatisfactory experience by an unknowing, fumbling young man, virtually unaware of the existence of a clitoris.

I can hear even my own old prejudices barking in the background, "Oh, if you discuss that in a sixth form class, you will excite an undue interest in sexuality and they will never leave each other alone!" Supposing some couples do, indeed, go off together at the weekend and practice some of what they have learnt, why exactly are we complaining? If they love each other, and are working on their sexuality, are practising appropriate safe sex, then surely this is precisely our aim, and not something to be feared.

This is a particular point in life where honesty about the real health risks can be extremely valuable. The young people should know exactly what the real risks are – a detailed Aids study, looking at the United Kingdom and the worldwide picture, the way that the disease manifests itself, the likelihood of mortality and the possible medical treatment that may or may not exist. They must know that we are being honest and open, lest they suspect, once again, that this is simply an authority figure's scare story. There has been a return, in recent times, to other forms of sexually communicable diseases and they need to be as aware of these. The discussion tends to be almost exclusively 'Aids', and this can be a radical mistake. Excessive sexual activity in under age girls can also have its medical risks.

I suppose that the fundamental message that comes home loud and clear to all of us is to remember the value of communicating at all levels, about any subject that truly matters.

FURTHER READING

Adolescence: the survival guide for parents, E Fenwick and T Smith, Dorling Kindersley, 1993

Coping with crushes, Anita Naik, Sheldon Press, 1994

Is everybody doing it? A guide to contraception. Family Planning Association, London

Let's talk about sex, Walker Books, London

The Period Book, Karen Gravelle & Jennifer Gravelle

Sex Ed, Dr Miriam Stoppard

35

Teenage Pregnancy

Our role as parents is to nurture our children through to adulthood. Sexual awareness dawns remarkably early. As we know, even babies find their genitalia fascinating. Most children pass through the "doctors and nurses", "you show me yours and I'll show you mine" phase of their development, which is all part of the childish fascination with sexuality and gender difference.

By the onset of puberty, young people are becoming increasingly sexually aware and concerned with the opposite sex and how they will interact verbally and physically. It is vital that we tackle sexual awareness in our children honestly and frankly. They must know exactly what is involved physically and emotionally. There are genuine physical and medical risks associated with excessive, immature sexual activity. The risk of infection, HIV, unwanted pregnancies, these issues must all be dealt with, but not as a 'scare' strategy. Boys and girls will find each other sexually attractive and exciting, will explore their mutual sexuality, and most will have had sexual experience long before they leave school at eighteen. This is part of the developmental process through which we must shepherd them. Hence, easy access, on a strictly confidential basis, to the family doctor is terribly important to the mid adolescent. Contraception is obviously much wiser than unwanted pregnancy. We cannot and should not hide our heads in the sand as far as the active sex life of our teenage children is concerned.

Diane

I spoke recently to bewildered and anxious parents whose daughter, Diane, still over a year away from her GCSEs, had 'fallen pregnant'. It seemed calamitous and, indeed, it was an issue that demanded the emotional and physical resources of all concerned, but it was not the end of life. There are far worse things that could have happened. Curiously, it can even be the beginning of an unexpected level of family bonding. If ever a family had to 'stand up and be counted' and pull together to resolve an issue, this was certainly it! The family agreed to help in the upbringing of the baby and to give Diane as much support as they could, but not before considerable anger and general family trauma had been resolved.

- I can well understand the heart stopping feeling at suddenly discovering that your daughter is pregnant. The first response is one of panic and anger. This is normal

147

and the youngster must give you time to adjust. However, the sooner a "right – let's sort this muddle out" attitude emerges, so much the better.

- As parents, you are probably not going to be able to deal with this on your own - you will need help and counselling support. However, the evidence suggests that, in the vast majority of cases, families come together in mutual support in the end.

- Let your General Practitioner know that your daughter may want an entirely confidential chat, the outcome of which will not be discussed with you.

- Give your daughter time to come to terms with the problem. This may take a while. Do not feel that her anger is a rejection of you or your support. You may even feel that in some extraordinary way you, as a parent, are being blamed!

- Guilt is never easy to deal with. Allow her space. Neither condone, nor criticise. It has happened – let's deal with it.

- Give her the National Hotline telephone number for LIFE – 01926 311511. They have offices in many districts throughout the country. LIFE will give your daughter non-directive counselling support, and, in extremes, they have hostels where young people can go to have their babies and be helped and supported, sometimes for many months.

- This is a worrying experience for you. Do not be alarmed by your own feelings of panic, uncertainty, and even guilt. Many doctors' practices have counselling available within them. This support will help you organise your thinking and come to terms with what needs to be faced. LIFE can also help you.

- Above all do not let your daughter make the decision to have an abortion without professional counselling, both before and after. It is an option to which women are entitled, but it is not free of complications, both emotional and physical. I have recently worked with a mother who still, at 31 years of age, carries the guilt of an abortion at seventeen, with which she has never dealt. This is affecting the way in which she manages her own two children and is having a complex impact on her psycho-sexual relationship with her husband.

- Daughters need to grow up learning that an abortion will not avoid a parental confrontation. Parents will find out sooner or later. They need to see their parents as allies. This is why confidential access to the family doctor needs to be made available while they are developing the courage to discuss their pregnancy and its implications with their parents.

What Next?

Interestingly, in three of the families that I have worked with recently where the teenage daughter has become pregnant, the first issue that has arisen, usually with the fathers, has been the involvement of the boy. Hostility and anger towards the young man concerned is a natural, if unhelpful, response. Was he really a sex mad, beer-drinking opportunist who is best kept away? Or does a warm and caring relationship exist between the boy and girl, leaving the boy with his own feelings of dread and guilt?

David and Carol

David was seventeen and Carol fifteen. They had been going out together for some nine months and felt that they were in love. Carol had wanted to go on the Pill, but was embarrassed to ask her parents and frightened to visit the doctor. David used condoms but was very inexperienced and less than efficient. It had simply "come off" at the wrong moment. It is important that sexually active teenagers are thoroughly aware of the variety of contraceptives that exist and their efficient use.

Carol, after weeks of anguish and two missed periods, knew she was pregnant and with the eventual support of her family, decided to keep the baby. David had become involved and eventually accepted by Carol's parents. He gave her a great deal of warmth and support and, now in a regular job, wants to make financial contributions towards the baby's care.

It took two to make this pregnancy and, given the right circumstances, I see no reason why two should not help deal with the issue.

- The conclusion reached by most families is that the teenager will have the baby. However, the issues of abortion, adoption or keeping the baby must be faced. LIFE can help here once again.

- Adoption agencies will give sound advice as to how this process should be managed and the degree of subsequent contact that is now allowed under the Law. What happens so often is that as the pregnancy develops the situation is slowly accepted by parents and other family members. Everyone rallies round to give support through the inevitable periods when the physical and mental demands of pregnancy seem to swamp the mother-to-be. There may be morning sickness, moods of depression or problems keeping up with schoolwork. The whole family unit becomes increasingly involved in the existence of this new life. Once the baby has been born, held and cuddled by its mother and grandparents, a bond is usually formed which becomes virtually impossible to break.

However, the entire issue of a 15-year-old, going through an adult experience at a totally inappropriate stage of their own lives needs counselling and careful thought. It is a time for the young mother to develop a sense of responsibility beyond her years and accept that she has created a new life which will depend on her for love and nurture. It is equally important that the new mother's parents become a part of the support team. Their 15-year-old daughter has her education to complete. This may be a difficult time for busy parents, already established in their own careers. It may be necessary to work out compromises and make plans for the future which will allow for shared responsibilities, especially while the student completes her education. Counselling for both the new mother and her own parents can give great support for what is an important life event, quite beyond their experience. A new pillar of identity for the whole family has appeared and will now establish its role firmly over the years to follow.

Families should be given the chance to be supportive. They are certainly the most therapeutic group available.

36
Young People and Alcohol

What do you do when your child comes home drunk for the first time?

Unfortunately, alcohol abuse by young people appears to be rising. For parents this presents a series of new problems which can start as early as primary school, but more often become apparent in the teenage years.

Jenny

We saw Jenny last summer, largely because she was dyslexic and might need extra time in her examinations. However, she was looking very sorry for herself and, on closer enquiry, we found out that she had been very drunk only two nights earlier. Her parents had come home to find her in her bedroom with her boyfriend. She rose staggering from the bed, teetered across the floor and when accused of being drunk, simply said: "Who me? – me – drinking?" and fell down on her face in what amounted to a coma! The boyfriend had simply been keeping a frightened eye on the girl, who had been becoming more and more violently sick.

Not a pretty sight. Any parent's immediate reaction may be a mixture of disgust and fury, even a touch of panic at having 'allowed' this circumstance to arise. Even more, what on earth might the two of them have been up to while they were drunk? Recall your own youth. I would suspect most parents have been through a similar experience themselves. Remember, they are practising the early stages of adulthood and on this occasion have got it badly wrong.

First and foremost, almost every drunk is eventually sick. The first ground rule established from the very earliest moment is, "The next time this happens, it will be left and you can clean it up, complete with your hangover!" However, rows, remonstrations, requests for explanations and so forth are completely pointless while the youngster is still drunk. At this point, treat them as being ill which, indeed, they are. Put them to bed, make them warm, give them a bowl because they will almost certainly be sick again and a glass of cold fizzy water, or possibly cold Coca-Cola. They will be dehydrated and often the bubbles in the fizzy drink help to settle a turbulent stomach.

In the morning, catch the youngster still subdued by a mixture of guilt and hangover. The deal should be that there will be no further recrimination, providing they sit down and discuss the issue quietly and sensibly.

We must hope that your child was not driving on the evening concerned, but, if they were, this must be regarded as an extremely serious offence. Far too many people are killed every year by drunken drivers. Quite apart from losing their licence, it is patently unfair to the people they hurt. I would suggest that for even a first offence, if they were drunk while driving a car, their driving licence should be removed by parents for at least three months.

The first question must be, "What did the booze actually do for you?" "Why, how and where did you drink it?" If it was in lonely seclusion, possibly with one other friend, listening to the internal buzz and bodily changes taking place, then we are talking about alcohol abuse. If this were to continue, there is no reason why it should not stray into other forms of substance. This attitude is not a 'social' use of alcohol at all, but a mind and body changing experience. I would suggest briefing your family doctor and joining your child in the surgery while the GP explains about the dangers of substance abuse and the ease with which this attitude leads on to far more serious problems. It may even be necessary to refer the child to a centre skilled in dealing with substance abuse. It is the attitude of mind while the alcohol was being consumed that must concern us.

The vast majority of people drink to relax, have fun and to become disinhibited. If this is what your child says, then this is entirely natural and in many ways a perfectly normal use of alcohol, for the first drink or two. I am not suggesting that we condone this in under-age children, but the real risk to your child is the abuse of alcohol, in drinking far too much and making themselves not only disinhibited and drunk, but very vulnerable.

Get them to reflect on the risks. There is a gender difference. Girls become pregnant - boys do not. It is all too easy for a girl of 15 to wake up in the morning and realise that she has had sex, often with a boy whom she does not particularly like, but she lost control and simply allowed it to happen or, indeed, it may have been forced upon her. Encourage the youngster to reflect on 'being out of control' and, therefore, by definition, allowing other people to control them. Who needs to be a puppet whose strings are pulled by others? We need to instil an awareness that loss of control inevitably brings personal vulnerability with it.

We worked with a teenage boy some months ago who may well find himself losing his freedom because he had been pushed, for a second time, into breaking into shops, having allowed himself to become drunk and easily influenced by his friends.

Point out to youngsters that a man, woman or child drunk never looks remotely appealing or attractive. Their humour often goes, as well as their ability to talk sense. Youngsters unable to hold their drink have usually vomited and this does not enhance their image any further! We all have a need to protect our self-image and are aware of the way others see us. Most teenagers are concerned about their peer group image. Drunkenness and vomiting does little for the 'street cred'.

Why do we get hangovers?

The answer is simply because we have poisoned our systems with alcohol. Most of us, if we felt the way we do with a hangover, without the excuse of alcohol, would report to the hospital outpatients without delay! It is nature's way of saying, "Your system did not like that and would like it even less if you did it too often." Youngsters seldom realise that alcohol abuse, taken to excess, can lead not only to brain damage and liver damage but has even caused heart failure. Dying while you are supposed to be having fun seems extraordinarily absurd.

We are not condemning alcohol; it is part of our culture. It is important to encourage a youngster to see alcohol used in a sensible and balanced fashion.

David and Tony

David and Tony, 11, both still at primary school, were found drunk in a ditch at the back of their school playing field, having consumed an entire bottle of Vodka. One of them had to be taken to hospital and resuscitated. Both commented latterly that they enjoyed the 'buzz' the alcohol gave them, a slightly 'narcotic' approach to alcohol abuse.

The need to reduce the glamour and mystique associated with alcohol became dramatically apparent in a letter I received from a concerned parent.

This has led to a parents' forum, to examine the use of alcohol in our culture, and how children should be brought up to understand and appreciate it. Alcohol is now a permanent part of our environment; no amount of denial will remove it. Hence, it is both a pleasure and a threat to which our children will be exposed, sooner rather than later, and about which they must learn in a rational and positive environment. The forum accepted that alcohol is a great social 'loosener', and makes us feel at ease with our environment. Chat and laughter flow much more easily and the tensions of the day are rapidly left behind. Connoisseurs were keen to highlight the sheer pleasure of drink on the pallet. The whole group concluded that a proper introduction to an acceptable, manageable, and, above all, legal 'drug', allows children to feel that this is not only socially acceptable, but is often fun. The de-romanticising of alcohol allowed parents to talk rationally about alcohol abuse, and the abuse of other drugs. It is important that children realise that there are more work hours lost per year through alcohol abuse than any other single factor and that it is frequently directly responsible for the abuse of women and children and the cause of much family unhappiness. The balance between use and abuse is vital to strike.

Our group also felt that it was important to be aware of the law related to alcohol, and its use by minors. After the age of 5, there is no limit on the introduction to alcohol within the home by a parent. It is the use of alcohol in public places that is a matter of law. Whatever our own attitudes may be to alcohol and its introduction to our children, for their own sakes, and the sake of the Publican or Restauranteur, it is vital that the law is observed strictly.

In general, the use of alcohol as part of everyday life by parents is a healthy introduction for even very small children. However, its abuse by a parent is a hopelessly negative and damaging experience. A parent who becomes drunk, loses their temper, experiences violent mood swings, will simply alienate the family and teach nothing about the socially acceptable use of alcohol.

Over the age of eight, it is helpful to introduce children to occasional pub meals. They begin to realise that a pub is a social gathering place and not a centre for alcohol abuse. An increasing number of pubs are prepared to have back rooms where children can eat, especially the countryside pubs with gardens and play areas. Restaurants will often allow children to join their parents. However, as we expand our horizons in terms of children's access to pubs, restaurants and hotels, the onus is on us to see that they behave properly. Any new environment of which children become a part will have its customs and rules. If you are old enough to be part of this environment, you are old enough to respect the norms that apply. Properly managed, this removes the mystique and aura of a pub and makes it what it should be, a social centre within a community, where people can relax, often with their families.

Much depends on the maturity of a child. There are many eleven year olds who are perfectly capable of coping with a half pint of shandy, should they wish to do so in the privacy of their own home. It is important not to force alcohol upon them or expect the children to drink it. However, if they show an interest, and would like a taste of Dad's beer, or a sip of mother's wine, this does no harm at all at this stage.

This is the time to look carefully at the criteria of use and abuse. Youngsters can look at the pleasures, social benefits of drink, but must also look carefully at the risks, not least of which is driving a motorcar while under the influence of alcohol. They will also need to be aware that their mood and behaviour may change dramatically when they are disinhibited by alcohol. Girls, particularly, should be aware of the sexual risks that will be heightened by this level of disinhibition. However, the very existence of alcohol can open the way to healthy discussion of various aspects of teenage development.

By 13, most youngsters will want to experiment and I see no reason why they should not join you at a meal with a small glass of wine or, again, a half pint of shandy.

By 14, a glass of wine or a half pint of beer would be normal and indeed many young people will have been introduced to alcohol at parties by this age. It helps to casually monitor its use in a rational, sensible and controlled atmosphere within the home, in order to give them a balance by which to judge abuse.

By 16, many of the youngsters in this country will have left school and others will be moving into the serious world of A Levels. It is time for them to practise the early stages of alcohol use in an adult environment. Throughout a lengthy meal, two glasses of wine or a couple of half pints of beer would seem to be totally acceptable. It is very helpful if their parents react by following this pattern of use. The example of 'don't drink and drive' must be set by parents.

I was talking to a family recently, who quite deliberately had only two glasses of wine when out to dinner with their sixteen-year-old twins, but still ordered a taxi to take them home. This set an excellent example to the young people.

By 17, we have twelve months left until 'adulthood' strikes. I would suggest that throughout this year, you treat youngsters exactly as you would treat yourself, and make no particular allowances. Clearly, do not encourage alcohol abuse, but let them follow exactly the same pattern of alcohol usage as yourself, with the exception of spirits. It can be great fun discussing wine and helping youngsters to enjoy the experience, against a background of normality.

CONTACTS

ALCOHOLICS ANONYMOUS

Your local telephone directory will give you your local branch., or contact:

>Alcoholics Anonymous
>PO Box 1
>Stonebrow House
>Stonebrow
>York YO1 7NJ
>Tel: 01904 644026

AL-ANON FAMILY GROUPS UK & EIRE

For families and friends of alcoholics:

>61 Great Dover Street
>London
>Tel: 020 7403 0888; Fax: 020 7378 9910

ALATEEN

For young people 12 to 20 affected by a problem drinker:

>http://www.hexnet.co.uk/akabib/alateen.html
>(Includes a helpful list of questions)

DRINK LINE

Information and advice on sensible drinking and alcohol misuse, and support for anyone concerned about their own or someone else's drinking. Free literature and referral to local agencies.

>Tel: 0800 917 8282
>(Mon–Fri 9am to 11pm; Sat & Sun 6pm to 11pm)

ALCOHOL CONCERN

>Waterbridge House
>32–36 Loman Street
>London SE1 0EE
>Tel: 020 7928 7377

37

Leaving the Nest

At times, there seems to be a bewildering difference between our role as parents and our parental instincts. Our instinct is to nurture and protect our offspring. However, our 'role' may be somewhat different. Youngsters pass through so many different phases, and each has its own rules. However, the ultimate target is to bring them to maturity at eighteen and then help them leave home, stand on their own two feet, become adults in their own right and produce their own new generation. It is at this point that our responses to young people are often in conflict.

Sharon

Troubled parents rang me up to discuss their daughter, Sharon, who had left school at sixteen and was now nineteen. She had never worked and had no intention of doing so. She was using their home as a hotel. She came and went as she wanted. She felt that as an adult, she was entitled to run her own life. There were vicious rows when she did come home if a vegetarian meal was not available for her. She was abusive, brought noisy friends home late at night, and often played her loud music till the early hours of the morning. Her parents both worked and had to be on the move by 7.30am. How on earth were they to cope? "She is our daughter, after all", they explained.

Firstly, would any parent accept even 10% of this behaviour from anyone else, a friend, or other relative? The answer is "certainly not". Secondly, we established a concept, which they found helpful. Sharon must be regarded as a 'young adult in the herd'. Sharon's parents' role was to encourage her to become independent and therefore if she stayed within their home, she had to begin to assume an 'adult mantle', at least in part. They began to see what their role had to be and to accept that there was absolutely no need for this continual abuse or for them to feel powerless to do anything about it. However, Sharon's mother said, "She will make our lives a misery if we attempt to stand up to her". They went off to a counsellor, specifically for assertiveness training. They finished the first stage of their counselling, and reached several fundamental resolutions. First and foremost, they had control over Sharon's money, her food, domestic support, clothing and, ultimately, the front door key. They could not avoid a confrontation with Sharon, realised it would be painful, but that they must strike a deal – each of them were members of the same team and must therefore contribute. Withdrawal of the front door key, and even changing the locks, might prove necessary. Sharon had to believe that they would do this, if necessary. Never threaten the impossible, or threaten and then fail to follow through.

Sharon had six perfectly good GCSEs, and quite capable of getting a job. A friend had already offered to share her small flat with Sharon but she would have to make a small financial contribution. They knew that Sharon had somewhere to go, but were more than prepared to let her stay at home for the time being, providing she 'played the game by the rules'. A difficult confrontation that takes considerable courage. Counselling gave them the conviction that they were right and that they would, in fact, do Sharon increasing harm by almost encouraging her to play her aggressive, parasitic role.

Charlie

Charlie was a somewhat more sensitive case. He was nineteen, rather depressed, quite unable to get a job or even tackle an application form. Two years ago, he was offered a job at a wage which he felt would be consumed by rent and travel. He still lived at home where he was on disability allowance and therefore, he felt that there was no need to make any contribution. In group counselling, Charlie and his parents arrived at the conclusion that he needed to make some contribution to the effectiveness of the team.

The first step for Charlie was to deal with his depression. He saw a psychiatrist on a monthly basis, was on anti-depressants and began to feel much better. We worked towards planning three fortnight modules of work experience in the autumn, which he began to look forward to. This would reintroduce Charlie to the world of work. More importantly, it helped to deal with his totally miss-set body rhythm. He found it difficult to get out of bed at 7.30am in time for work. This first fortnight of work experience was tough going. However, once he had established a new biological rhythm and was beginning to develop some self-respect, he went from strength to strength. Charlie's contribution to the team was, "Get yourself fit, begin to look at the world of work, and then we will discuss more tangible contributions when you are fit enough to make them'.

Mike

Mike, who was seventeen, was perhaps rather more typical. He was in his first job and being given the minimum wage. He lived at home and claimed to be unable to afford to contribute because he did not earn very much and he needed what little money he did earn.

It was true that Mike was not earning a great deal but he actually had twice as much available cash per week as either of his parents. We can all understand the excitement of being an earner for the first time and suddenly having cash available. Human beings are naturally selfish and Mike could see widening possibilities for spending all this newfound wealth. He naturally resented parting with any of it, to the Taxman, National Insurance, and certainly not his parents, who had to reflect, once again, on their fundamental role in helping the young person mature. It was ultimately decided that if Mike was to remain at home, he would contribute 10% of his weekly earnings. This would pay for his roof, heating, food, use of the television and so forth. He continued to buy his own clothes and fund his own social life. Holidays would remain at the family expense.

Somewhat to Mike's chagrin, we also felt that some practical input to the management of the home was necessary, if he was to truly be a young adult 'team player'. He has now agreed to make his own bed, tidy his room and walk the dog each evening. Not onerous tasks, but at least his parents felt he was making a real commitment. Curiously, during the weeks that followed the establishment of this contract, Mike seemed to grow in maturity and his relationship with his parents was far more friendly.

A family, of whatever composition, only truly works as a team if each member has a role and makes a contribution, however small. This rule only alters if for some very exceptional reason of disability, they are quite unable to do so. None of us should expect to be a passenger, parasitic on those around us.

Part 4

Collaborating to Manage Academic Stress

38

Homework

There are few topics that cause greater stress and upset in many families than homework. I worked with the family of a youngster of average intelligence, placed in a school for which he was, frankly, unsuited. To survive even in the bottom quartile of his class group, he had to spend two hours a night accomplishing what peers achieved in thirty minutes. There was no time or emotional energy for any serious quality of life in this family throughout the working week. This was living a 'lie'.

Homework should be a rather more productive experience than simply finishing off schoolwork. This would suggest either a badly structured teaching session or a lazy attitude in the child, who feels "Oh, I can easily dash this off later".

It is also a time for developing, from the earliest days, a degree of independent study. Once children become literate, they learn to use books as sources, visit libraries, cull information from newspapers and use the Internet. As they become increasingly academic the quality and depth of independent study increases. Time and again, concepts are discussed in Mathematics, for example, which can only be practised briefly in class. The newly learned concept will quickly drift if it is not consolidated.

In the literacy-orientated subjects, especially with the older child, it is often appropriate to discuss sources and characters as part of the basic framework around which an essay will evolve in a class period. It is then entirely appropriate that the student works at home in peace and quiet to draw these threads together.

Jane

Jane's mother felt that homework was beginning to wreck family life. Both parents worked and Jane's mother returned home in the evening tired and then had to galvanise herself to see Jane and her older brother through their homework commitments. Subconsciously Jane had decided that this was a marvellous vehicle for attention seeking. She took hours to settle, her mind constantly wandered, the work was seldom finished and if her mother left the room nothing happened at all. Jane ensured that she trapped her mother's attention for the maximum amount of time every evening.

161

"Why have homework at all?"

Unfortunately, life is not quite so simple. We all have responsibilities and these gather in number and complexity the older we get. Homework gives a child a chance to consolidate and practise skills that have been learnt in class, in peace and quiet. Above all, it teaches children to cope within their own resources. This will become an increasingly important part of their lives the further up the academic ladder they climb.

Fabian

The school suggested that Fabian, aged 9, needed help with his homework. His mother seldom left his side. The result was that the homework was always completed, beautifully presented and of a level of sophistication that Fabian could never manage on his own. Fabian undoubtedly loved his mother's attention, but seldom had to focus his own mind for any length of time as his mother did this for him. Fabian was being kept out of trouble in school, his work was of a high standard, attracting very positive reports.

However, he was beginning to develop a reputation for being very 'scatty' and distractible in class. With the evidence of the homework, staff were becoming more and more disenchanted with the lack of effort he was apparently making within the classroom. Even worse, elements in the homework that Fabian frankly did not understand were never re-taught in class because the teacher assumed that Fabian knew what he was doing.

In the first two or three years of school life, homework should be very brief and usually accomplished in some ten to fifteen minutes. However, even at this early stage, a pattern must be established. Decide on a time, a place and a routine which will be the same every evening, if possible. I would suggest that the child should come home, have an appropriate drink and snack to boost their energy level, and then embark on homework. In the early terms it may well be necessary to be 'in contact', so that the child has a feeling of family support, without too much distraction. At the kitchen table while a parent potters with the evening meal would be perfectly appropriate at this stage, but not with the radio or TV in the background. Do not sit with the child and 'police' them through the exercise, but allow them to come to you for support and advice. Where a child has clearly not understood, be sure the teacher knows the following morning. This is no disgrace. Teachers want to be aware of exactly what needs to be re-taught.

From eight or nine years of age, up to secondary transfer, homework may become rather more intense and the volume will increase. This is the time when children need a quiet study area, possibly in their own bedroom. Work will require far greater concentration, well away from the television, radio, doorbells, telephones and so forth. Above all, a child should not be crouched using the coffee table, with a television noisily in the background. Serious consolidation of class work and enriching of skills are now part of the experience.

I would suggest that, at this stage in their development, you should give your child a five-minute warning before homework starts. They should then settle down to their homework at the appointed time. It is vital that you know from the class teacher just what subjects are involved and how long each homework module should take. Where children are having difficulty disciplining themselves, arrange a kitchen timer in the room set for the amount of time prescribed by the teacher. When the timer rings, they should bring their homework to you. Write a brief comment on the bottom of the homework describing the maturity with which they have settled down to their work. They should only be allowed to come to you for support if they are stuck. If the work has not been finished within the appointed time a comment should be made to this effect. It is very important that children learn to work within the constraints of time and to settle down quickly when the need arises. You are not a teacher, you are a prescriber of regimes and a supporter. If they have not coped it is up to the member of staff to deal with this issue in class the following day. Homework should not become a battleground, and, of course, children also need their free time in the evenings. So get homework out of the way quickly and efficiently.

By secondary age, a pattern should have been established. The children are now old enough to realise that homework is their responsibility and should not inflict 'pain' on other family members.

Tom

Tom, 14, very dyslexic, struggled with essays. His mother had recently come up behind him as he sat, hunched shouldered and scowling, as he did his homework. She read the essay question, and realised to her horror that Tom had completely misinterpreted the essay subject, so pointed out exactly where he had gone wrong. Tom stormed out of the room and slammed the door behind him, "I would do much better if you didn't always interfere!"

She spoke to me of her disappointment, hurt and frustration. We looked at his negative reaction to help. As is the case with so many youngsters, especially dyslexics, homework is a nightmare. As parents we are used to homework resistance, but it can easily become a battleground. In Tom's mind the bedroom door opening behind him and his mother coming in, was a prelude to criticism and faultfinding. Remember that the words we use, our body language, and, even more importantly, the behavioural history over the years, will dictate the way in which our communication is interpreted. Her opening remark over Tom's shoulder had been "Oh, for goodness sake ……." already disparaging, critical and provocative. Tom had been conditioned to look on parental support as negative intervention.

It is important to accept that struggling and the search for strategies, was part of the learning process for Tom. It was easy for this youngster to drift into an attitude of mind – "As soon as the going gets rough, somebody will help me out".

Do not make it too easy for our children. Above all, do not actually do the homework for them. By all means explain strategies, techniques, help them understand what is required of them, but let them complete the task for themselves. As in Tom's case, it was also important for teaching staff to be aware of the difficulties, that he had not fully understood the subject, and, therefore, further explanation was needed.

Helping our children with their homework depends on setting up a framework within which this work is accomplished, with a clear understanding that parental support is available, but only if necessary. Fundamentally, the request must come from the child.

Sarah

Sarah, twelve, had been completing her homework far too late at night when she was tired. This caused an emotional confrontation almost every evening. She and her parents sat down one Saturday lunchtime to discuss the strategy for the following week. Interestingly, most children will agree more readily to a commitment that is still days ahead, rather than today! The 'team' agreed a time and a place when her commitment would be completed. They reached a clear understanding that the homework was Sarah's commitment. Her parents were to withdraw, in a large measure, and to stop nagging! She would come home from school, change out of her uniform, have something to drink, and begin at 5.30pm. It was also accepted that she anticipated working for two thirty-minute modules each night. These would, therefore, be completed by 6.30pm.

Her mother agreed to give Sarah a ten minute warning before homework time which allowed her to collect her books, arrange a drink and set about her work. The kitchen timer was placed at the back of Sarah's room. Sarah realised, with exams in the offing, that it was important that she learnt to work against the constraints of time. Furthermore, her homework commitment would be finished in reasonable time, without trailing on into the evening.

There was a firm commitment from her parents to avoid 'policing' the homework. At first they struggled to accept that homework was now Sarah's commitment, and that they must let her cope on her own. They arranged a meeting with the staff in the school and explained that from now on, Sarah's homework would be completed largely independently, and so there might be a period when her work may appear to deteriorate, in the early stages of having to cope entirely without any help.

I explained to Sarah that she could, at any time, use her mother as a source of advice if she needed it, but must then return to complete the work for herself. What we had established was a 'link' with her mother which was totally within Sarah's control. She could use this resource as and when she felt it was required. It is important that youngsters take on this early academic responsibility for themselves.

In the early days, when conflict is still perhaps just around the corner, wander into the youngster's room once, in the middle of the homework period – be supportive and then go. Do not be critical or inquisitorial, or in any way challenging. Remember the child will be expecting the 'inquisition' and will tense up as soon as you come into the room.

If you are aware of a build up of stress and anxiety then this is 'support time', but, remember, say nothing. The overture must come from the child if you are to be successful.

Dwayne

Dwayne, who is now fifteen, discussed how much he valued his mother's new adult/adult problem solving approach. They now sat down together, analysed the problem and searched for strategies for resolving it. He wished his father could do the same. His father could not avoid lecturing him, often on a subject about which he knew very little, becoming excessively critical and angry. It is not surprising that the 'shutters' come down with Dwayne.

Sam

Project work is the major exception to this general rule. Sam produced a magnificent project on dinosaurs. He and his mother went down to the library and local bookshop and scoured the shelves for useful material. The family took the opportunity to make a trip to the National History Museum, bought post cards and talked to the curators and, in general, researched in great detail, while having a marvellous day out.

They then discussed how best to present the material, but the boy eventually set about the task for himself. His parents helped him answer the basic question "Where will I find resources and information to help me answer these questions?" He looked at his mass of information and considered how best to make it appealing to a reader, with enthusiastic parental support.

At each stage of the exercise, it is important that the parent is an encourager and facilitator, but that the eventual product truly belongs to the child.

Know your children and their differing needs

What constitutes success in terms of our developing children? Know your child – provision, expectations, homework, etc. must all be geared to an understanding of the individual's strengths and weaknesses. Because a notional contract exists between a parent and the school, it does not mean that all children of a given age can actually cope with the prescribed amount of homework.

We need to rid ourselves of the myths and look at the realities that face our children. It worries me when those in authority comment on the needs of our children starting with – "Children in the United Kingdom should ...".

Gary

Gary, who was ten, had a marked Attention Deficit Disorder (ADD) and was dyslexic. He often came home from school white faced and exhausted. His older brother, Shane, who was bright, articulate and academic, teased his younger brother mercilessly. Shane was now in a very academic school where he was coping at the top of his group. He coped easily with an hour-and-a-half's homework every night. Not so Gary.

We must accept that the homework demands made on these two youngsters should clearly be modified to suit their individual needs. We were having wet beds and nightmares from the younger of these two boys – never under estimate the quality of anxiety and depression that can so often follow this type of stress. This was not to say that both boys should not cope with homework of some sort. It simply clarifies their colossally different needs.

Nevertheless, let us not sacrifice our children on the altar of academic obsession. Homework has its place, but the enrichment of our children's lives needs to be very much more broadly based. Be sure they have time and space to develop family relationships, and, above all, to just be 'kids growing up'.

39

Can Our Children Work Too Hard?

For many of us, encouraging our children to settle down to their schoolwork, is only a daily chore. For others, it is an area of considerable stress and concern.

Avril

Avril, now 16, was working towards her GCSE exams. The youngster had lost her appetite, was no longer sleeping well, and matters had recently come to a head when her mother found her pacing fretfully back and forth in her bedroom, unable to settle down to her revision. Avril had allocated herself four hours a night for her revision, and, apart from a lie-in on Saturday mornings, was revising between eight and ten hours a day, over half term, and then throughout the Easter holidays. She was becoming increasingly frustrated. No matter how hard she worked, the information did not seem to penetrate, and she saw 'vast mountains' of work still stretching ahead of her.

The long hours and resulting mental exhaustion had induced a state of panic, which was impairing her capacity to process complex information and needed careful rationalisation.

Avril and I looked at the need to restrict her revision sessions to two-hour modules, and she received help in school on the more efficient use of this time. We also insisted on proper thirty-minute breaks between sessions.

Natasha

Natasha, who was also 16, posed a particular problem. She found it very hard to leave her books alone, was up at six in the morning, and was white faced and exhausted long before lunch. She realised the importance of her GCSE exams, and knew that good grades were vital if she was to succeed, in due course, in A Levels. She became obsessed with filling every minute of every hour throughout the waking day with homework. She was quite unable to give herself permission to take time off.

I advised her parents to take her away for a long weekend over the Easter holidays and forbid her to bring any books with her. After a moment or two's disquiet, Natasha relaxed visibly, thoroughly enjoyed her weekend, spent time discussing a more realistic approach to the hours she put in, and was happier and more effective thereafter. Breaks, relaxation, proper sleep and nutrition are essential elements in dealing with exam stress.

June

June is only 14, still a long way from her GCSEs, and has gained a place in a relatively academic grammar school. She is struggling to cope with her Maths and Science for which she is having extra coaching. Her parents rang me because they were concerned that the school had suggested she should drop drama, which was "wasting too much of her time", and was surely a subject that she could pursue in her spare time.

This raised two fundamental issues. Firstly, for June, drama was her one true area of excellence, and she badly needed this 'platform of success' to give her the confidence and courage to deal with the rest of the curriculum. Secondly, creativity adds a breadth and a quality to education and is, in reality, a vital ingredient in the academic process. It should not be regarded as "an additional extra, if there is time". Not surprisingly, June moved to a new school which valued drama, art, design and music very highly, while still being academic in the rest of the curriculum. She will do GCSE Theatre Studies, and hopes to pursue her drama into A Levels, and eventually to university.

In essence, it is vital, as parents, that we look clear-sightedly at the academic pressure that our teenagers face. We need to prescribe the fundamental boundaries of discipline. However, our aim must be to encourage the youngster to be self-disciplined, while we remain supportive in the background. For the public exam candidate, two-hour modules, with breaks between, are usually ideal, but it is vital that proper rest periods are also built in. These are therapeutically necessary. The mind and body need time to recuperate. Evidence suggests that excessive stress and fatigue produce diminishing results. Sit down with your youngster, if necessary with an expert to guide you, and work out a timetable of exactly when revision sessions will start, and, above all, when they will finish. The youngster then has a licence to stop, relax, enjoy television, meet their friends or follow other interests.

Marion

We had a curious time with Marion, who was 18. She was a gifted girl with an IQ in the 140's, but had become obsessed with perfection. Her essays took hours to complete, when one hour was all that was required of her, but they were of almost textbook quality. She found, once mock A Level exams came into view, that she simply could not cope with the 'imperfection' of a time related response.

She refused to return to school in the early spring, and was going to abandon her A Levels. I helped her to review her approach to exams. She began to realise that the refining of information, was, in itself, a skill and an intellectual challenge. Having dealt with her stress, Marion returned to school and went on to Cambridge the following autumn.

From a parental point of view, it is important that we look at the stress associated with academic achievement, long before matters come to a head. You will know the hurdles that face your child. At the first sign of a report reflecting, "David has worked hard through the year, what a shame about the poor exam results." Look for a tutor to help with revision strategies, note taking and exam technique. Far too often, youngsters are mis-reading questions, producing less than relevant replies, overwriting and failing to finish papers. Better technique produces better results and infinitely less stress for the individual. Be well prepared academically and look after yourself physically, is the message for our children.

40

Controlling Exam Nerves

Stress, to some degree, is a normal and perfectly healthy facet of examinations from which we have all suffered, but undue anxiety and unhappiness can be avoided. Every year during the spring and early summer, young people feel the twitch of adrenaline as important exams approach. Has revision been sufficient? Am I going to make a terrible fool of myself?

David

Poor David was becoming greyer, loosing weight, unable to sleep or eat properly and was now quite unable to face his books. He needed some weeks of counselling and, at last, began to deal with the run up to his A Levels.

Curiously, David was a first class athlete and began to recognise that he felt equally 'stressed' in the hours leading up to a major athletic event. In the same vein, his sister took part in school plays and could never eat before a production. It was important for David to come to know his body and the way in which it worked. Adrenaline is an extremely valuable part of our system – it prepares us for 'fight or flight'. We really do run faster when we are being chased by the proverbial bull! Maximising our performance depends on the effective use of this adrenaline.

David's first step was to examine his own bodily reactions to adrenaline, which he was able to do easily enough with the advent of the athletic season. He began to realise that without the symptoms of 'butterflies in the stomach', tension, and nausea, he was not, in fact, ready for the event and would under perform. He now recognised the symptoms as a positive sign, building up to examinations, and not as an indication that he was falling apart and unable to cope. The symptoms are so like those associated with anxiety and panic that the subconscious mind readily interprets inaccurately. As an athlete, he also acknowledged the tremendous importance of a proper routine of sleep and diet. He had never before seen exams in this light.

It is when the whole system is being put under physical and emotional pressure, to examine and observe and 'professional' routine. Eat, even when you do not feel like it, to ensure that nutrition is kept adequate and the blood sugar level is not allowed to drop unnecessarily. It is easy, especially on the morning of an examination, to abandon breakfast. This is a bad mistake, as a drop in blood sugar level will take its toll by mid morning. The same is true of a sunny lunchtime when it is tempting to lie on the grass with final revision, rather than bother about lunch. David has now been persuaded to know how his body works and to be systematically organised in the way he controls his day-to-day life leading up to the exams.

David also looked at proper breath control. There is a tendency, when we are anxious, to hyperventilate. Many cultures exploit hyperventilation – before battles; to raise arousal levels before competitions; to induce trance states during religious festivals. In sport, it is often described as 'focusing' or 'being in the zone'. The result upsets the vital balance of carbon dioxide in the blood so that its level begins to drop. If this situation persists, the entire body metabolism becomes less efficient. Exhaustion and a chronic sense of tiredness follow, and, occasionally, even depression. The reverse may occur where people take such shallow breaths that the brain fails to oxygenate appropriately.

The rule for David was, in the moments before an exam, to take four deep breaths which he held and let out very slowly. This re-oxygenated the brain, raised his arousal level and encouraged the effective use of his adrenaline. He also learned to control his breathing to a steady, moderate, rhythm, which created exactly the right balance of oxygen and carbon dioxide. It also gave David a feeling of being in control.

David was now physically ready to tackle revision. The first step was to design a proper, appropriate, revision schedule. He divided the day into four revision periods. Two hours in the morning, two one and a half hour spells in the afternoon and a two-hour session in the evening. He was in the final two to three weeks run up to examinations. It was also vital to build in proper breaks. If David allowed himself breaks between these sessions, had Wednesday and Saturday evenings off and did not begin work until 11 on Sunday morning he found he reduced the stress on himself and yet had plenty of time to study. I also advised him to be sure that he spent his breaks with his friends and not twitching in a solitary state on his own. In his time off, he should "have a laugh"!

When he reached the examinations themselves, he had learnt to time his attack properly, assessing exactly how much he could write in a given time, so that he need not worry that the papers would remain unfinished.

David was also taught to develop a clear-cut strategy for tackling the literacy-orientated papers. Read the instructions carefully – is there a new part 'C' that has never been there before, for example? Read the questions and decide on choices and order. Read the first question carefully, preparing the skeleton of the reply. Then challenge this outline for total relevance. Only then, flesh out the answer. Sound technique does wonders for confidence and stress management.

Sue

Sue complained that she was feeling lonely, edgy and depressed, working upstairs on her own. She too had to learn about proper breath control and management. I asked her mother pop into her daughter's room, say nothing to distract Sue, bring an appropriate drink, put a gentle hand on her shoulder for reassurance and then leave quickly.

These are also times when family meals are of particular importance. During meals, there can be the normal bubble of interaction to break up the routine of revision. Try to avoid allowing young people to take their supper upstairs on a tray "because I want to get on with my work". Breaks are therapeutically necessary.

In essence, you cannot avoid stress but you can use it productively to maximise your performance. You can also minimise unnecessary and unhelpful stress. It is fascinating how often a 'professional', business-like approach to revision and exams has an impact on overall maturity. It certainly enhances performance.

TECHNIQUES FOR DEALING WITH EXAM NERVES

Have you ever found yourself yawning inappropriately?

Have you ever taken great gulps of air when you haven't really exerted yourself?

Do you find that if you are nervous or worried, you take in more air than normal – and may do so by yawning?

Most people have experienced this from time to time. It is called 'hyperventilation' using the lungs to move more air in and out of the chest than the body can deal with. It can be triggered by:

- Sudden exertion – leaping out of the way of a speeding car, for example, if you were ever chased by a bull, you really would run faster than ever before!

- Sitting exams

- Going for an interview

- Intense emotion – love, rage, pain.

Bodily responses:

- The body becomes primed for action.

- Adrenaline pours into the bloodstream

- Heart and breathing rates speed up

- Eyesight and hearing sharpen

- Pain thresholds drop and pain is less intense. Think of the wounds soldiers seem to be able to cope with whilst in battle.

What happens?

Normally our lungs breathe in oxygen and breathe out carbon dioxide and this is balanced in a natural way by steady breathing. Hyperventilation upsets this vital balance because more carbon dioxide is breathed out than normal, so carbon dioxide levels in the blood start to drop.

This upsets the normal acid/alkaline balance (pH) of the blood.

Nerve cells can react – with dizziness, pins and needles or numbness. If the hyperventilating continues, the carbon dioxide levels in the blood fall further and body cells begin to produce lactic acid in an effort to balance the body's pH. Metabolism becomes less efficient – exhaustion and chronic tiredness follow – sometimes with feelings of physical and mental depression. Natural anxiety about these symptoms increases the tendency to over-breathe; this increases the above symptoms and leads to more unpleasant or frightening symptoms.

How do we learn to cope?

Breathing retraining:

- Be aware of faulty breathing – a feeling of panic often accompanies fast, shallow breathing.

- Learn to nose-diaphragm breathe.

- Suppress upper-chest movement during normal breathing.

- Reduce breathing to a slow, even, rhythmic rate. Approximately twelve breaths per minute. (2–3 seconds breathe in; 3–4 seconds breathe out).

    1. Put a hand on your chest, on your breastbone (just below your collarbone). Now, take a deep breath, without raising your shoulders.

    2. Notice which part of your chest moved first/moved most?

    3. Did you breathe in through your mouth or nose?

If you breathed in through your nose, your stomach expanded first – this is the natural and correct pattern.

If you breathed in fast through your mouth, your upper chest heaved first and your stomach drew in – you are a disordered breather.

Practise:

1. Lie comfortably on your bed or a sofa, with your head well supported. Take three deep breaths and let them out very slowly and you will find that this re-oxygenates the system, and is already serving to make you feel more relaxed and positive.

2. As you let the air out of your lungs, your shoulder and the upper part of your chest should remain relaxed.

3. You are trying to encourage yourself to breathe through your nose, so keep your lips together, your jaw relaxed, and draw air slowly through your nose.

4. You breathe out slowly, let the air seem to 'fall' out of your lungs, through your nose, without making any conscious effort.

5. Time your breathing rate over thirty seconds, with a breath in and out counting as one breath. Your aim is to control your breathing to twelve breaths a minute. Keep an eye on the even relaxation of your breathing.

Practice this technique for six or eight days and then begin to adopt the same process when you are sitting, standing, and even walking around the house.

You will find, ultimately, that you can use your three deep breaths, let out slowly, as a very helpful and convenient relaxation technique before you face any adrenaline provoking situation, such as when as you sit waiting for the papers to be handed out in the examination hall, moments prior to major physical exertion in an athletic event, or as you stand, hovering in the wings of a stage waiting for your entrance, wondering why on earth you ever committed yourself to the play! Understanding your body is a part of dealing with your life, as a whole, and particularly in managing stress.

Preparing for the exams themselves

Proper, thorough preparation is the very best form of stress management in examinations. Only a minority of would be academics know instinctively how to set about revision, deal with note taking, designing of revision schedules, and so forth. Particularly, if having struggled with an examination, results have been disappointing, ask for help with these fundamental skills. Six to eight one hour tutorial sessions should be plenty in the hands of an experienced tutor. It is vital that, when you develop a revision schedule, you stick to it, and you must be certain to allow yourself the appropriate amount of time off to allow both your body and spirits to re-kindle. Students need to be aware of sources of support and know exactly when and how they can be contacted if help is needed. Asking for help, at an appropriate time, is the sign of a winner, not a loser.

Some students find that working against the clock and the pressure that results, contributes to a sense of panic. Timed essay work and further mock examinations all help to desensitise the individual to this type of stress. For example, in a tutorial hour, it might be possible to be offered three mathematical problems, and be asked to solve one of them for which a limited time would be allotted. Or possibly, three complex history questions, to be sorted and sifted, a decision made, and the outline skeleton of a reply planned. It is then that the relevance of this plan should be attacked robustly by the student. This is a vital exercise in preparing an essay style examination answer, and it is this link between question and the student's interpretation of what is required, that is the most frequent stumbling block, and it is this very vulnerability that often causes the stress and anxiety.

Essentially, an amalgam of effective relaxation techniques, preparation, and possibly a programme of desensitising to working against the clock, help the vast majority of people to cope with examinations. Remember that adrenaline is a key ingredient. It is also important for the individual to know exactly how adrenaline works on their system, and what the symptoms are. Be pleased about the symptoms. Welcome them as a sign that you are ready for action.

The more pro-active the young person is, in preparing for examinations and looking after their physical and mental welfare, the more in control they feel and stress is less likely to take over.

PARENT'S EXAM NERVES

I was talking to a friend recently, whose son had been sitting A Levels. The results were due very shortly. He and his wife had been awake until the early hours of the morning, night after night, fretting about the results. Infuriatingly, their son was partying with equal vigour! I remember so clearly that envelope falling on the mat with our own daughter's exam results. She was away from home, and we had to wait for several days before being allowed to open it and put our minds at rest!

Being exhilarated by the successes of our loved ones, and sharing their disappointments, is a normal part of love within a family. We must look very carefully at precisely what our role is in the world of a rapidly developing eighteen-year-old. We have been working for many years towards maturity in the child, and helping them reach a stage at which they can stand on their own feet, make their own decisions and carve a niche for themselves in life. Our responsibility as parents is to give support, affection and backing. We should not be bullying an 18 year old into studying. A Levels are their first major 'adult' responsibility.

If we look back over our shoulders, did we help them with their choice of subjects, relate these to their GCSE results, particular interests, as well as their choice of possible college course? If their GCSE results were modest, did we encourage them to avoid overload in A Levels and choose sensibly? The beginning of their fifth form year was the time to establish a study regime, a peaceful, private place in which they could work and a timetable which allowed the work to be covered, but, equally, allowing for time off. Other than this, our role was to nurture and support. If, as a parent, you feel you can 'put a tick in the box' in each of these categories, then there is no more you could or should have done for your 18 year old.

Results time

If targets have been hit, then share in the young person's joy and a 'dinner out' is usually the best vehicle for this. If, in your view, the youngster has made a very fine effort, but has just fallen short of targets, then this, too, should be regarded as a 'success', celebrated and not regarded as any sort of failure. There is plenty of time to discuss re-sits, or even a change of college course, but none of us can do more than our best.

David

Last year, David produced a B and two Cs in his A levels, when he was hoping for three Bs and yet he had not achieved a single A grade in any of his GCSEs. With his 'track record', this was a phenomenal performance at A Level. It only took a single session of counselling for both parents to realise that there was plenty of cause for celebration – he had 'beaten the system'.

Disappointing results

There is an issue to face. The child has not failed you as a parent. You have not failed. They must not be left feeling that they have let you down or that the family feels, in any sense, betrayed.

The 'rule of thumb' for dealing with any emotional crises is invariably 'let the dust settle for a while'. Never make vital decisions in a tired, wound-up state, or late in the evening. The same applies if exam results have not turned out quite as had been hoped. Much that is positive can mature out of what may seem, at first, to be a disaster. However, it does need a very adult/adult approach between those involved.

The whole concept of 'failure' concerns me somewhat. Devastating disappointment needs warmth and accepting support. So much anguish and unnecessary unhappiness can be caused by over-expecting and over-demanding. This is then followed by the crash of disappointment at what may well be, in fact, a superb performance, but perhaps not quite good enough in the light of what may have been unrealistic targets.

Ask yourself a few pointed questions: What exactly went wrong? Were they simply unlucky by a single grade, but performed perfectly adequately during the mocks? It may well be that their exam technique was poor, and half a dozen sessions with a tutor should resolve this issue and increase their performance significantly at the next attempt. Are they efficient, methodical revisers, and are their notes competent?

Sarah

I remember working through Sarah's Biology notes, shortly before her A Levels, only to find that many of them were inaccurate. Her final revision was based on totally faulty input. On repeat in the autumn, she was much more methodical, was guided in efficient note taking, and produced the B grade that she badly wanted. Remember, this is a team approach to problem solving, not a recrimination session.

What is their next target in terms of a college course or career? What are the basic requirements? Far too many students are hugely overloaded and would be far better coping comfortably in two or, possibly, three A Levels, rather than struggling through four. There is no 'magic' about A Levels. They are simply a lever into the next stage of education or career development. Encourage them to go for what they need. Are these subjects ones that they really enjoy and want to pursue in far greater detail?

Now that you have had a chance to reflect on GCSE results, mock exams and the current results, has the youngster chosen a college course or a university degree which expects grades that ask far too much of them?

Jonathan

Jonathan has not made it to Veterinary College because he failed to get the three A grades that he required and was devastated to achieve 'only an A and two Bs. What a shame that such a magnificent performance was regarded as a failure.

If the decision is to re-sit, then talk to the school authorities. They are well informed and briefed to deal with exactly the dilemma your family is facing. Use them as consultants. Should the young person return to school to re-sit? If not, where and why? Could they, in fact, achieve their ends by moving on with the grades that they already have, without wasting another academic year?

Avoid being obsessional in target setting.

One cannot avoid looking at the issue of maturity of approach. On reflection, was sufficient effort and time put into the A Level programme as a whole and, particularly, into the stressful run-up to the exams over the last two or three months? Look hard and long at the next step. Does your youngster really want exam success? Is there a hunger to achieve targets?

If not, they might be far better moving into career development. It is only worth considering re-sits or a repeat year if the attitude is mature and workman-like. Countless youngsters, all over England, who adopt this approach, succeed and finish up with very creditable degrees. These discussions need to be adult/adult. Any tendency to drift back to the hectoring parent and resentful child is fruitless. If they really have been lazy and uninterested, face this issue head on. There is only one sense in persisting academically if the student is prepared to be honest, objective and construct a new, more mature approach to study.

Quite apart from 'patchy' motivation, there are two key issues that arise time and again. For some bizarre reason, both we as parents and the education system, as a whole, assume that the ability to deal with sophisticated information processing, under pressure, comes by a 'process of osmosis', some sort of natural instinct.

The refining of complicated information into accurate, readable note form is a skill in itself. To further refine these notes in the weeks coming up to an exam and, ultimately, possibly arrange them in a cardex, is a skilful technique that often needs to be taught. Far too often, young people spend endless hours slumped in a chair reading and simply hoping that they will recall. They forget the huge difference between reading and processing. You can read, but if the information is not processed into the left hemisphere of the brain, accurate recall is extremely difficult.

Hence, the tremendous value of detailed note taking. It forces the individual to process what is involved and, of course, produces an *aide memoire* for the final revision. However, notes need to be a personal summary – not simply a copying exercise.

An investigation into poor GCSE results suggested two fundamental flaws in young people's performance. Firstly, they misinterpret the longer, wordier questions, producing what amounts to their own version of what has been asked. This may, of course, be entirely appropriate, or may be wildly off the point. Work on question interpretation can yield massive dividends.

There is a tendency to lose sight of time, and therefore overwrite. The result may be that only three and a half out of five questions are completed and one has missed the point. It is hardly any wonder that the result is compromised.

Disappointing exam results may simply indicate a change of direction and need not be seen as a failure, but a proactive family conference is important, whatever the outcome.

41

Gifted and Talented Children

The gifted and talented are a fascinating, challenging group of individuals, but that does not always free them from their own special dilemmas.

Katie

Katie had been referred to me because the very caring Head Teacher wrote: "I love Katie dearly. But I don't know what on earth to do with her now." Katie had a stunning use of vocabulary and linguistic subtlety beyond her years. Katie and I worked through our standard IQ tests, but my scoring manuals simply could not cope. She produced scores that would have given a full grown adult an IQ in excess of the 130*. I then spent half an hour sitting at the back of a mental arithmetic class and, on three occasions, watched Katie's arm shoot up to answer her teacher's question, only to see her withdraw it in some embarrassment, lest her friends think she was showing off! Unlike some gifted children who find their peers a bore, Katie loved her friends but was becoming increasingly apt to hide her 'giftedness'.

*IQ of 100 is average IQ of 130 is superior.

I suggested to the head teacher that Katie should be regarded as having a very special need. My appeal caused outrage at the very suggestion that so delightful a child should have a 'problem'.

Delightful though it may be, 'giftedness' can be a significant problem. We must accept that true 'giftedness' puts those concerned under considerable pressure – both the children themselves, the parents and those teaching them. The normal activities in an age appropriate classroom are seldom enough. Fortunately, the National Association for Gifted Children, among others, are working hard to fill the vacuum, but why do these children not have statutory support?

Howard Gardener, an American, has introduced the concept of 'multiple intelligences'. He would tell us: "We must regard the talented violinist, who will one day make music their livelihood, as a 'gifted' and 'talented' individual." One must include the artist, actor and sportsman in this same category. Gifts are so rare. It is vital that they are fostered when they do occur.

THE FAMILY STRUGGLE WITH 'GIFTEDNESS'

The 'gifted' have their own special problems. Normal enterprises that take an average child 6 months to master, may well be dealt with competently in weeks. The gifted are often unfulfilled and frequently find fools difficult to suffer. Unfortunately, even parents may be included in this category of 'fool'. They may develop a bored and patronising attitude towards their peers. At primary level, for example, they are able to cope at eight with the work of 11 year olds and, therefore, class-time is less than stimulating and the topics of conversation in the playground seem immature. They are regarded as 'odd' and 'quaint' for using vocabulary way beyond their years.

However, a gift in one area may not be matched by gifts in others. Frequently, the intellectually 'gifted' child is not especially strong on the sports field, or they may be ham-fisted in Craft, Design and Technology. This discrepancy in performance can be especially unsettling for a sensitive and alert young mind. Equally, it can offer targets for teasing.

Gareth

Gareth, who is now 10 years old, has an IQ of 149, is an extremely talented violinist and has the manipulative language skills of a barrack room lawyer! He can manipulate his peers, his parents and his teachers with his clever use of language. He has become arrogant, self-opinionated and demands instant gratification. He is extremely impatient with his 8-year-old sister and will simply not tolerate his 4-year-old brother in the same room. He will not even 'allow' him to have tea at the same time!

We cannot allow gifts to be a route to the arrogant and neurotic control of others.

We all need to live in the real world. 'Giftedness' needs to be fostered and developed, but each of us has our own needs and this applies as much to the 'gifted' child as it does to other members of the family. There is no reason why they should not learn the same rules of conformity and mutual respect. I frequently meet 'gifted' individuals who are extremely sensitive and pleasant. There is a great danger in making undue allowances for the 'gifted' child, almost as though we are afraid of them.

Gareth is beginning to learn that he is no more entitled to instant gratification than anyone else and that sanctions will follow his rude and abusive demands, if they persist. 'Gifted' sportsmen cannot be permitted to break the rules of their game because they feel that their gift entitles them to. The same applies to life.

What to do?

- Treat them as perfectly normal members of the family, as far as attitude and behaviour are concerned.

- Make an accurate assessment of the level of their 'giftedness', and here the National Association for Gifted Children may prove particularly helpful. They will also advise on facilities that may be available in your area to provide the extra stimulation that your child may need.

- Keeping the child as close as possible to age appropriate development is infinitely better than pushing them to work with children much older and more mature than themselves. Remember that physical, social and emotional maturity do not necessarily correlate positively with IQ. Gifted children can often undertake a second or third foreign language, a further musical instrument, more extensively researched project work, or develop a hobby. Meanwhile they live and work with their physical and emotional peers.

Dave

Dave decided that archaeology and, particularly, Egyptology fascinated him. He explained to me exactly how Ancient Egyptian culture worked. He could give a detailed account of their weaponry, how they stopped their armour rusting, what they ate, how they lived, how they heated their homes and so forth. He spent a great deal of time at the local museum and library. The family have twice been on holiday to Egypt to help him pursue his interest, while having a good time as a family. However, he is also in the school play at Christmas, on the Second XI soccer team and was thrilled to grab five wickets in one innings in a cricket match last summer.

Do not let children's youth be taken away too soon. The gifted are too often robbed of the benefit of childhood experiences, frequently sacrificed on the altar of parental ambition.

I worry about the 15 year old, sitting in an upper Sixth Form, albeit coping academically and intellectually with A-levels. Let them progress through the school with horizontal development and perhaps cope with an additional A-level. Children with gifts often have areas of the curriculum where they are not nearly so strong and where an A-level would be a considerable challenge.

Deborah

Deborah has decided to tackle a Sociology module from the Open University during her Sixth Form years, while coping with the 4 A-levels prescribed by the school. This gives her the flavour of university education and its intellectual demands, without having to cope with the social pressures.

I remember a young man of barely eighteen, about to do his finals at Durham University, whose parents became anguished because he had now found girls and beer! Being so much younger, he hated his first two years where the other students had no time for him. Suddenly, now 18, he discovered that fun could be combined with studying. His fellow students warmed to him and he began to develop the social skills which would make him a more rounded personality. It should not have been necessary to face the stress which for two years he found isolating and depressing.

Some gifts have inevitable risks that go with them. The violinist may well want to join a major orchestra and this creates a challenging way of life for a developing young adult. The brilliant sportsman may have a career that extends barely past his 30th birthday. Actors, talented though they are, may struggle to make a living. These are realities, but gifts need fulfilment and expression. None of us want to wake up at 60 years of age, crying: "Why on earth did I not at least give it a try – an entire part of me has never been fulfilled?"

THE GIFTED SPORTSMAN

The gifted and talented are a very special group who need a great deal of fostering and encouragement if their special abilities are to reach their potential. In America, they now talk of 'multiple intelligences' and with some sense. Why should academic, intellectual giftedness be the only criterion? Surely a brilliant musician, or a startlingly talented sportsman should be of equal status in our society. Fortunately, at long last, increased funding is being found for our young sports men and women. However, it has become quite apparent that talent, in itself, is not enough. It must be backed up by time, consistent encouragement and all round dedication, let alone resources.

It is not good enough to foster the odd, brilliant youngster, and hope that others will appear as if by magic. Of those with the drive and the talent, only a small number ever rise 'like cream to the top'. The amount of 'cream' clearly depends on the volume of input lower down the system.

However, if your son or daughter is truly athletically talented, what will be involved and what impact is this likely to have on the child and your family? We must remember that to develop abilities at this level, we are competing against the very best and anything less than total commitment will not be enough. Success at this level demands a single-minded obsession with the chosen sport and a great deal of extremely hard work on a regular, time-consuming basis. This may sound alarming but without it there is no point in aiming at the very top. Furthermore, if it is an obsession, the hard work should come easily because the young person is spending their life working in the field that they love.

From a parental point of view, we need to accept that development for the child will be narrow, with very few peripheral interests and a limitation in a choice of peers.

Martin

Martin is an extremely talented tennis player, who has begun to develop an interest in girls and partying. At sixteen, this is perhaps hardly surprising, but his parents are extremely concerned. They feel that this is distracting him and he is making excuses to avoid training and often turning up less than fit after long, rather late nights. Martin has had to make the choice between an active social life and the considerable sacrifices that will go with choosing his sport as his paramount interest.

After many turbulent, and, at times, tearful confrontations with his father, Martin has accepted at last that the issue is not parental coercion, but a personal decision affecting his entire life style. He has decided to be a first rate amateur, to struggle for his A Levels and, hopefully, earn a tennis 'Blue' at Cambridge. It has taken his father rather longer to come to terms with this conclusion.

I was speaking to a representative of a major league football club recently about a boy that I was due to see. The boy sounds as though he may be a little dyslexic, but able academically, in a local grammar school. My adviser at the football club made it quite clear that if he eventually moves from an early youth programme into the serious 16–19 group, his days and weeks will be all football, with very little time for study and, certainly he can abandon any ideas of A Level study. Indeed, it was made quite clear that A Level studies and a desire for professional football were simply not consistent with one another. Much will depend on his aspirations in other directions, but, if he sleeps, dreams and plays nothing but football, and it is to be his whole life, then this may well be the direction in which he should go. At least he can never feel in the future that he has squandered his talent.

I was given specific advice about the Youth Training Programme of major football teams. "Encourage your talented youngster to join a first class local amateur team, with a competent youth side. The scouts from major clubs watch these youth groups for possible talent and may invite your child for trials and may sign them on into their Youth Development Programme. From 16–19, many clubs have rather more serious youth groups that may lead on to professional contracts". It is at this point, particularly, that the world becomes a total absorption with football, and academic life necessarily takes a second place.

The commitment is almost as great for parents in the provision of equipment, transport, time to support and being there to help and encourage, especially when times are difficult.

If you suspect that you have a youngster with sporting or, indeed, theatrical or musical gifts, the first step must be a highly professional assessment of skill levels and potential. It takes an expert to spot true talent and not just the 'rose tinted spectacles' of an adoring parent. Secondly, does your child have the all-consuming drive to become supremely fit and to accept endless training, advice and improvement of skills? Drive without sufficient talent can be as heart breaking as talent squandered because the drive does not exist.

As a parent, it is perfectly normal to enjoy the excitement of living through a youngster's sporting career, but we need to keep our egos firmly in check. It is their skill, not ours. We provide the support and encouragement.

Only a few make it to the top and, at the beginning of the adventure, both the child and parents need to be well aware that most will face disappointment. It is very hard to accept that your dream has been shattered. It is important for youngsters to remember that although they may not have made it to the pinnacle of professionalism they are still young people with immense ability in a particular area. It is often as much fun being an endless winner and star, much sought after in the serious amateur ranks, as floundering to cope among talented professionals. Vitally, encourage the youngster to remember that their skill has brought them so far and how much it has meant to them and still means. Coaching qualifications and the chance of passing on the enthusiasm that they have felt so strongly to the next generation is a very real contribution they can make to the world of professional sport.

The development of young talent is a considerable enthusiasm within the Lawn Tennis Association. I was very impressed by the increasing number of tennis centres all over England and the extent to which youngsters go to tennis camps abroad, in Spain, for example. I was staggered to hear that by the age of ten, the average youngster plays approximately sixty competitive matches a year! At times, they even move schools to be closer to their tennis centre, to cut down the fatigue of travelling. The opportunities are there, the equipment is there, the coaching is there, and the talent exists in this country. However, it must become an all-consuming passion. Saturday afternoon coaching sessions are not what professionalism in sport is all about. Rather like our young footballers, by sixteen their sixth form studies have become the early stages of the international tennis circuit, endless tournaments in far flung centres, learning to deal with the rough, tough world of the professional tennis circuit. They are exposed to a myriad of different climates, tennis surfaces and opposition, but not A Levels.

What is clear is that your youngster will need far more than talent. The drive, enthusiasm and hard work are clearly vital, but so too, is the psychological preparation for competing at the highest level. Abandoning sixth form studies and A Levels is a major issue, but if tennis is your child's true love, only total commitment will give them the chance of reaching the top.

CONTACTS

GIFTED CHILDREN'S INFORMATION CENTRE
Tel: 0121 705 4547

NATIONAL ASSOCIATION FOR GIFTED CHILDREN
Tel: 08707 703217

Part 5

Is Your Child Struggling at School?

DIGSLEGSIER

ROOLS KO

42

Dyslexia

"Could do so much better if he tried" – "If only he would concentrate ..." – "You really must concentrate on your spelling, John." "You need to finish your work?" The list is endless. For the psychologist working with children with specific learning difficulties, there are so many presentations. The one constant is that the children are failing, not reaching their potential and often becoming very distressed as a result.

Nevertheless, dyslexics include some very famous names – Churchill, Einstein, Susan Hampshire, Jackie Stewart and Michael Heseltine. Dyslexia is no respecter of persons, background or intelligence.

But what exactly is it? It is fundamentally an information processing disorder, largely to do with the processing of language and, particularly, symbolic language. The classic dyslexic finds reading and spelling difficult, but even when these difficulties have been addressed, may still find comprehension and, even more so, the organisation of their own written replies, a labour.

In essence, reading is simply the decoding of symbolic language, produced, usually, by somebody else. It is a code that allows us to communicate with people whom we may never meet. It is a marvellous, sophisticated medium for the transmission of ideas, stories, poetry – indeed, an 'Aladdin's Cave' of language. For some, this code is difficult to break.

The encoding process of producing written information is more complex still. It is, of course, processed rather differently in the brain and involves skills and sensory inputs not required for reading. This explains the typical dyslexic gulf that often occurs between comparatively competent reading and poor spelling and written work. There will often be a three or four year gap between these two skills. With little or no phonic skills, poor visual memory and very awkward fine motor skills which make the coordination of a pen difficult, the wonder is that youngsters ever communicate in written form at all.

On the next page we have the most obvious and clear-cut manifestation of dyslexia. This young man's work produced classic examples of letter reversals, bizarre, inappropriate spellings, very awkward letter formation and disjointed, rather staccato written expression as a whole.

The hidden information-processing deficit

Unfortunately, for dyslexic sufferers, their disability extends much further than the mechanical **185**

A classical example of
dyslexic writing

Wen yoo are dicklasiek yoo can run and doo enee fing Wat a nom cid but we sum tims have difadlt Reding and Spelling. We are gust as smrt as enee cid.

interpretation or production of letter symbols in word-making combinations. It also affects the processing of the underlying information contained in these words, sentences, paragraphs and chapters. This tends to be especially true of the youngster whose reading has made rapid and dramatic progress. Their visual scanning of material and apparent fluency often masks a total inability to process the content of the passage. One can well imagine the dramatic effect that this difficulty will have on the older, brighter dyslexic, who is attempting to cope with the rigours of examinations.

The confusion often extends into the planning and organisation of creative writing. It is typical to find a bright youngster of ten years of age producing an essay describing 'my favourite holiday', only to find the family actually reaching Devon in the last paragraph!

Initial remedial input may be aimed at grasping the mysteries of letter symbols and their organisation, whether this be in reading or spelling. However, we must look still further at an individual's capacity to comprehend and access or, indeed, communicate the information underlying these symbols. Mechanical reading that means nothing to the reader, and chaotically disorganised written information that fails to communicate, are both frustratingly worthless endeavours.

The search for a diagnosis

At the outset of our quest into the realms of dyslexia and an exploration of the way in which youngsters process information and, indeed, perceive the world about them, it is vital that the psychologist is well armed with a battery of initial information. Far too often the process is regarded as being almost on a par with 'reading the tea leaves'.

It is crucial that we all regard ourselves as part of a team attempting to reassemble a complex jigsaw puzzle, each of us having a clear, distinct and vital role to play in this process.

Before a psychological assessment takes place, a family questionnaire is dispatched to the child's parents. This may often seem like a cross between adult homework and a penance for producing a dyslexic child. However, its true purpose is to give us advance understanding of the child's early developmental history, especially their language development and early mobility. Ear, nose and throat difficulties, often in the pre-school years, can be very significant in a child's auditory processing. For example, a family history of specific learning difficulties suggests a hereditary factor and, of course, a brief outline of school history to date, with the problems that the child has been experiencing, provides useful clues. Finally, a 'thumbnail sketch' is helpful, describing exactly how the child's parents perceive the problem about which they seek information and understanding.

From a psychologist's point of view, it gives us our fundamental starting point. There are often reports available following previous investigations by other Educational Psychologists, Speech and Language Therapists, Occupational Therapists, a variety of medical specialists, Orthoptists and, even more frequently, the remedial teachers who have begun the struggle.

Current school reports are also invaluable and earlier ones must not be forgotten as they elucidate the developing pattern over a period of terms and sometimes even years. Furthermore, they not only give us a clear indication of the problems as perceived by the school, especially the class teacher, but also to what extent the underlying dyslexic phenomena have been recognised and are being treated.

Test scores, statistics, numbers – all have their purpose but nothing quite takes the place of typical examples of the work that children are currently attempting. These will demonstrate levels of success, the way the child uses written language, coordinates the use of a pen, organises work on the page and understands the concepts under discussion, quite apart from the spelling errors which frequently occur. If we add to this a photocopy of a page or two of the book which the child is currently working on, together with a page of current mathematics, we are able to create a much clearer image of exactly how the youngster is coping, against which we can make assumptions based on the norms that apply to this particular age group.

Administering the tests

It is vital that testing is not undertaken until the child is put at ease. It is crucial to remember that we are assessing a child's capacity to process a wide variety of different types of information, both verbal and non-verbal, and then comparing the outcome with the norms for the child's age group, and, therefore, stress must be minimised.

The test information is obviously extremely helpful in making a diagnosis and prescribing treatment, but it would be wrong to assume that IQ test results are 'writ on tablets of stone'. We are simply describing human experience and the information processing of a comparatively young child. There are so many factors affecting a child's performance, quite apart from their attitude to the experience.

For example, a rather distractible, attention-deficit, dyslexic boy was assessed one summer on a very hot, humid afternoon. There was no doubt that towards the end of the afternoon, the combination of the weather, the fact that the child tired, as well as the noise of distant traffic, all affected his performance and this must be allowed for in the discussion following the test results.

What to watch for

Untreated, dyslexia usually results in 'critical academic under-functioning'. Between 5% and 10% of our entire population experience some degree of specific learning difficulty, (dyslexia). What a waste of so much of the country's talent.

Warning signs
Preschool
- Before children even begin formal schooling watch for

(i)   language is late to develop

(ii)   they have constant ear infections

(iii)   they tend to be distractible

(iv)   their drawings are very untidy and immature

(v)   keep an eye on early literacy development.

School age children

- By seven the vast majority of children have made early inroads into literacy. If your child is not keeping up with their peers and work is drifting further and further behind their classmates, then questions should certainly be asked.

- The key signs – apparent potential not showing through in: reading, understanding, spelling or producing written language. Number skills may also present a problem.

- Many dyslexic children find spoken language difficult to process and become easily muddled in class. Early on, rhyming is often difficult to grasp.

- Fine motor skills are usually untidy, reflected in poor handwriting.

- They seem to forget alarmingly easily what they have been told, or what they are shown. Instructions are frequently confused. Copying is very error-prone.

- Learning tables and spellings can be frustratingly difficult – learnt one day, forgotten the next.

- They may have little idea of the management of time.

- Their personal property is easily forgotten or lost.

- They have difficulty in linking letter sounds to letter symbols. Equally, they may struggle to use phonics in their reading and find it difficult to break words down into their sounds and blend them into effective words. Spellings are often bizarre and letter and word reversals are not uncommon.

- The concepts of sequence and direction, and handedness as a whole may prove a complete mystery.

The next step

If you feel that most of these pointers fit your child, the problem should now be discussed with the Special Educational Needs co-ordinator in the school, and the early stages of an 'in school' assessment put in place. This will identify areas of difficulty that the child is experiencing, the extent to which they are indeed behind their peers, and a programme should be built around these findings, based on an individual education plan (IEP) which will be reviewed regularly. However, if progress after a term or so is insufficient, then a thorough diagnosis may need to be made by an Educational Psychologist. Within the State system, there is a School Psychological Service provided in each area, but referral will normally have to be made via the Head of the child's school. There are a number of educational psychologists practising privately and they too can be consulted, but liaison with your child's school is a very important part of the process.

Diagnosis

It is the pattern of discrepancies that makes for the dyslexic diagnosis. It is important to know exactly which areas of the dyslexic spectrum affect your child. It varies so much from individual to individual and seldom does any dyslexic sufferer experience all the symptoms. Once this pattern is clear, we can move on to treatment.

The management of dyslexia should be in the hands of staff trained, qualified and experienced in the teaching of the children with a specific learning difficulty. It is a skilled business and there are a range of rather special techniques available. It is vital to give the child the adequate phonic skills and, ultimately, literacy skills, to allow them to access the curriculum and proceed at an appropriate pace with their education.

There is no reason why investigations, if a child is seriously behind, should not begin as young as six years of age – the earlier the better in many ways. The more we can pre-empt the failure and misery that dyslexia can cause, the better. Why allow four or five years of failure if it can be avoided?

You will need to be patient. Progress can be slow and at various stages of a child's development you may need to return for further support. However, learning to use the basic skills of reading and writing are the vital first steps, but later on we may need to look at the more sophisticated world of written information processing, certainly leading up to examinations.

Increasingly, word processing is opening a wonderful new window into written communication. Keyboard skills, once firmly established, allow an individual to process written ideas more fluently, and, above all, legibility, hand fatigue in exams, and so forth, are no longer a concern.

Special arrangements in examinations

Once specific learning difficulties, dyslexia or dyspraxia, have been diagnosed, the educational world becomes increasingly sensitive and supportive. The examination boards in both GCSEs and A Levels, have a variety of special arrangements that they are prepared to make, providing the child's case is appropriately documented – usually supported by an Educational Psychologist's report. The Head Master/Mistress of your school should have a document entitled "Joint Council for General Qualifications, Regulations and Guidance Relating to Candidates with Particular Requirements", which they should be prepared to discuss with you, if you feel it might be relevant.

The two most frequently granted special arrangements are extra time, which can be as much as twenty five percent additional time in examinations and word processing. Increasingly, young people are using word processing in their public examinations and for course work. The evidence is extremely encouraging in terms of significantly enhanced performance.

A 'reader' who will read the questions to the candidate can occasionally be made available where there is a danger that the youngster will be unable to understand the examination questions, and, therefore, will have little chance of producing an adequate answer. This may also necessitate the use of a 'scribe' or 'amanuensis' to copy down the young person's responses.

Understandably, with the exception of extra time, all these concessions will be mentioned on the eventual certificate. The aim is to encourage the young person to absorb the necessary information, to have it available to them and to be able to communicate it in another medium. Even voice-activated word processing is beginning to appear on the horizon as an examination medium.

However, do remember that your child must have a learning difficulty to justify these concessions. This will need to be diagnosed by an appropriately qualified Educational Psychologist, and the report conveyed via the head of the relevant exam centre to the examination board for approval. Some children, especially those with a marked attention deficit or physical difficulty, may need short breaks during the exam.

The schools themselves and the Local Education Authority should be able to offer helpful advice.

CONTACT

There is a variety of sources which you might feel useful if you feel the time has come to pursue the matter of dyslexia and your child a step further:

- The British Dyslexia Association, 98 London Road, Reading, Berks RG1 5AU

- The Dyslexia Teaching Centre, 23 Kensington Square, Kensington, London W8 5HN

- The Dyslexia Institute, 133 Gresham Road, Staines, Middlesex, TW18 2AJ

- The Dyslexia Computer Resource Centre, Department of Psychology, Hull University, Hull, HU6 7RX

- The Helen Arkell Dyslexia Centre, Frensham, Farnham, Surrey GU10 3BW

- The Hornsby Centre, 71 Wandsworth Common West Side, London, SW18 2ED.

FURTHER READING

Dyslexia: A Multidisciplinary Approach
Edited by Patience Thomson and Peter Gilchrist – Stanley Thornes, Cheltenham

Dyslexia: The Pattern of Difficulties
T Miles (1993) 2nd edition, – Whurr, London

Dyslexia: A Cognitive Development Perspective
M Snowling (1987) – Blackwell, Oxford

Developmental Dyslexia: The Nature, Assessment and Remediation
By M Thomson (1990) 3rd edition – Whurr, London

Feingold, B.F. (1976) Hyperkinesis and learning disabilities linked to the ingestion of artificial food colours and flavours. *Journal of Learning Disabilities*

Snowling, M. J. Stockhouse, J and Rack, J (1986) Phonological dyslexia and dysgraphia – a developmental analysis. *Cognitive Neuropsychology*

The Dynamic Assessment of Retarded Performers.
Feuerstein, R, Rand, U and Hoffman, M.B. (1979) University Park Press, Baltimore.

43

Dyspraxia

A few years ago dyspraxia was seldom diagnosed and usually only by Speech and Language Therapists. It rapidly came to include the 'clumsy child syndrome'. Now it seems to have become the current educational fad, somehow allied to dyslexia, but different. Parents are left in great uncertainty as to exactly what is actually wrong with their child, much less what they can do about it.

In 1985, Dr Ayres, defined dyspraxia as "a motor planning disorder and a disorder of sensory integration, interfering with the ability to plan and execute skilled motor tasks". This infers difficulty in co-ordinating, planning and executing tasks which involve physical action. Quite often this refers particularly to relatively familiar tasks. For most of us, these tasks are automatic, but the dyspraxic individual has great difficulty in actually planning how the task should be accomplished. At the simplest level, this may involve planning how to move across a room and out of a door, without bumping into furniture. It is hardly surprising that, in times gone by, a dyspraxic was loosely described as 'a clumsy child'.

In essence, these children have difficulty in organising their bodies. At home, this is often reflected in clumsy, rather chaotic behaviour. They are often very messy, untidy eaters, sitting awkwardly at the table, and tending to sprawl. Food often misses the mouth and as much food is scattered around the plate as is ever eaten! It is almost as though there is insufficient strength in their shoulders to keep them sitting in an upright position. We instinctively encourage our left hand to co-operate with the right, in performing a complex task, but dispraxics find this extremely difficult. In class, you will see them writing, but failing to steady the page with the opposite hand, with the result that the paper shifts and moves making the written work even less tidy. It is not difficult to be critical, even angry, with a child who seems to be making no effort, is scruffy, untidy, awkward and whose work is limited.

They are often very bright, articulate children, usually boys, who sound as though they could be doing much better, and parents and staff are even less forgiving as a result.

However, if you think consciously of how you move to orientate yourself in preparation for writing a letter, you suddenly become aware of what a complex series of motor actions this actually involves. For a dyspraxic, each has to be a conscious, separate movement, which makes integrating the actions much more difficult. Where they do not bother to concentrate, they become even more chaotic and haphazard.

Frequently, the child's problem is also reflected on the sports field. They have little or no hand/eye co-ordination and, even at eight or nine years of age find catching and throwing a ball difficult. School ties, shoelaces, riding a bicycle are all inexplicably difficult tasks.

Diagnosis and treatment will usually be in the hands of an occupational therapist, who will give advice as to how to handle the problem, domestically and academically. Referral is usually via an educational psychologist, or occasionally a family doctor, Paediatrician or Head Teacher. As a parent, you will find yourself given exercises to carry out with the child most nights, ahead of the next occupational therapy session.

These children are often very fidgety and restless, and may even be described as 'attention deficit', (having a very short span of concentration) as well as dyspraxic. The two syndromes may overlap. However, a remarkable number of apparently attention deficit difficulties are improved via occupational therapy. If a child is constantly struggling to find a position for their body in space and a comfortable position in which to sit, it is hardly any wonder that they are fidgeting endlessly. Once therapy has been successful, they become much more relaxed, less restless and tire less easily.

Written work is usually poorly organised on the page in the first place, and handwriting is invariably untidy and almost illegible. While therapy will certainly help, remember these youngsters are borne in an information technology age. A treatment of choice, especially for the bright, articulate dyspraxic, is keyboard skills. Not only is legibility no longer an issue, but they begin to take pride in their written work for the first time.

David

David, 16, now types at thirty-five words a minute, and the quality of his written responses is in a different league from anything he can ever produce with a pen. The keyboard frees him to think more clearly, to use a richer vocabulary and far more sophisticated syntax and grammar. The exam boards have allowed him a concession to use word processing skills in his GCSE exams next summer, following his detailed psychological evaluation.

In this boy's case, he was also mildly dyslexic and with the two overlapping disabilities, the exam boards will also be prepared to allow him extra time in which to complete his papers. Properly documented, the schools can make this facility available within their own remit, but the assessment of an educational psychologist is usually sought.

Donal

Donal never knows where his clothes are and he has been dropped from the school football team because he constantly forgets to bring new laces for his boots. His mother has had to replace numerous school jerseys, and there is a noisy row at the beginning of each day as the family attempt to get him to school.

We have initiated a new regime in the evenings. His dirty laundry is put away, by Donal, in the laundry basket. He then has to put out his clothing for the following day, in the same order, and on the same chair each night. Finally, he has a chart on the back of the bedroom door, with the days of the week along one axis and everything he might need listed beneath each day. His final act before getting into bed is to check the list and ensure that everything is in his school bag ready for the following day. In this way, 65% of the information that would otherwise be processed in a rush in the morning is to hand before he even gets into bed. The mornings are now more placid, and a better organised. Dyspraxics are never good at being caught in a rush. Forward planning is a vital technique to learn but it will never be instinctive.

Formal exams will appear on the horizon next summer for Donal. At present, he has no idea of how to set about revision, organise his books and prepare adequate notes, exam technique is a complete mystery. As a result, questions are often mis-construed and papers are almost never finished. This makes exam results a complete lottery. However, by this time next year, personal organisation should be in hand and he should be far more 'professional' in the way he approaches the build-up to the examinations and copes under pressure in the exams themselves. There is no reason why dyspraxia needs to be critically disabling. However, remedial staff need to help devise coping strategies and the youngster has to be mature enough to adopt them.

Mike

Finally, social naiveté is often a part of the dyspraxic profile. Mike, eleven, came thundering into the sitting-room. He needed £5, saw his father, rushed up and asked for the £5 and to his horror, found himself being slapped and told to leave the room. In reality, there was a mass of information available to him, including the look on his Father's face. He failed to absorb these signals and simply rushed up to the person he knew would have the money.

Mike needed a period of counselling in his middle teens, to help him perceive the body language of the world around him, and work out how others were reacting to him. He was not processing sufficient information before responding.

We have become increasingly aware that this hidden syndrome exists, and the unhappiness it can cause if left untreated. It is easily interpreted as rude, clumsy, chaotic behaviour to be addressed by punishment. 'Punishment' simply exacerbates the problem. Insight and management should allow a dyspraxic youngster to perform on equal terms alongside his peers.

An educational psychologist should be able to establish basic intellectual levels so that academic expectations are kept appropriate. These youngsters are such patchy, unpredictable performers that 'could do better if he tried' is an almost inevitable 'cri de coeur'. The assessment will also highlight the specific areas of vulnerability in the child's profile, reflecting dyspraxia or its absence.

The hallmark of the dyspraxic reflects the statistically significant discrepancy between their various skills in life, as well as in tutoring. The psychologist will explain in detail the precise areas in which the child struggles, and, as importantly, where their strengths lie. In each case we are always searching for areas of excellence to foster which will then give the child the confidence to deal with facets of life that are far less easy.

It is important to remember that processing different types of information at such radically different levels of efficiency can be very distressing. Self doubt and poor self esteem are hardly surprising. Swift diagnosis and a clear appreciation of the difficulty and its management in the minds of both the dyspraxic and those managing them, is a vital first step.

Properly managed, the prognosis is usually very positive.

FURTHER READING

Developmental Dyspraxia – A Practical Manual for Parents and Professionals
Madelaine Portwood, Durham County Council

Handwriting: Theory, Research and Practice
J. Alton and J. Taylor (1987) Croom Helm, London

Ayres, A. J. (1969) Deficits in sensory integration in educationally handicapped children. *Journal of Learning Disabilities*

Amundsun, S, J, C, (1992) Handwriting evaluation and intervention in school settings. In: *Development of Hand Skills in the Child* (eds. J. Case-Smith and C. Petroski), American Occupational Therapy Association, Rockville, MD.

44
Attention Deficit with or Without Hyperactivity Disorder (ADD/ADHD)

Attention Deficit Disorder with or without the hyperactive element is a worryingly misunderstood phenomenon, frequently misdiagnosed, and seldom adequately treated. Far too often, distraught mothers seek advice, only to be lectured on their inadequate parenting strategies. The child's behaviour can vary from irritating to oppositional and defiant, challenging to the point of constant family explosions. Where it coincides with the bi-polar syndrome of massive mood swings it can become devastating for the entire family, disrupt marriages and compromise the emotional, social and academic life of other siblings, let alone the sufferer.

At the basic level of ADD or ADHD, uncomplicated by other issues, it is 'selective attention' that is difficult. We all have an extraordinary mechanism for trimming out redundant sights and sounds around us that we do not need for the particular problem solving in which we are involved. With the ADD individual, this is almost impossible unless they are at a 'high' state of arousal and totally 'locked in' to an activity. This often happens for only very short periods of time, or with materials that particularly excite them. Often this is true, especially of computerised and televisual input. Even then, they form an almost impenetrable 'glass wall' around themselves to force the concentration. A parent arriving to announce that a meal is ready may seem to be completely ignored because the instruction fails to penetrate the 'glass wall'. This may require that the television is turned off and the resulting hostility dealt with. However, it is so important to be sure that a much-favoured TV programme is not interrupted inappropriately.

It is impossible for most of us to imagine what it must be like being constantly distracted by sights and sounds of no real relevance. ADD adults at social gatherings when called upon to concentrate often ask if the conversation can be moved to a quiet corner where they can limit the distractions. ADD and ADHD affect adults as much as it does children, often with equally disturbing consequences, to work, marriages and interpersonal relationships. An occasional individual can be surprisingly successful. We are all aware of the 'human dynamo' factor that

196

has sometimes made politicians, diplomats, and businessmen hugely successful, but they are the tiny minority.

If a child constantly rushes in 'where angels fear to tread', either at home or in the playground at school, they will face constant rejection and apparently inappropriate responses because they have failed to account for half the information that was available, had they been able to take the time to assess it. ADD/ADHD is a readily diagnosable condition. It is very real. It undermines the social and, particularly, academic performance of the individual and can have a shattering affect on parenting. None of the management strategies that seem so appropriate for the other children in a family appear to work for the ADHD child.

A drug called Ritalin can be hugely effective in managing this disorder and, indeed, there are times when paediatric and/or child psychiatric advice should certainly be sought, especially when the problem is severe and the disruption to family and school life has become intolerable.

However, I have an understandable reticence about strong medication and children and would always wish to start by looking at the possible implications of diet in a child's behaviour. I have been increasingly heartened at conferences and in recent literature by the acceptance of even the most hardened cynic that, for an occasional individual, diet does have a dramatic influence.

We have been following change in behaviour through diet for some fifteen years now. I worked for three very productive years with Marianne Williams, a Consultant Dietician, looking very carefully at the possible implications. For a small number of children there is no doubt that factors in their food change their behaviour.

Stuart

Stuart was particularly fascinating. He was a placid, normally functioning boy two or three days a week and a difficult, distractible fidget on the other days. We looked at family background; his life proved chaotic. Several times a week the whole family shot out of the door with shirt tails flying, and a slice of toast in one hand. This, I thought, was the answer. A turbulent start to the school day. I could not have been more wrong. It was the other days that caused the problem. These were days when his breakfast consisted of chocolate-coated cereals and a half pint of fresh orange juice.

These were removed from his diet and his behaviour stabilised within a week.

Mark

Mark, at six, visited my office, then refused to come out from under the desk. He took everything from my shelves, scattered them round the room and was almost impossible to test. We took Mark off fresh orange juice. Six months later, at an amateur drama event, he sat still throughout the hour-and-three-quarters. On review, it was impossible to imagine that it was the same boy.

I am not suggesting that all hyperactive behaviour can be cured by diet, but of every five children that I see, at least two are dramatically different as a result of diet change, and a third improves so much that no further action is necessary. We also often advise visiting the family doctor to arrange sweat tests so that mineral levels can be assessed. In a small number of individuals, low levels of zinc and/or magnesium are making a dramatic difference to activity levels. Supplementation is straightforward.

Things to avoid:

- Cola drinks, etc., including diet varieties

- Fruit juices, both apple and orange

- Blackcurrant cordials

- Dairy products, but only in excess

- Chocolate products, including sweets, biscuits, spreads, drinks, et cetera

- Excess sugars

- Over flavoured and highly coloured sweets

- Flavoured crisps

- Wheaten or chocolate content breakfast cereals

The following common additives should also be avoided:

- Tartrazine (E102),

- Caramel (E150)

- Benzoic acid (E210)

- BHA (E320) and BHT (E321).

In recent times, I have had positive feedback from parents who have taken homeopathic advice for their overactive children. Cranial osteopathy also seems to have brought benefits. However, more robust remedial intervention is sometimes necessary...

David

For David, a lively 15 year old, facing the traumas of GCSE exams at the end of the year, more robust medical management had been vital. He was now busy, active, on the go, represented the school in various sports teams, and even study, while not especially easy, was far more productive than it had been in the years prior to treatment. What a success story!

I first met David, years earlier, shortly before his tenth birthday. It is hard to imagine so dramatic a difference, socially and academically. At that point he was being invited to leave yet another school. Progress was minimal. He was still struggling to learn to read, was constantly in trouble and attention seeking in class, never finished a piece of work and even his friends were becoming heartily sick of him. At home, he was restless, found it difficult to sit still even through a family meal, was constantly picking fights with his younger brother and his parents. Even simple requests from his mother would be met with a defiant "No". David's impulsivity had led to his being thrown off the school football team because he lost his temper with an opposition player once too often and was constantly leaving his kit at home.

David had alienated virtually everyone in his world, apart from two other boys with a similar problem. The three of them were in constant mischief. The change in David, now aged 15, suggests that he had not been simply a naughty, malad-justed delinquent. He had an attention deficit hyperactivity disorder (ADHD). The diagnosis led to a referral to a child psychiatrist who prescribed a drug called Ritalin. The pill lasted for four hours and it was important that there was an overlap from one dose to the next. The world became a dramatically different place for David, not to mention his parents and his younger brother. He is, at last, beginning to fulfil his potential, and there is no shortage of friends.

Susan

Susan was a delightful nine year old who, during a classroom observation, seemed compliant and involved, until you watched a little more closely. She did not fidget physically as David had done and, apart from being an irritation to her teacher because work was never finished, she was a pleasant little girl. However, her mind wandered like a constantly restless butterfly. Even the slightest sights or sounds distracted her. She often found these distractions more absorbing than the task she was meant to be facing. For Susan, it was not a matter of refusing to concen-trate but being quite unable to do so. Constantly her work would begin well and then deteriorate as the time passed. In testing with me she was often successful for thirty to forty seconds, at which point her information processing capacity would plummet and she would become inefficient and would even dismantle tasks that had begun successfully. Interestingly, computers, television and even playing with Lego absorbed her attention and her mind wandered less during these activities. Susan was diagnosed as experiencing an attention deficit disorder (ADD). Most of us can run relatively successfully in 'third gear', but not the ADD individual. There were some tasks, usually only for a short period of time, which would enhance Susan's arousal level, during which she functioned perfectly normally. She simply could not cope with the mundane or, indeed, any task that lasted for too long. Nevertheless, with an IQ of 138, Susan was already under functioning at nine years of age. She had a Reading Age of 8.5 and her written work was extremely immature. A bright mind was being wasted.

She was referred to a Paediatrician who prescribed Ritalin and Susan began an appropriate regime. Within two terms her school reports were encouragingly different and she had become a more self-contained, happy, well integrated girl. It took four years for her to begin to really fulfil her superior IQ, but she is now in an academic school, coping in a way that would have seemed impossible a few short years ago.

As a parent, I am concerned at the prospect of any young child being put on a strong medication. I would want to know exactly what the implications were.

- *Would my child become addicted?* There is no evidence in the literature of either addic-tion to Ritalin or any tendency to go on to addictive behaviour thereafter. Indeed, the untreated sufferer is statistically more vulnerable to seeking out clinical support for their often vulnerable social relationships.

- *Are there worrying side affects?* Very occasionally there is a slight growth delay which almost always balances itself out before long and, in any event, the programme should be kept under regular medical review, including checking appropriate weight gain.

- *Am I using an experimental drug to 'tame' my child?* No, the drug is simply improving your child's arousal level, so that they can stay on task, exactly the way they already can, if only for a few short minutes. You know what they can be like at their best. Imagine if this could persist for most of the day.

- *Do they have to be on it all the time?* Most consultants advise on a regime and make it quite clear that 'holidays' are perfectly acceptable, often for many weeks, especially when the child is not having to concentrate intensely. This also suggests that addiction cannot be taking place.

- *Are there medical conditions which suggest that Ritalin is a bad thing?* Yes, there are one or two and these would need to be discussed with the Consultant concerned.

- *Ritalin is not simply a 'chemical cosh' to subdue our children!*

- *What exactly is Ritalin?* Ritalin is a stimulant drug that raises the individual's arousal level. As we have already discussed, the problem for ADD and ADHD sufferers is that while they can often function perfectly normally when sufficiently alert and aroused, once their arousal drops below the level of equilibrium they can no longer function effectively and become extremely distractible and often very fidgety. The purpose of the Ritalin is to increase the arousal level over a period of four hours, allowing the individual to function normally.

- *How long will they have to take medication for?* So much depends on the severity of the problem. Most children can come off it at weekends and holiday time, which reassures us that they are not becoming addicted. However, it often persists through adolescence, and helps greatly with concentration on revision, exam performance, and so forth. There are now an increasing number of adults who are also maintained on Ritalin and whose success in the workplace may well be dependent on the management of their ADHD.

- *How do I know if my child actually has ADD/ADHD?* The following is a useful checklist, recommended and referred to by many of the agencies involved in helping and supporting these children. There is no specific psychometric assessment battery available for assessing children with ADD. Hence, conclusions need to be drawn from clinical evaluation, self-report questionnaires, and questionnaires completed by the parents and those managing the children in class. Observations are required in a variety of settings, and need to address the following issues:

    1. Is the child able to work independently, without a major degree of teacher support?

    2. Is the child able to interact effectively with their peers?

    3. How does the child perform in a variety of different school orientated environments, such as the gym, assembly, playground, lunchtime, and, of course, in class?

4.   Is work often left incomplete, or does it tend to deteriorate constantly after an initial burst of enthusiasm?

Key criteria: "developmentally inappropriate degrees of inattention, impulsivity, and physical hyperactivity".

ADD refers to children with no great physical implication, whereas ADHD includes the hyperactive/impulsive group of children. If your child fits the majority of these criteria, then the possibility of ADD/ADHD must clearly exist. You would be wise to discuss this with your family doctor, and if matters persist, you should ask to be referred to either a child psychiatrist or a paediatrician for diagnosis and the discussion of treatment. It is equally important to keep the school informed, because it is vital that they monitor progress when it begins to occur, following treatment, and that they are aware of the steps you have taken. It often helps a great deal for them to realise that the concentration difficulties that they have been observing, which they have been largely unable to help, were not of their making or yours. It is likely to make them a great deal more sympathetic and supportive so that you can work together as a parent/teacher team in helping your child.

- *What causes ADD/ADHD?* The cause is difficult to identify. Suffice to say that there is a very considerable genetic link with at least one other family member, often a parent, experiencing the same difficulty. However, it is a physiological disorder which could arise in any family, however well managed. Poor management can make it worse, and, following treatment, can delay progress, but does not in itself cause it. A mother with an ADHD child is far from being a bad mother. She is a mother with a great deal to contend with, who needs considerable support.

- *Incidence.* The research suggests that approximately 5% of the population experiences either ADD or ADHD, and the number may well be more, bearing in mind the difficulties of diagnosis and how many children's problems are missed.

DSM IV Draft Criteria for Attention-Deficit/Hyperactivity Disorder (Diagnostical Statistical Manual of Mental Disorder, published by the American Psychiatric Association in 1994) gives us useful guidelines.

CONTACTS

THE HYPERACTIVE CHILDREN'S SUPPORT GROUP
Tel: 01243 551313

ADD INFORMATION SERVICES
Tel: 0208 9069068

ADD/ADHD FAMILY SUPPORT GROUP
Tel: 01373 826045

LADDER
Box 700, Wolverhampton, WV3 7YY

OSTEOPATHIC CENTRE FOR CHILDREN
Tel: 0207 4866160

FURTHER READING

ADHD/Hyperactivity: A Consumer's Guide For Parents and Teachers
Michael Gordon. GSI Publications, PO Box 746, DeWitt, NY 13214, USA

Bakker, D.J. van Leeuven, HMP and Spyer G (1986) Neuropsychological aspects of dyslexia. *Child Health Development*

Attention Deficit Hyperactivity Disorder
Barkley, R (1990) Guildford Press, New York

Dyslexia – A multidisciplinary approach
Patience Thomson and Peter Gilchrist (eds) Nelson Thornes Ltd

45

Asperger's Syndrome

Increasingly, over the last ten years, our practice has been presented with youngsters who fall into the relatively recent category of Asperger's syndrome, a disorder on the Autistic spectrum, which is thought to be largely a milder offshoot of autism. However, although this association can be made, it is important for parents to be aware that the prognosis is very different. There are many Asperger individuals who marry, hold down worthwhile professional functions and lead relatively normal, if often somewhat eccentric, lives. While autism has been described for over forty years, it was not until 1981 when Lorna Wing published a detailed account of thirty-four cases that interest began to re-emerge in Asperger's syndrome. Wing based her diagnostic criteria on Asperger (1944) as follows:

i. Pedantic speech

ii. Non-reciprocal social interactions which lack empathy

iii. Little facial expression, monotonal voice, inappropriate gestures

iv. Poor gross motor co-ordination. Clumsy

v. Skills/interests – very circumscribed. Good rote memory

vi. Resistance to change – enjoy repetitive activities

It is undeniable that the same impairments emerge over and over again. A label is often useful in helping us understand the problems that people face, and possible treatment regimes that may prove helpful.

Daniel

Daniel, who was nine, was typical of the mildly Asperger child. The 'absent minded professor' would have been a very suitable description! He had an immense vocabulary, produced some very high scores on his IQ test but was physically comparatively ill co-ordinated, and showed no interest, whatever, in

203

sport. He had an obsessional passion for dinosaurs and was totally encyclopaedic in his understanding of both the creatures, their habitat and their history.

Daniel was totally self-centred; everything that was said or discussed was always related back to Daniel and how it might affect him. He was obsessional at home and became extremely angry if anybody moved his belongings in his bedroom. His parents even had to control his desire to manage the furniture and ornaments in the family sitting room. He seemed to feel much safer if these obsessions could be fulfilled. Denial or obstruction made him angry. When he left his bedroom, he had to return, usually three times, to open and close the door again to ensure that it was properly shut. He was sometimes given to talking to himself and wandering around the school playground looking totally absorbed and was even found, on one occasion, seeming to talk to plants at the back end of the school playground.

We all rely heavily on a small number of individuals who make up the pillars of our identity, but for the Asperger's child these pillars can become threateningly uncertain.

Unusual for an Asperger's individual, Daniel's work was immaculate, especially his mathematics for which he had a particular flair. His creative writing was eccentric, disjointed, demonstrating little or no understanding of the world around him, but, nevertheless, obsessionally well presented.

The most striking feature of Daniel revolved around his communication skills, and this is very much the essence of Asperger's syndrome. He had a first class vocabulary, but when questions were long, wordy and involved and he had to process and organise what was required of him and prepare an articulate response, he was less adept. He seldom seemed to understand a joke, although within himself he had a good sense of humour and would often chuckle, but it was never quite clear what exactly he was chuckling at. Linguistic subtleties in jokes, irony, sarcasm, etc. were either misunderstood or went straight over his head.

Most worryingly, he had little or no understanding of body language. He would often close down social space between himself and someone to whom he was talking, making them feel very awkward and embarrassed. He would crash in on groups uninvited and then be hurt when he was rejected. His complaints appeared perfectly rational, until one observed the circumstances in which Daniel had found himself. In class, he often looked totally disinterested and even turned his back on the teacher, but when questioned it was quite clear that he had been listening and had absorbed a great deal.

Visitors to the family home were often upset and felt that Daniel was very rude as he seemed to be quite unable to deal with the ordinary social courtesies. In general terms, Daniel was extremely disorganised and chaotic, often leaving his dirty clothing lying all over the house. On one notable occasion, when he went to visit friends of his mother's, he got himself soaked in the pouring rain because he had forgotten his raincoat. He simply took off his soaking shoes and put them on the cooker, leaving his socks hanging from the radiator in the sitting room. This, needless to say, both perplexed and irritated his hostess.

With Daniel, his academic life was progressing as well as could have been expected, although one would anticipate that once he reached the sixth form of secondary education he would find the organisation and discipline involved extremely difficult and would need a great deal of support. However, the intellect was available to him but he would need very careful support, both academically and at a pastoral care level, throughout his education, if he was to fulfil his potential.

Therapy, in the short term, involved considerable work on Daniel's communication skills. Not only was he not terribly efficient with the spoken word, but he had little or no idea what body language meant. Work with our counsellor on understanding the world around him and what made it work, how and why people reacted the way they did, what facial expressions and body postures meant, all built gradual insight. Daniel returned to a session on one notable occasion, with his eyes wide with amazement, because the counsellor had suggested that with every adult he met he should shake their hand, ask them how they were and smile. He was stunned to find that almost everybody smiled back at him! His comment was, "Why is the world so happy all of a sudden?" It began to give him an inkling that the way he had acted had triggered a happy response in other people.

We also involved him in drama therapy, where role-playing exercises in a small group of four youngsters proved extremely valuable. Mime, without spoken language, often played a part in this process and after a confused and bewildered beginning Daniel began to realise that so much can be communicated without a single word being spoken.

So what is Asperger's syndrome?

- It is a disorder that comes under the umbrella of autistic spectrum of disorders.

- Asperger's syndrome affects the development of a wide range of abilities and is seen predominantly in boys, but occasionally in girls.

- We have to remember that children with Asperger's syndrome have a different perspective on the world from anyone else, and we must try to see the world through their eyes to help understand their responses.

- It can certainly be managed, although it cannot be cured. Even university professors are ranked among the numbers of successful Asperger's sufferers, and many marry and have children.

Features of Asperger's syndrome

- Their principal vulnerability is one of impaired communication. They are usually quite unable to empathise with other people and may even respond totally inappropriately to other people's pain or suffering. This does not mean that they are callous, but simply that they have not understood or empathised.

- As their social interactions are usually one sided, often inappropriate and demanding, they find friendships extremely difficult to make and keep. They often have superior vocabulary but their speech patterns, in themselves, are rather pedantic, and they repeat themselves endlessly.

- As we have already said, they have little or no understanding of body language, and their non-verbal communication, as a whole, is immature. Their social maturity lies significantly below their chronological age level, let alone their intellectual capacity.

- They are usually uncoordinated, clumsy, awkward, and may have either a casual disregard for bodily hygiene, or alternatively, be obsessionally over clean.

- Obsessions for certain objects or subjects are familiar, and these may be accompanied by rather irritating mannerisms. Generally, if one obsession is removed or discouraged, another will quickly take its place.

- Change of any kind, even minor, may cause considerable stress. However, major changes such as a move of home, or change of school, may prove distressing and may need careful management. It is important to anticipate these changes and prepare the child well in advance.

FROM A SCHOOL TEACHER'S PERSPECTIVE

In the classroom, teachers and classroom assistants may observe the following:

- Lack of eye contact

- Does not respond easily to group instruction

- Does not respond to non-verbal messages

- Is unaware of the effect on others of their own facial expressions and body language

- Can read well and use language competently but without complete comprehension

- Socially unaware and insensitive to social interaction

- Blunt and often tactless and rude, unintentionally

- Cannot understand jokes, sarcasm, metaphor, or body language

- Slow response to questions

- Odd and ritualistic behaviour

- Inappropriate voice levels

- Uncoordinated, clumsy and generally hates PE and changing into sports kit

- Poor personal organisation

- Cannot visualise and predict

- Easily hurt when rejected by peer groups

- Very high level of anxiety and stress – leading to outbursts of frustration

- Lack of confidence and over-anxiety to please

- Need consistency and predictability in their school day

Social interactions

The social life of the Asperger's individual can be a lonely and frustrating affair, let alone irritating to peers, parents and teachers. In an effort to encourage more effective social interactions, there are a variety of steps that both parents and teachers can take. Fundamentally, Asperger children need consistent help to see into the world of those around them, and begin to learn how others feel, what hurts and excites them. There are many signals that people give, both verbal and non-verbal that are totally misinterpreted by the Asperger child.

These youngsters need a great deal of help in recognising even basic facial expressions, body postures and the way people move in certain circumstances. This can be greatly helped with role-play, pictures and even stopping to discuss the motivation of characters in a popular soap opera. For example, they need to learn not to close down the space between themselves and someone with whom they wish to communicate, as this makes other people feel threatened and possibly even angry. Role play, especially watching the role play of others in their group, should help, given time, and can assist them to develop the idea of space between communicators. I recently observed an Asperger's group working with a therapist who made very clever use of a video camera. The children were then able to watch their performance on video and after some eight or ten sessions were beginning to discuss their body language much more effectively. It will also help them learn useful introductory remarks, comments and phrases that help break the ice on meeting somebody new. Even when the children try hard to make their new techniques work, they will often go badly wrong and become upset. This is the time to discuss how it went wrong and how they might try differently on the next occasion.

The same applies to hurtful remarks, teasing and even verbal bullying. It is important for them to realise how the other person may feel, and, above all, how foolish it is to rise to the bait. They need to learn, albeit painfully, that if you reward a tease, the behaviour will continue.

If you are trying to encourage friendships, be sure that you do so where there is a common interest like computers, so that instant dialogue is possible without having to indulge in social chat.

Finally, remember how difficult Asperger individuals find unstructured time. School lunch clubs and after school clubs can be immensely valuable and it is important to keep them gainfully occupied at breaktime, in the evenings and on holidays. Indeed, holiday time can be stressful and Asperger's children need to know exactly what the plan will be for tomorrow, and precisely what will be expected of them and of those around them. Remember, they will be obsessional about timing and upset if the plan does not work out as prescribed.

James

James was a young man in a special school for children with behavioural disorders. He was very bright and, in many ways, comparatively successful, but it was quite clear from his case study that life was far from easy for the boy.

James had typical Asperger features, rather strange, large nose and mouth, arms and legs all over the place. His head often seemed to be slightly wobbly and he worked his fingers constantly around his mouth and nose. His hair was invariably dirty and he regularly smelt and had to be told to have a shower. This, however, was not enough; to make sure he washed, someone had to instruct every move from outside the shower curtain. Even then, there was no guarantee that the soap had been used to any great degree. There was no question of invading his privacy as he would become very distressed and bend himself double.

Totally disorganised, James had to be reminded of timetables, appointments and commitments. (He was never late for meals!) He hated to be touched physically, and if he was, would squeal and curl himself up into a ball, often pulling his jumper over his head, leaving his parents and teachers to wait for the ball to uncurl. This problem was overcome to a great extent by regular, light touching and he eventually would respond favourably to this. He had several obsessive interests, one being computing in all its forms, the other, war-gaming. He could spend all day on this and was a brilliant strategist. He was quite a snob, looking down on those peers he thought had inferior intellect (these were many, since he was highly intelligent), he was generally racist and inflexible in his views, but surprisingly moral.

Getting James to work in the classroom was a difficult task. However, once the teacher had won his respect by being understanding and encouraging (not to mention demonstrating superior knowledge on the subject), he was prepared to begin to absorb knowledge. The use of a computer was essential and once he started he could concentrate on a task for considerable periods. However, if he disliked the teacher or subject his response was hostile.

James responded to a firm but understanding attitude. He had great respect for knowledge and an encyclopaedic memory. He was successful at GCSEs with a great deal of support and pushing. The more independent learning at sixth form level, however, was disastrous. He would not organise or discipline himself even to attend lessons, much less attempt coursework without supervision. He was very aware of his failings, quite ambitious, but sadly, could not succeed on his own. This caused anxiety build-up and depression.

Resistance to change

Change, anxiety and stress are hugely linked in the life of the Asperger individual. They depend heavily on life being predictable, and within their own control. They quickly become anxious, sometimes agitated, even angry, and occasionally depressed, if they are unable to cope with change.

Coping with minor levels of stress, distraction, achievement and relaxation are the keys

Encourage Asperger individuals to become involved in a project with which you know from previous experience, they will be successful. Demonstrate their success. Reward and praise it. They need this confirmation that all is well, and that the world around them can be relied on, after all.

Keep life as quiet and low key as you can. They often enjoy music and particularly low level music, which creates a gentle ambience, and is not so loud as to obscure communication. Quiet games that involve them with other children and help to distract, are extremely valuable, as are simple and manageable jobs around the house or classroom. Also remember the fascination for Information Technology in Asperger children – a return to the computer may solve all your problems!

For the agitated or hyperactive child, a physical activity like cycling, walking, trampolining – works well. Remember that having to socialise is extremely stressful for a child with Asperger's syndrome. Allow some solitary and relaxing time.

If major changes are necessary

It is vital to anticipate major needs for change and to prepare the child thoroughly by introducing them to the various facets of the change that will occur. Photographs, chats to a grandparent over the phone, a visit to a new school, even the introduction of another child who has already been through the experience, may all be extremely valuable. If it is to be a change of home, describe how their new bedroom will be, have constant pictorial references to the new home around the house, begin to make it as real and three dimensional as possible before the move even takes place. Above all, avoid anxiety and stress by not leaving change to the last moment. Introduce it gradually or the response, while delayed, may well be far more violent.

This is also a time when predictable and anticipated routines that are clearly recognised and identified by the Asperger individual become particularly important. They need a massive amount of security to help cope with change. Involve them at all stages and look enthusiastic and excited about the impending change yourself so that they begin to sense that there is something desirable at the end of the road.

If the child becomes angry or unduly distressed, do your best to avoid direct confrontation and raised voices. If you become angry, this is likely to make matters much worse. You may find that the uproar will continue for a long time. However much pressure you may feel you are under, the child must feel that you are relaxed, in control, know exactly what is going to happen next and will see them through this stage. Appear totally neutral, relaxed and unperturbed. This will bring out the actor in us all!

If the child refuses, becomes defiant and unwilling to cooperate, pretend not to have heard, ignore the apparent confrontation, go off and make a cup of tea, and then try again a few minutes later. The defiance may well have been nothing more than a symptom of anxiety and panic and not a challenge to you as a parent.

Parental response

If you feel that your child, or one with whom you are working, answers the characteristics described, seek the advice of an Educational Psychologist, Child Psychiatrist or Paediatrician to confirm the diagnosis, and then work through your Local Educational Authority so that appropriate management can be put in hand. You will need support, and your child will need considerable help with communication skills and understanding in the school environment, where inappropriate behaviour may alienate him from his peers and make classroom management far from easy. It is important to remember that the prognosis can be encouraging, providing management is professional and robust.

Many Asperger children are proving largely successful in their environment, but they do need a great deal of help, understanding and support. Fortunately, there are increasingly useful help lines for parents.

CONTACTS

NATIONAL AUTISTIC SOCIETY
276 Willesden Lane, London NW2 5RG
Tel: 0208 451 1114

> West Midlands Autistic Society, Birmingham
> Parent Support Groups – very active in all areas
> Websites: Search under 'Asperger's Syndrome'

NAS has many and varied information pamphlets for parents

TEMPLE GRANDIN (AUTISTIC)
Various books and articles, some on the Internet. Very insightful, and from the autistic sufferer's point of view

Special Needs Advisers in all Local Education Authorities can help with information, names, schools.

FURTHER READING

Asperger's Syndrome – A Guide for Parents and Professionals
Tony Attwood – ISBN 1-85302-577-1

Glossary

Asperger's syndrome This is best understood as a mild form of autism, demonstrating itself in inappropriate behaviour and emotional responses and a considerable naivety in an individual's capacity to interpret the feelings and body language of those around them. The majority of Asperger's individuals can be helped to adjust, at least to some extent, to relatively normal social interactions.

Attention deficit disorder (with or without hyperactivity) Characterised by individuals who cannot remain on task for more than a relatively brief period of time, who are largely incapable of coping with selective attention in that they are as distracted by redundant stimuli around them as they are by the task in hand. Their social responses are naïve, disinhibited and, at times, inappropriate. Those experiencing hyperactivity will find themselves constantly on the move, fidgeting restlessly as they struggle to process information.

Auditory acuity The ability to hear sound, sharpness of hearing.

Auditory perception The identification, organisation and interpretation of information through the ears, subdivided as follows:

Attention – the ability to know when to respond to sounds

Blending – the ability to blend together separate speech sounds to form words

Discrimination – the ability to distinguish between sounds and/or noises, e.g. between a car or lorry or individual speech sounds

Figure-ground – selecting specific sounds from an environment of many, e.g. picking out teacher's voice in a noisy classroom

Localisation – the ability to recognize the source/direction of a sound

Memory – the storage of auditorally presented information long enough to analyse it

Sequencing – reproduction of the correct order of sounds/information

Body image Awareness of one's own body and its orientation, position and movement in space.

Cerebral Pertaining to the brain.

Cerebral dominance The leading hemisphere, right or left, of the brain which appears to determine an individual's dominant hand, eye, foot, etc. See also hemisphere and laterality.

Cognitive Describing intellectual activity; knowing as opposed to feeling.

Concept An idea, abstract or concrete, mentally established through interpretation of experiences and usually embodied in a word, e.g. a young child learning 'hot' by association with fire, cooker, sun, etc. All language is built up this way.

Coordination Combination of different bodily actions to perform a functional task.

Bilateral coordination – coordination of both sides of the body simultaneously, e.g. catching a large ball, where both hands work together, or writing, where one hand writes while the other supports the paper

Gross motor coordination – coordination of muscle activity to carry out large movement patterns, e.g. running, walking, hopping, jumping

Fine motor coordination – coordination of small muscle groups for functional tasks involving precision and small movements, e.g. finger movements when writing

Visual-motor coordination – the ability to focus on the visual aspect of a task whilst carrying out the motor activities needed simultaneously, e.g. catching a ball involves hand-eye coordination and kicking a ball involves foot-eye coordination

Correlation The relationship between two sets of test scores. In statistics a perfect relationship gives a correlation of +1.0, complete lack of relationship is 0 and the exact opposite is −1.0.

Crosslaterality See laterality

Digraphs Two letters, vowels or consonants, which combine to make a single sound, e.g. th, sh, ar, aw, ee.

Discrimination The ability to perceive differences between two or more stimuli.

Dyscalculia A specific difficulty with mathematical functions.

Dysgraphia Difficulty with mechanical aspects of writing, i.e. poor letter formation and presentation of written work.

Dysphasia This implies a comparative disability in the capacity to process spoken language and to organise incoming language, frequently demonstrated in an incapacity to understand complex instructions or in inappropriate and at times even bizarre spoken responses.

Dyspraxia Fundamentally, a difficulty in interpreting spoken instructions in motor terms. It implies a lack of effective sensory integration, poor spatial organisation and motor planning. Individuals can appear awkward, clumsy and, in general terms, thoroughly disorganised.

Encoding The process of changing one form of symbol into another, as in transferring the spoken word into the relevant written form in spelling/writing.

Grapheme A written symbol representing a speech sound (phoneme).

Handedness The preferred hand which may differ for different activities or may be different from the preferred eye, ear or foot. See laterality.

Hemisphere One of the two halves, left and right, of the brain. The left hemisphere controls the motor activity of the right side of the body, the right hemisphere controls the left of the body. Many human activities require a preferred limb or organ, e.g. for writing, kicking, playing tennis, using a camera. In these instances one of the hemispheres is said to have cerebral dominance. Some functions are specialised in one or other hemisphere, e.g. the speech and language centres are normally in the left hemisphere, while appreciation of rhythm and music is specific to the right hemisphere.

Holistic Looking at a subject in its entirety and not just at its constituent parts.

Hyperactivity Excessive and often uncontrolled body movements or general activity.

Hypoactivity Below normal levels of physical activity, listless behaviour.

Hysterical This must be clearly differentiated from the popular image of the hysterical, out of control, weeping individual. Hysterical blindness, for example, will deprive the patient of effective vision and yet there will be no apparent organic causation. There are well-recorded cases of hysterical paralysis, including hysterical ataxia, as well as hysterical deafness. The condition tends to be associated with a personality type but the symptoms are real as far as the patient is concerned and may be totally disabling, but treatment will be directed more at stress and anxiety management then any organic disorder.

Kinaesthetic Perception obtained through muscle awareness and movement. Feedback to brain from muscle receptors in limbs and body when a movement is made.

Laterality Pertaining to the left and right sides of the body. Mixed or crosslaterality refers to mixed left or right side preference for certain activities, e.g. dominant right hand combined with dominant left eye.

Morpheme The smallest meaning-bearing unit in the language, which can be a single concept, word, root, prefix or suffix.

Motor movement

Fine motor – activities involving small areas of the musculature of the body, e.g. writing, cutting

Gross motor – activities involving large areas of the musculature of the body and particularly the large muscle groups, e.g. skipping

Motor perceptual – this describes the linkage between the child's brain and their body's capacity to respond physically to the environment

Multidisciplinary Implies the involvement of several different disciplines, often professions, in the resolution of problems.

Multisensory Using all the pathways – visual, auditory, kinaesthetic- simultaneously, with particular reference to teaching methods with dyslexic children.

Occlusion Means fundamentally an obstruction, a block, a closure. In the case of dyslexic children it normally refers to the patching of one eye to allow for the strengthening of the other.

Orientation The chosen direction, in terms of English literacy, of reading along a line of print. It can also refer to the direction of letters, where reversals and confusions may exist. It may also refer to the child's personal orientation in space, for example, their capacity to position themselves at a desk or even deal with their body appropriately in gymnastics.

Paired reading A shared reading exercise with child and adult. The adult can drop out when it is felt that the child has a good 'flow' and then come in again if the flow ebbs a little at any time.

Perception The process of organising and interpreting the information received through the senses.

Phoneme Smallest unit of speech sounds. It may correspond to a single letter (e.g. b, g) or digraph (sh, th, ai, oy).

Phonetics The study of speech sound, its manner and method of production and representation by written symbols, as in the International Phonetic Alphabet.

Phonics An approach to reading instruction where the emphasis is placed upon the sound value of letters as a means of word recognition.

Proprioception Feedback to the brain about sensations in the body and unrelated movement from muscles to joint receptors.

Psychosomatic Generally pertaining to that which is presumed to have both mental and bodily components. The individual may be considerably physically disabled, in the case of gastric ulcers, for example, and yet stress and anxiety may play a major part in the generation of the condition and its eventual management.

Reading age An individual's attainment in reading is expressed against the reading standard for the average child in a particular age group.

Reversal The turning back to front of a letter or word, e.g. 'd' for 'b', 'was' for 'saw'.

Scanning Glancing quickly through a text to find specific items of information.

Semantic Referring to the meaning of a morpheme, word, phrase or sentence.

Sensory Pertaining very generally to the senses, the sense organs, the sense receptors, the afferent neural pathways, sense data, etc.

Sensory discrimination – differential responding to different stimuli

Sensory integration – the neurological process of integrating incoming data from the various sensory channels, e.g. selecting and picking up an object following an auditory command, requires auditory analysis and interpretation leading to visual-motor activity.

Spatial orientation A person's awareness of how their body relates to the environment.

Standardised A test is said to be standardised when it has been administered to a representative population and its consistency and validity have proved satisfactory.

Tactile The ability to interpret sensory stimuli experienced through the sense of touch.

Tracking The visual pursuit of a stimulus in a prescribed manner, e.g. searching in a left-right direction along a line to pick out a particular letter.

Validity The extent to which a test measures the area it sets out to test.

Visual acuity The capacity to see the fine details of objects in the visual field. In clinical practice standard displays are used, for example the Snellen Chart, allowing for the measurement of the eye's capacity to discriminate fine detail.

Visual perception The identification, organisation and interpretation of a sensory data received through the eyes. It may be divided into separate features as follows:

Discrimination – the ability to discern similarities and differences within visually present material

Closure – the ability to identify a visual stimulus from an incomplete visual presentation.

Figure-ground – the ability to perceive objects in the foreground and background and to separate them meaningfully

Memory – the storage of visually presented information long enough to analyse and recall it accurately

Motor planning – the ability to reproduce from memory physical activities which have been previously demonstrated.

Sequencing – reproduction of information in the correct order

Vocabulary The number of words a child can recognise or use in speech or in written form.

Index